International Screen Industries

Series Editors:
Michael Curtin, University of California, Santa Barbara, and Paul McDonald,
King's College London, UK

The International Screen Industries series offers original and probing analysis of
media industries around the world, examining their working practices and the social
contexts in which they operate. Each volume provides a concise guide to the key
players and trends that are shaping today's film, television and digital media.

Published titles:
The American Television Industry *Michael Curtin and Jane Shattuc*
Arab Television Industries *Marwan M. Kraidy and Joe F. Khalil*
The Chinese Television Industry *Michael Keane*
East Asian Screen Industries *Darrell Davis and Emilie Yueh-yu Yeh*
European Film Industries *Anne Jäckel*
European Television Industries *Petros Iosifidis, Jeanette Steemers and Mark Wheeler*
Global Television Marketplace *Timothy Havens*
Hollywood in the New Millennium *Tino Balio*
Nollywood Central *Jade L. Miller*
Latin American Television Industries *John Sinclair and Joseph D. Straubhaar*
Video and DVD Industries *Paul McDonald*
The Video Game Business *Randy Nichols*

Localising Hollywood

Courtney Brannon Donoghue

palgrave

A BFI book published by Palgrave

First published in 2017 by
PALGRAVE

on behalf of the

BRITISH FILM INSTITUTE
21 Stephen Street, London W1T 1LN
www.bfi.org.uk

There's more to discover about film and television through the BFI.
Our world-renowned archive, cinemas, festivals, films, publications and learning resources are here to inspire you.

Palgrave in the UK is an imprint of Macmillan Publishers Limited, registered in England, company number 785998, of 4 Crinan Street, London N1 9XW. Palgrave Macmillan in the US is a division of St Martin's Press LLC, 175 Fifth Avenue, New York, NY 10010. Palgrave is a global imprint of the above companies and is represented throughout the world. Palgrave® and Macmillan® are registered trademarks in the United States, the United Kingdom, Europe and other countries.

Cover image: Alex Robinson / Getty Images

Set by Integra Software Services Pvt. Ltd.
Printed in China

This book is printed on paper suitable for recycling and made from fully managed and sustained forest sources. Logging, pulping and manufacturing processes are expected to conform to the environmental regulations of the country of origin.

British Library Cataloguing-in-Publication Data

ISBN 978–1–84457–687–6 (pb)
ISBN 978–1–84457–688–3 (hb)

To Brian, who gave me the world

Contents

Acknowledgments

This project is the result of many miles travelled, many hours of conversation contributed, and too many cups of coffee consumed. The tiny kernel of an idea for *Localising Hollywood* began with my first summer living in Brazil in 2005 and evolved over the following decade through conference papers, a PhD dissertation, publications, and finally this series of case studies. I want to thank the many people and institutions who supported me on this journey to explore the ever-changing nature of Hollywood's local operations.

First, I am indebted to my editors Paul McDonald and Michael Curtin and the BFI Publishing/Palgrave team for all their feedback and insights during this process. I will forever appreciate Paul and Michael's championing of this project through its various iterations. They will never know how much they influenced me as scholars and challenged me as editors while I developed this book. Also, a huge thanks to Paul for the cheery check-ins that kept me going.

I owe my deepest gratitude to the dozens and dozens of media professionals across many industries, institutions, languages, and borders who took the time to talk to this curious American scholar. These are the studio managers, executives, creatives, policymakers, civil servants, etc. whose contributions to the media industries are never acknowledged enough. This book was only possible due to your generosity in sharing your experiences and stories with me.

I received financial support from the Department of Radio-Television-Film, Teresa Lozano Long Institute of Latin American Studies, and the Graduate School at the University of Texas at Austin during my doctoral studies that made my first round of fieldwork in 2010 and 2011 possible. I am additionally grateful to Oakland University's University Research Committee, College of Arts and Sciences, Department of English, and Cinema Studies Program for their generous support of my continued research endeavours and various international and domestic fieldwork trips between 2013 and 2016. Since landing at my home institution, I have benefited greatly from a stellar and encouraging group of colleagues and friends. This work would not be possible without my lovely Cinema Studies and English colleagues and their ongoing support and encouragement. A special thanks to my lady colleagues across OU – Erin Meyers, Andrea Eis, Joanie Lipson Freed, Alison Powell, Andrea Knutson, Amanda Stearns-Pfeiffer, Erin Dwyer – who give me strength, inspire me to be bolder, and remind me not to apologise.

So many thanks to my PhD advisors Janet Staiger and Joseph Straubhaar and committee members Shanti Kumar and Thomas Schatz in the Department of Radio-Television-Film at the University of Texas at Austin. Your brilliant guidance helped me to develop my dissertation into a transnational comparative study about Sony's local-language production strategy. My time in Austin was forever shaped and influenced by my fellow RTF graduate students who pushed me to be sharper inside and outside the classroom and stood by me as we climbed out of the ABD trenches – Kevin Bozelka, Manuel Aviles-Santiago, Sharon Shahaf, Assem Nasr, Tarik Elseewi, Lisa Schmidt, Andy Scahill, Colin Tait, and so many more. To Kristen Warner, Matt Payne, Kevin Sanson, and Anne Helen Petersen – thank you for the late nights, writing sessions, real talk, therapy sessions, and laughs. We started from the bottom, now we're here.

Additionally, the media studies scholars who helped to mentor me along the way – Aswin Punthambekar, Serra Tinic, Timothy Havens, Derek Johnson, Daniel Herbert, Alisa Perren, and Kevin Sandler – thank you for the stellar feedback, savvy advice, and professional opportunities. For all my fellow academic friends and extended cohort – Ross Melnick, Erin Copple Smith, Elizabeth Ellcessor, Racquel Gates, Hollis Griffin, Allyson Field, Peter Alilunas, Alyx Vesey, Jade Miller, Aymar Jean Christian, Ethan Tussey, Karen Petruska, Ben Sampson, and many more – y'all are an amazing support group and I cannot wait until the next SCMS reunion.

Along the way, I have had the fortune of stumbling across friends in the academy and industry who have become my family. To the folks who are always there for me, who make me laugh until I cannot breathe, and who will not let me get away with being anything but myself – Kristen, Erin, Amanda Ann Klein, Anna Froula, Faye Woods, Dana Och, Melissa Lenos, and Kirsten Strayer. And to the Cannes family that is Bryan Sebok, Ericka Friedrick, Lucy Hanke, and Mark Horowitz, I adore our endless debates over movies, long dinners, and never-soon-enough reunion trips.

To my wonderful parents, Emily and David Brannon, who ignited my love of learning and supported every academic endeavour and wild passion I pursued. Thank you for passing along your love of history, teaching, old movies, writing, and wanderlust. You taught me to reach the highest heights and always believed in my success. And to my sister and academic partner-in-crime, Jessica Brannon-Wranosky, you blazed the way for the Brannon girls. Thank you for the real-world advice and savvy strategy as I struggled to write that undergraduate film history paper once upon a time to finishing this project.

Brian, I can never express what your endless love and faith in me means. You've supported and witnessed every accomplishment and struggle with me as a plucky undergraduate film nerd to newly minted junior scholar. Your quiet strength, passionate spirit, and timeless wisdom inspire me daily. You are the perfect partner and fellow adventurer for exploring this big, crazy world. After every far-flung journey you have been, and always will be, the lighthouse calling me home.

The author and publisher would like to thank the University of Texas Press for permission to reproduce a portion of the article "Sony and Local-Language Productions: Conglomerate Hollywood's Strategy of Flexible Localization for the Global Film Market," by Courtney Brannon Donoghue, in *Cinema Journal* Volume 53 Issue 4, pp.3–27. Copyright ©2014 by the University of Texas Press.

1

Introduction: Hollywood's Global Footprint

Universal Pictures had a good year in 2015. By summer, the studio's annual film slate resulted in a string of mid-budget theatrical hits including *Fifty Shades of Grey* and *Pitch Perfect 2* that complemented blockbuster series instalments *Jurassic World* and *Furious 7* performing record-breaking numbers (McNary, 2015a). Anne Thompson credits Universal's strategic targeting of wider demographics with films focusing on female, African-American, and Latino audiences domestically as well as broader global markets (A. Thompson, 2015). Even as industry analysts and scholars bemoan twenty-first-century Hollywood as the age of blockbuster franchising and 'sequelitis', for some Universal's film slate may signal a larger shift in an industry production and distribution cycle towards more culturally specific content and targeted audiences (Levin, 2010; Goldstein, 2011). Universal is not alone in this move to specialise, as Sony, Fox, Warner Bros., Paramount, and Disney have also been developing and experimenting with strategies to reach new markets and audiences. Particularly in the past two decades, the majors have expanded their approach to markets outside North America and English-language territories. Through an array of production and distribution models to localise and adapt their content for key territories, Hollywood is actively changing the way it thinks about the international film business.

The importance of the global marketplace for major American film companies coalesced around World War I. The studios have maintained a consistent, albeit constantly evolving, presence in local markets outside North America for over one hundred years. However, in recent decades, filmed entertainment divisions of Sony, Warner Bros., Fox, Paramount, Universal, and Disney increasingly have come to rely on worldwide theatrical revenue (Balio, 2013; K. Thompson, 1985). In an annual theatrical market report, the Motion Picture Association of America (MPAA) illustrated that the North American market (US and Canada) has plateaued around $11 billion, in contrast to the continued growth across European, Middle Eastern and African (EMEA), Asia Pacific, and Latin American regions, which increased from $22.4 billion in 2011 to $27.2 billion in 2016 (MPAA, 2016). International film markets out-earn domestic by more than two to one, and successful studio tentpoles now make most of their theatrical gross abroad.

This stark ratio also breaks down on the individual film level. One of 2015's top-grossing summer releases, *Jurassic World*, earned $652 million in North America; international receipts topped $1 billion (B. Lang, 2016).

Common studio logic works to explain the waning domestic box office and increased reliance on international markets. A 'battle of the theatrical box office' narrative drives industry and popular press coverage of Hollywood film divisions and their conglomerate parents. US-based trade headlines, such as *The Wrap*'s 'Why America Doesn't Count at the Box Office Anymore' and *Variety*'s 'Hollywood B.O. Rides O'Seas Boom', abound (B. Lang, 2011; Stewart, 2012). Anyone working on a studio's financial side will insist the reality of box-office returns is more complicated than 'the rest of the world is just profits' lore, particularly since accounting is always creatively opaque. Yet these discursive patterns mark shifting institutional and industrial priorities around the importance of international film markets outside North America for Hollywood's operations and bottom line.

Industry lore that contrasts emerging international markets with a stable domestic market presents a mutually exclusive binary, where media circulation within these regions often seems to have little relationship or interaction with local industrial conditions, content, or cultures. How this data and market logic are framed raises a number of questions. What do scholars and industry professionals mean by the term 'international'? Mike Goodridge argues the 'foreign' designation is 'a vaguely derogatory term, of course, relegating the 50 or so significant territories outside the US with all their different tastes, audience demographics, and exhibition landscapes into one lumpen market' (Goodridge, 2009). This vague category diminishes the scope, span, and intricacies of European, Asian Pacific, Middle Eastern, Latin American, and African media markets under a problematic 'Othering' reminiscent of the West versus the rest. Box-office data and splashy headlines offer little insight into how a film circulates within an individual territory or how a particular studio approaches localising content market by market. These regional markets may make up the lion's share of studio box-office gross, yet what happens when we look beyond the numbers and vague 'international' category in order to understand the complex picture of how media content is produced and circulated outside the Anglophone market?

BOOK OBJECTIVES

Localising Hollywood explores, and complicates, the dynamic interaction between Hollywood film entertainment divisions and individual media markets: namely, how their position, partnerships, and practices operate in an era characterised by globalisation, digitisation, and convergence. The book's objective is to move beyond universal and surface-level box-office reporting that so often character-ises international operations of Sony, Fox, Warner Bros., Disney, Universal, and

Paramount to examine the macro-level forces and micro-level contexts at play. I offer a multifaceted discussion of studio activities that should be understood as translocal: partnering and circulating local-language and English-language content within and across a handful of territories. I ground my understanding of translocal processes in Patrick D. Murphy and Marwan M. Kraidy's conceptualisation that emphasises the importance of adding 'trans', which 'lies more in its capacity to comprehend the articulation of the global with the local, than its supposed ability to understand the local in isolation of large-scale structures and processes' (Murphy and Kraidy, 2003, p. 304). My approach considers questions of locality and connectivity as inextricably linked, where industrial forces and institutional power cannot be separated from individual agents and cultural specificity (Hepp, 2009, p. 3). I am interested in interrogating earlier notions of a 'global Hollywood' and globalisation, where media conglomerates were viewed as economically rational or logical organisations.

What does a translocal study of contemporary Hollywood's international operations look like? My approach challenges earlier theoretical frameworks and expands methodological practices towards understanding the globalisation of Hollywood. Local studio activities may involve territory managers overseeing local offices and teams, developing infrastructure, and making creative and financial decisions in nuanced and specific ways for each individual market. Often, how a studio tentpole film is released or a local-language film is developed varies from territory to territory due to political, economic, sociocultural, technological, and industrial conditions.

My study is based on extensive international fieldwork and interviews with Hollywood executives and managers, co-production partners, policymakers, film commissioners, lobbyists, financiers, independent producers, and distributors across Brazil, Spain, Germany, France, Belgium, the UK, and US. This mid-level approach serves as the foundation of my methodology and is complemented by consulting trade and popular publications, box-office data, policy reports, and marketing and promotional materials. I acquired access to studio country managers, local directors of production, and international executives through years of building contacts and gaining introductions. I conducted more than fifty interviews over a six-year period representing a broad range of individual personalities and positions. Each interview offers a range of voices: I heard from individuals developing and implementing plans to distribute and market Warner Bros.' products like *Man of Steel* (2013) in the German theatrical market, and I learned about how Sony implements its local-language production strategy of partnering with local co-producers in Brazil. How do these media professionals understand and navigate studio cultures, corporate and creative strategies, and their own role at the intersection of Hollywood's local presence and global network?

Rather than trying to provide an exhaustive account of each Hollywood studio's international operations, I gathered and selected a series of case studies exploring dominant strategies among a diverse set of managers, executives, producers, and distributors. I aimed to understand networks and partnerships, how studio professionals and partners interacted on various levels. Because I explore different roles, practices, and priorities at the six studios in vastly different local territories, the localised perspective sacrifices some breadth (the expansive intricacies of Asian, Latin American, and European markets) for depth (how studio activities intersect with local media climates and conditions in a handful of markets). This approach was intended partially to make the project manageable, since each studio has dozens of local operations worldwide. Although Sony, Warner Bros., and their peers may maintain local production and distribution operations across Europe, Latin America, and Asia, I limit my focus to a handful of territories in the former two regions.

Additionally, my decision to focus on five or six key territories evolved from my own cultural, linguistic, and professional access in these markets. The scope of this project emerged from my earlier work on the Brazilian film industry and the success of Portuguese-language studio co-productions beginning in the 1990s. Depending on who I asked in the local industry, whether studio country managers or independent producers, I received a different answer for classifying these film products. Were they Brazilian or Hollywood? Local or global? Commercial or state-supported? This questioning led me to other markets in order to understand how the major studios approach local production and distribution in increasingly different ways. By focusing on studio-specific case studies, this book explores the forces involved and different priorities of the various local players alongside how studio content is increasingly localised for mid-size markets around the world. In turn, I offer a close analysis of lesser-known localisation strategies to cultivate audiences, adapt franchises, manage industrial relationships, and promote Hollywood activities worldwide.

CRITICAL APPROACHES

The historic presence of Hollywood studios outside North America is a centrally debated and contentious area of film and media studies. Three key areas of research characterise work on studio international operations – historical, political economy, and, more recently, critical media industry studies. First, a historical and largely archival body of work maps Hollywood institutions' growing dependence on global audiences from the classical studio system to conglomerate era. Thomas Schatz, Tino Balio, and Alisa Perren trace institutional histories of studios such as Universal, United Artists, and Miramax during pivotal industrial moments of transformation wherein the authors directly or indirectly identify the increased reliance on international markets. Other industry scholars such as Jennifer Holt and Paul McDonald explore how shifting policies and technological platforms resulted in structural changes for global ownership and distribution patterns. Kristin Thompson and John Trumpbour directly link how the international market developed alongside the emerging studios from the 1900s to their post-World War II heyday. These broader industry studies offer insights into the diverse institutional practices and cultures of production that facilitated a long-term steady growth in international activities for the Hollywood studios. Additionally, a recent wave of international studio history is emerging and includes works by Ross Melnick on theatrical ownership and exhibition, Nolwenn Mingant on local territory offices in the Middle East, and Daniel Steinhart on the first wave of runaway European productions in the 1950s (Melnick, 2015, 2016; Mingant, 2010, 2015; Steinhart, 2013).

Political economy serves as the second approach to understanding Hollywood's global footprint. Namely, the legacy of scholarship by Thomas Guback, Janet Wasko, Eileen Meehan, Douglas Gomery, and Toby Miller cements a distinct conversation regarding Hollywood activities expanding beyond North America and is vital to understanding questions of ownership, capital, and distribution monopolies in the twenty-first century. In arguably the most influential work on the movie industry's political economy, *Global Hollywood 2*, Toby Miller, Nitin Govil, John McMurria, Richard Maxwell, and Ting Wang utilise a Marxist framework and interrogate Hollywood's hegemonic position as central to the unequal flow of media worldwide in a globalised moment. They contend: '"Hollywood" appears in nearly all descriptions of globalisation's effects – left, right, and Third ways – as a floating signifier, a kind of cultural smoke rising from a US-led struggle to convert the world to capitalism' (Miller *et al.*, 2005, p. 51). Grounding their critique in histories of colonialism and imperialism, the authors characterise the state of film industry studies as apolitical empiricist archivism and uncritical celebration that gives too much power to an active audience (Miller *et al.*, 2005, p. 4). *Global Hollywood* offers a critical view of American media and telecommunications industries and contributes to a discussion of policy, economics, and labour practices benefiting the studios' international activities through what they call an increasingly mobile and flexible New International Division of Cultural Labour.

However, *Global Hollywood* takes an overly deterministic view of the studios as global institutions. Hollywood is presented as a monolithic entity, and not as what I argue represents a handful of film companies operating inside diverse transnational media conglomerates constantly in flux due to shifting institutional structures, management roles, economic resources, and cultural practices. Furthermore, Miller and his co-authors assert that, due to the pervasive nature of studio content, 'we are all experts at understanding Hollywood movies ... [global] audiences are mostly watching fiction conceived, made, and owned by Hollywood. It symbolises an invitation to *replication* and *domination*, an invitation both *desired* and *disavowed*' (Miller *et al.*,

2005, p. 1, emphasis added). From this viewpoint, the six major studios maintain an unshakeable grip on power, a one-way flow of productions to media markets and audiences worldwide. In turn, I raise the question of exactly what, beyond this limited viewpoint, Hollywood signifies today. And what does Hollywood mean in a translocal media climate? All films involving a major studio are not conceived and made the same way for a vague global audience. This is not Henry Ford's automatic assembly-line, stamping out identical studio strategies or products for unquestioning audiences to consume in the same manner worldwide. Instead, we find ourselves in a post-Fordist moment where the decentralised studio units are scrambling to address increasingly localised media tastes, cultures, and processes. Therefore, what happens when we move from the broader global view of Hollywood activities to understand how content is produced and circulated more locally?

In this aspect, *Global Hollywood*'s approach offers a limited view of media con-glomerates as unified, coherent, and all-powerful entities dominating local media industries through vast financial resources and ideological concerns. The authors provide little insight into the specific organisational or individual activities of these diverse companies operating across multiple continents. At best, assumptions are made about the individuals and teams working within and partnering with Hollywood studios inside various industries worldwide; at worst, these industry agents are not considered or are completely ignored. Again, as with trade press dis-cussions of the global box office, we find ourselves back at a place where Hollywood studios are powerful players in a vague space and place known as the international market. The nature of film practices on a transnational level is more complex and multifaceted than the earlier, one-way-flow model assumes. *Localising Hollywood* offers a different perspective on studio divisions cultivating and negotiating rela-tionships across Latin America, Europe, and increasingly Asia Pacific. While this project acknowledges the historically hegemonic position these studios hold inter-nationally, I do not give unyielding weight to the political and economic might of these organisations.

How can we as media industries scholars best understand how local production and distribution divisions and strategies are set up and operate to develop local part-nerships and content? Earlier conversations about Hollywood's global influence and footprint relied heavily on broader notions of globalisation. A slippery and abstract concept, globalisation is understood as unified global time or simultaneity, involv-ing the increased emergence of transnational institutions and agencies, destabilised nation-states, the development of further forms of global communication, and a change in standards of citizenship across local, national, regional, and transnational spaces (Featherstone, 1990, p. 6). While many of these factors directly shape Warner Bros. or Sony's territory offices in Spain, Brazil, or Germany, focusing solely on these macro-level issues also clouds the day-to-day interactions and complexities of micro-level processes. Michael Curtin argues:

globalization of media therefore should not be understood reductively as cultural homogenization or Western hegemony. Instead it is part of a larger set of processes that operate translocally, interactively, and dynamically in a variety of spheres: economic, institutional, technological, and ideological. (Curtin, 2007, p. 9)

Dismissing Hollywood's local production and distribution activities as universal or monolithic ignores these rich and complex translocal dynamics. Instead, I work to situate 'local Hollywood' as the site where transnational studios and local industry priorities intersect as an opportunity to unpack the so-called media industries 'spheres'.

The final approach, and the central framework of this book, is what Timothy Havens, Amanda D. Lotz, and Serra Tinic call 'critical media industry studies'. In the tradition of media industries scholarship, Curtin and others employ fieldwork and ethnographic methods to explore the dynamics and processes of international institutions and professionals on a more local level. I adapt Havens, Lotz, and Tinic's call for a mid-level approach for this institutional and industrial research based on understanding the role of media professionals as individual agents. The authors position what they categorise as a 'critical media industry studies' approach through 'a "helicopter" level view of industry operations, a focus on agency with industry operations, a Gramscian theory of power that does not lead to complete domination, and a view of society and culture grounded in structuration and articulation' (Havens, Lotz, and Tinic, 2009, p. 246). The authors emphasise mid-level research as a way to understand corporate business cultures and how particular media texts and practices arise from and reshape industrial practices. This approach focuses on media professionals – producers, distributors, managers – making day-to-day decisions and negotiating relationships with their corporate executives and creative partners. As Havens, Lotz, and Tinic contend,

the way in which institutional discourses are internalized and acted upon by cultural workers is an important missing link between political economy's concentration on larger economic structural forces and much of cultural studies' analyses of end products such as media texts and audience interpretations. (Havens, Lotz, and Tinic, 2009, p. 247)

Institutional discourses and cultural workers' levels of negotiation and participation are vital to analysing local production and distribution processes within Sony, Fox, Warner Bros., and the other studios.

The authors continue by arguing

the imperative of case study methods that shed light on the ways in which members of the media industries define the conventions of production and distribution based on their assumptions of the prevailing cultural values and issues of the time. (Havens, Lotz, and Tinic, 2009, p. 247)

In other words, institutional and individual case studies can reveal the contradictions and fissures between how media professionals' day-to-day processes and decision-making are negotiated with institutional priorities and strategies and local industrial conditions and media cultures. In their seminal cultural studies work on the Sony Walkman, Paul du Gay, Stuart Hall, Linda Janes, Hugh Mackay, and Keith Negus introduce the 'circuit of culture' framework, which is particularly helpful in this instance. The authors argue against privileging one condition or factor in order to understand cultural products. They propose a 'combination of processes' in their articulation, specifically the connection or 'linkage' across a variety of cultural texts – representation, identity, production, consumption, regulation (Du Gay *et al.*, 1997, p. 3). Therefore, instead of privileging merely the economic or political factors of globalisation and media, I am concerned with how local studio professionals, strategies, and relationships are 'represented, what social identities are associated with it, how it is produced and consumed, and what mechanisms regulate its distribution and use' (Du Gay *et al.*, 1997, p. 3). A significant contribution of this book to critical media industry debates is my consideration of management identity formation, industry lore, and individual agency alongside the constantly evolving studio practices and partnerships inside these local markets. My methods contribute a unique, on-the-ground perspective missing from current conversations about Hollywood's international operations by offering privileged information, institutional memory, and personal insights unavailable from trade and popular press coverage and earlier scholarship.

CHAPTER SUMMARIES

Localising Hollywood offers the reader an unprecedented industrial overview of Hollywood international operations since the 1990s that engages with key scholarly and industrial debates. I incorporate first-hand accounts gathered from extensive fieldwork and research about the wide scope of international operations, from creative partnerships and production strategies to promotional and distribution processes. By exploring how decision-making processes and creative negotiation between Hollywood media executives and local forces operate, this study reveals the complex picture of film-making and circulation in an era often characterised by the forces of conglomeration, digitisation, and globalisation. Chapter 2 traces a broad history of Hollywood global operations from the rise of the studio system to the first wave of conglomeration in the 1960s and 1970s. What emerges is the central importance of international markets during industry-wide cyclical shifts. Studios relied more heavily on global audiences during significant times of industrial transformation such as the coming of sound or the crumbling of vertical integration.

By focusing on the international market from the 1980s to 2016, Chapter 3 explores how the second wave of conglomeration reshaped film studios into diversified entertainment divisions inside expanding global media companies. I briefly outline Sony Pictures Entertainment's early international expansion, particularly into the Latin American television market, as an example of early division-wide localisation. The remainder of the chapter examines dual globalisation and localisation strategies for international film operations. First, I map Hollywood's changing 'international market'. The increased importance of global audiences for tentpole films has led to reimagined production and circulation patterns on the local level. This results in local studio units becoming more involved in the distribution of English-language studio films. Second, the local-language strategy emerges during the 1990s as an industry-wide attempt at localising content on a smaller scale for a number of mid-sized territories. Beginning with industry pioneers Sony and Warner Bros., I trace how the local-language production strategy (LLP) – a Hollywood commercial co-production between a local studio unit and independent partners intended for an individual market – becomes an experiment for all six filmed entertainment divisions, with varying results, by the 2010s. Shifting from a broad industry discussion of local production and distribution, the next chapter is the result of dozens of conversations with local studio management in offices across Brazil and Europe. This access provides unparalleled first-hand observations of local studio operations, country manager system, and LLP strategies. Specifically, Chapter 4 describes the management structure, or country manager model, driving many local studio operations. In challenging earlier scholarly and popular notions of studio management as top-down suits, I argue how managing directors for local offices of Fox, Warner Bros., Sony, and their peers function as cultural intermediaries. Country managers, also known as managing directors, utilise dispositional and tactical strategies to manage relationships in local industries as well as show their value internally. The other case study in this chapter considers the role of local production directors and their processes for pitching, co-producing, and releasing LLPs in individual markets Brazil, Germany, and Spain. Similar to their country manager bosses employing circumscribed agency, directors of production must balance creative and financial negotiations and distinct priorities among local unit operations, independent producing partners, and international home office.

Chapter 5 explores local Hollywood's increased operational footprint across a network of international media hubs worldwide. I examine the complex dynamic of studio production sites, offices, and business operations as they navigate particular industry spaces and places. An important aspect of Hollywood's presence and positionality within local media centres is a reliance on specific locational factors, everything from the material to symbolic resources available from Europe to Asia. Whether developing international co-productions or investing in local studio infrastructure, the majors rely heavily on financial, physical, geographical, and labour resources inside key creative clusters. First, I engage with scholarly debates around runaway productions in an effort to extend the conversation. I consider how studio operations intersect local media sectors in the case of Rio de Janeiro as a growing international hub. Next, Germany's regionalised studio complexes and infrastructure have become a key site for international co-productions, with the Berlin-Brandenburg region home to Studio Babelsberg. The complex facilitates partnerships between big-budget productions and the country's growing support services like the VFX sector and also housed Sony's early attempts at an LLP unit. Finally, through on-site observations, I examine UK's Leavesden Studios as a historic site of international production purchased and reimagined by Warner Bros. Nestled inside the working studio complex and located on a handful of soundstages, 'The Making of *Harry Potter*' tour simultaneously operates as a promotional space for the franchise and works to legitimate Warner Bros.' position within the London area creative sector.

Chapter 6 offers a unique discussion of the Motion Picture Association [MPA], the international division of Hollywood's trade alliance, the Motion Picture Association of America. My goal is to complicate scholarly views of the organisation as merely a monolithic entity operating under a central agenda. I take a close look at MPA regional operations (Latin America and EMEA) through three priorities – policy and market regulation, piracy, and promotional activities. What emerges is an organisation dealing with internal changes, with a strategic shift away from 'confrontation' to 'cooperation', and the external challenges posed by the rise of piracy and competing studio member interests. In talking with former and current MPA executives and territory managers, a broader view of their roles in expanding local studio operations and how they understand their positionality in working with other industry groups for advantageous policy emerges.

The last chapter considers how studios employ franchising practices and convergence strategies with local-language productions. Through their massively successful *High School Musical* (*HSM*) property, Disney almost immediately began to localise marketing and broadcast efforts for the English-language films. Through its local operations, Disney also developed a handful of *HSM* LLPs in Latin America and Asia that illustrate the company's long-time investment in 'total entertainment' and tightly controlled brand management. Additionally, through one of its most successful LLP units, Warner Bros. developed a co-production strategy in Germany based on star power, prominent producing partners, and family entertainment films. Originally a rom-com star vehicle, *Keinohrhasen* (*Rabbit without Ears*, 2007) evolved into a cross-media family franchise driven by its paratextual toys. The two case studies, which illustrate two different strategies for Disney and Warner Bros. that both rely on franchising and cross-media practices, illustrate the difficulty of managing property extensions on a localised level.

Conversations with media professionals making day-to-day production and distribution decisions and negotiating relationships with their corporate executives and creative partners provide a critical window into the management cultures, business models, and power structures of a twenty-first-century globalised Hollywood. This study considers the competing visions, financial and creative decisions, and daily industry processes involved in films operating simultaneously as local media and Hollywood products. In turn, my research relies on unparalleled access to studio executives and management. My ability to achieve introductions and network with high-level professionals at Warner Bros., Sony, or Fox reinforces the closed nature of studio culture. In general, once I gained access to an international division or local operation, most of these individuals were open and accommodating to my questions, at times showing production slates, sharing budgets, and speaking critically of their companies and competitors. While my fieldwork process shows how precarious understandings of studio 'power' can be, I also discovered how invisible most of the international mid-level management and practices are to the academic community and general public. Many of these individuals were eager to champion their role in the local market and help contextualise current studio activities.

International operations are not totalising examples of Hollywood power within the global film industry. This work illustrates something the studios themselves learned in recent decades: there is no clear formula or strict rulebook for localising and adapting their business for an individual territory beyond North America. Instead, my attention to fieldwork, interviews, trade and press coverage, and studio promotional materials from various angles – international executives, local managements, diverse institutional partners – reveals how management and production cultures, financial and creative investment, and public and private priorities swing widely from alignment to conflict to negotiation. In speaking with local operations, it becomes remarkably evident how value and knowledge circulate differently depending on which part of a Hollywood conglomerate is examined. A studio's local management and projects must be understood within a dynamic of shifting translocal contexts and internal studio cultures. *Localising Hollywood* is not just the story of one industry's global expansion and adaptation; it also reflects local industry cultures and histories often seen as separate or disconnected from domestic operations. The book offers a new approach for understanding Hollywood's local presence and practices, whether successes or failures, against the backdrop of constantly evolving media industries.

2

History of International Operations (1900s–70s)

Since the 1990s, Hollywood's increased reliance on international markets outside North America has provoked waves of celebratory and critical attention. As the central focus of this book, the contemporary period marks a moment when media properties, financing, professionals, and cultures circulate globally with increased ease and mobility. Yet it is important to understand that the flow of Hollywood content and investment in international activities outside the English-language market is not a new phenomenon. In fact, the major studios have actively developed strategies – with varied success – to capture local markets across Europe, Latin America, and Asia Pacific since the early days of the American film industry.

This chapter offers a historical overview of Hollywood's international operations from one-reelers in the 1900s to the first wave of conglomeration beginning in the 1960s. Significantly, key institutional and industrial strategies from production to exhibition emerged during this period, many of which will be adapted and reimagined as contemporary media conglomerates work to capture and adapt to local markets in the twenty-first century. Four earlier periods – which I will call Early Cinema (1900s–1914), World War I to Early Sound (1914–31), the Classical Studio System (1931–49), and the System's Decline and First Wave of Conglomeration (1950s–70s) – highlight the global expansion and cycles of international activities beyond the highly documented Anglophone region.

Through a broad historical overview, I show how studios approach international operations during key moments of economic, industrial, and technological change. In general, cycles of financial instability or sweeping structural changes distinguish these periods when international market activities become more important to the studios. Whether due to the economic impact of the world wars or to industrial shifts after the post-Paramount theatrical divorcement, clearly it is the case that Twentieth Century-Fox, Warner Bros., and their peers' approach to specific regional and local industries as well as production and distribution strategies systematically evolves. This shift illustrates the historically globalised nature of the film business. Early institutional strategies and assumptions about international film markets, or how the studios essentialise the entire world's media market into the 'foreign box office', operate under assumptions about

- how audiences worldwide engage with Hollywood content
- how these films travel locally, nationally, regionally, and transnationally
- how localisation efforts reflect the way larger industry lore or discourses operate and continue to circulate today

In addition to larger structural and institutional trends, this chapter summarises and engages with shifting scholarly conversations and theoretical approaches to Hollywood's international operations and activities. A politically economic-determinist framework or cultural-imperialism lens frames much of the earlier scholarly work covering silent cinema and the studio era. I outline the key debates and concepts that serve as the foundation for the remainder of this book, which are structured in dialogue with my overall research objectives.

EARLY CINEMA (1900s–1914)

From its emergence in the 1890s, the film industry operated as a global network of creative professionals, industry practices, technologies, and cultural products. In addition to the exchange and influence of early production practices and hardware development, the flow and regulation of cinema as a business became a key issue almost immediately. Early film-making pioneers and entrepreneurs such as Thomas Edison focused on the restricted dissemination and licensing of their technological inventions, which ranged from cameras to projectors. Most famously, in 1908, Edison and a group of American and European film businessmen including George Méliès, Max Selig, and Siegmund Lubin formed the Motion Pictures Patent Company (MPPC) cartel (Sklar, 1994, p. 35). This organisation resulted in a transnational network as well as a way to regulate and control the flow of their films, cameras, and projectors worldwide (K. Thompson, 1985, p. 2). These early efforts proved an opportunity for expanding into international markets and building partnerships through a centralised and controlled manner.

Prior to the emergence of the multi-reel feature film around 1907, American film companies hired agents, or middlemen, to sell their prints outside the United States. By the 1910s, London served as the international headquarters for most film firms, whereas American film companies opened offices there to sell distribution rights and supply prints to local companies (K. Thompson, 1985, pp. 3, 29–31). Timothy Havens and Amanda D. Lotz define media distribution as 'both the physical (or technological) transfer of a media text to an exhibitor and promotional activities that distributors engage in to convince exhibitors to stock or show specific texts' (Havens and Lotz, 2012, p. 147). While the following chapters discuss the diversification of distribution practices emerging with digital technological changes in recent years, theatrical distribution was the central method of film circulation and exhibition for the first half of the twentieth century. Theatrical distribution practices beyond North American until this point were fairly hands off for US-based studio executives. They did not adapt their sales strategies to local market conditions and, as described by Kristin Thompson, represented an 'unorganized export business' (K. Thompson, 1985, p. 40).

As the domestic production of features grew and new US film companies during this period mobilised away from the East and towards the West Coast, the circulation of films within international markets also expanded. According to Thompson, the 'American film industry emerges as a dominant presence internationally in the mid-1910s' (K. Thompson, 1985, p. 1). The emergence of film companies such as Universal, Famous Players-Lasky (later Paramount), Loew's, and Fox during the 1910s coincided with a systematic move into European, Latin American, and Asian markets. Trade journals advised film executives how to export films to other local markets more effectively. For example, a column in a 1914 issue of *Moving Picture World* advises readers on how to enter a new market:

> The film companies should combine in sending a representative to Latin America to prepare the ground for importation of American films on a much larger scale than would have been possible before the war. He should be a man that understands the South American countries and people, and who speaks their language. He should also be a man who is thoroughly acquainted with the motion picture business from every angle. (A. Lang and de Csesznak, 1914, p. 468)

At first, the early studios did not have the infrastructure or distribution network available to enter local markets in this way. In the case of Latin America, a number of studios began to establish offices in the region. For example, Fox's first office outside North America opened in Rio de Janeiro in 1915 (K. Thompson, 1985, p. 72). Not until the end of World War I, and then the coming of sound, did the studios attempt more localised and industry-specific production and distribution strategies.

WORLD WAR I TO EARLY SOUND (1914–31)

World War I brought a number of changes to the global film market and to American film companies' approach to international production and distribution models. First, due to the political and economic upheaval in many European countries, local film production was greatly weakened by the late 1910s. Whereas France had been a leading producer and distributor, the war 'redirected the international flow of capital' (Guback, 1969, pp. 388–9). Paramount, Fox, Warner Bros., and their contemporaries outlived the MPPC cartel. Survived and strengthened by World War I, the emerging studios capitalised on the opportunity to expand and internationalise their business. Second, the war also brought the decline of London as the headquarters for worldwide film distribution and the rise of New York as the industry's business centre. American film companies shifted away from the middleman-agent approach in local markets and instead began opening subsidiaries run by studio employees and overseen by US-based executives (K. Thompson, 1985, p. 68). As this centralised strategy evolved over the next decade, a more direct approach to overseeing international operations and film distribution would shape the following century of major studio business practices and institutional structures. Finally, by 1917, local revenue was a predictable share in many markets. International sales outside North America began to be factored into production budgets. This signals the increased importance of international box-office revenue for the studios' production and distribution model (Gomery, 1986, p. 12). Significantly, studio production and distribution practices evolved from a global network of audiences just as much as from domestic viewership.

The industry's development into a centralised studio system coincided with an increasingly internationalised distribution network. Many of the independent film companies that fought for market share against the Patent Trust only a decade earlier gradually expanded their operations and formed their distinctive structure as vertically integrated studios by the 1920s. Companies such as Warner Bros., Universal, Twentieth Century-Fox, and Columbia bought real estate, built studio lots, and began to systematise production (Gomery, 1986; Schatz, 1988).

Furthermore, the most powerful studios owned their own theatre chains in an effort to control the process from production to exhibition. Internal growth and diversification for these film companies were key to subsequent international expansion. Ross Melnick identifies how the major studios aggressively began to build and open movie theatres worldwide during this period. Twentieth Century-Fox, Paramount, Warner Bros., and MGM acquired and operated film theatres internationally beginning in the 1920s. For example, Paramount purchased a theatre circuit that included Cuban cinemas in 1929, while Warner Bros. had invested in its first international theatre in London by 1938 (Melnick, 2015, p. 157). As the majors expanded their business activities internationally, investing in local cinema chains across Europe, Latin America, and the Caribbean – and later Asia, Africa, Australia – signalled a strategy to control exhibition of their films by building vertically integrated local operations. From décor to shop-window cinema architectural design, the studios worked to localise and adapt theatrical experiences to the specificities of urban moviegoing culture in Rio de Janeiro or London (Melnick, 2016). Until this point, the studios did not prioritise adapting content for local markets beyond producing English-language content intended to travel. Besides intertitles, however poorly translated, the same film versions circulated across international markets.

Paramount opened this Brazilian film theatre in São Paulo in 1928

Douglas Gomery determined that 'overseas rentals accounted for approximately one half an average feature film's taking' by 1925 (Gomery, 1986, p. 12). The studios already distinguished various European, Latin American, and Asian markets by language for distribution sale purposes, yet they made little effort to adapt or localise their English-language content for these audiences. However, the transition to sound technology led many studios to experiment with localisation efforts. American film executives initially resisted the conversion to sound, especially for the international market. In order to incorporate sound into the film-making process during this transitional period, the studios had to overcome a number of technological, cultural, economic, and regulatory issues. The first major industry-wide experimentation in localising studio films coincided with the coming of sound technology (K. Thompson, 1985, p. 163). Pioneered by Warner Bros. and Fox, sound films began to be exhibited around 1927. As well as their efforts to incorporate and overhaul domestic production practices and exhibition conditions due to this new technology, the studios also had to reimagine their approach to the international market, specifically non-English-language audiences. Challenges included sound patents, screen quotas, cultural specificity, and additional production and distribution costs outside the United States (Crafton, 1999, pp. 419–20).

Dubbing was introduced in Hollywood around 1927, yet the recording and playback techniques and equipment were unable to support wide-scale conversion at the time (Crafton, 1999, p. 425). The most expensive and audacious option for converting talking films outside English-language markets was the multi-language version (MLV). This strategy, adopted by all the prominent American studios at some point between 1928 and 1931, involved adapting and reshooting an existing English-language project in Spanish, French, or German (K. Thompson, 1985). The productions employed émigré casts, film-makers, and creative professionals. Warner Bros. became the first studio to experiment with MLVs. For example, the studio produced an English-language adaptation of *Moby Dick* (1930) and shot subsequent French and German versions at their Burbank studios (Crafton, 1999, pp. 425–7). MGM, Fox, Universal, RKO, and Columbia each formed multi-language film units. Yet Paramount proposed the most ambitious operation with a $10 million budget to produce ninety films per year in six different languages (K. Thompson, 1985, pp. 160–1). Production units were not limited to Los Angeles. Both Warner Bros. and Fox produced a number of MLVs in European studios, including studios in Berlin (Crafton, 1999, pp. 427–8). Two of the most famously documented MLVs are Universal's Spanish-language *Dracula* (1931) and MGM's *Anna Christie* (1930), starring Greta Garbo in both the English and German versions. In the case of *Dracula*, the English-language version directed by Tod Browning was shot on the studio lot during the day. After wrapping for the day, the Spanish-language production took over. With a different director (George Melford), cast, and crew, Universal utilised the same set and equipment for separate night and early-morning shoots. The Spanish-language *Drácula* was seen less as an individual film and more as an extension of the English-language version.

Although introduced as an industry-wide strategy for tackling diverse geolinguistic markets, primarily in Europe and Latin America, the MLV model proved expensive and short-lived. By the middle of 1931, studios including MGM and Warner Bros. began to shut down these units. One issue was cost, since an MLV version ranged anywhere from $30,000 to $80,000 above the English-language production's initial budget. To put this in perspective, subtitling on average cost only $2,500 above the negative cost of producing an English-language film (Crafton, 1999, p. 437; K. Thompson, 1985, p. 160). As dubbing techniques improved, the studios saw 'capital-intensive' units as superfluous to their central operations of producing English-language content for the domestic market that also travelled internationally. Additionally, with the struggle over investing resources and systematising local-language intertitles for specific linguistic markets during the silent era, cultural blunders and the lack of specificity were problems. According to Donald Crafton, 'dubbing and subtitling enabled studios to sidestep many of the cultural and political pitfalls that had made foreign-language production so risky' (Crafton, 1999, p. 438). With the standardisation of dubbing and subtitling, these two methods eventually became the central model for the circulation of Hollywood films

Greta Garbo as *Anna Christie* in MGM's 1930 multi-language versions (BFI Stills Collection)

globally.[1] As this book argues, Hollywood studios would not attempt an industry-wide local-language strategy again for almost seventy years. Much of the resistance to linguistic and cultural localisation efforts came from institutional memory, the solidification of studio operations, and industry lore surrounding the international market. At the height of the classical Hollywood system, studio executives found different approaches for expanding and capturing a larger market share of theatrical audiences across Europe, Latin America, and Asia.

THE STUDIO SYSTEM'S HEYDAY (1930s–50s)

The 1930s mark the maturation of classical Hollywood cinema as defined by David Bordwell, Janet Staiger, and Kristin Thompson (1985). Until its eventual decline by the 1950s, distinctive industrial structures, institutional cultures, and crea-tive and economic practices characterised the studio system of this era. Basically, an oligopoly of studios dominated the American film industry – the majors (Warner Bros., MGM, Twentieth Century-Fox, Paramount, RKO) and the minors (Universal, Columbia, United Artists) – through means of cooperation and control (Schatz, 1988, pp. 9–11). While each studio vertically integrated production and distribution, only the majors, or 'Big Five', were fully integrated in the sense that they owned first-run theatre chains and directly controlled the exhibition of their films. In addition to the structure of the industry and individual institutions, a contracted labour pool powered the factory assembly-line mode of production that characterised the studio system. A studio head and handful of executives ran each studio according to a strict hierarchical decision-making process from greenlight-ing to releasing their pictures. While Warner Bros., Columbia, and Fox each had their own corporate identity or brand, the goal of these institutions was economic and creative efficiency (Schatz, 1988). As the following chapters illustrate, certain systematic structures and practices continue to this day, yet the continuation of the studio system culture and centralised decision-making process is overestimated within today's diversified media conglomerates.

Given this focus on streamlined production and economically efficient operating costs, after the MLV experiment, the studios largely reverted to wide-scale production and distribution models that conflated or combined domestic and international markets. In other words, audiences outside the North American market were treated to the same stars, genres, and stories as US-based audiences. This strategy represents the studios' larger imagined global audience with homogenous tastes and moviegoing habits. During the studio era, Thomas Guback argues, 'the foreign market did not warrant enough attention to force Hollywood to modify significantly the content of its films to suit tastes abroad, nor to induce the film companies to maintain elaborate overseas organisations' (Guback, 1969, p. 3). The dependency on markets outside the United States grew, whereas Western Europe continued to be the most important international market for circulation of English-language studio pictures over the next three decades (Guback, 1969, p. 165).

The majors' ambitions to expand into theatres worldwide were aided largely by the trade organisation the Motion Picture Association of America (MPAA; formerly the MPPDA, or Motion Picture Producers and Distributors of America, prior to 1945) and its international counterpart, the Motion Picture Association (MPA; formerly the Motion Picture Export Association of America, MPEAA). The original 1922 formation of the MPPDA/MPAA marked the 'beginning of government and industry cooperation' through self-regulated censorship and lobbying efforts (Gomery, 1986, pp. 11–12; K. Thompson, 1985, p. 94). Described as the 'little State Department', the MPEAA/MPA served as the 'watchdog' over international business activities. On behalf of its members during the studio era, the MPEAA worked to keep local film markets open and to expand studio distribution networks by fighting against screen quotas, regulations, and import barriers imposed on Hollywood films. Additionally, the trade association helped to negotiate treaties within national industries and recover frozen earnings (Guback, 1969, p. 395).[2]

One of the most direct impacts of MPPDA and MPEAA activities involved Disney's Latin American-themed films during the 1940s. Made under the Good Neighbor Policy, a goodwill cultural agreement between the US and Latin American countries, this cycle of films reflects the complex intersection of foreign-policy interests alongside the growing international ambitions of American film companies. Often described as 'Donald Duck diplomacy', films such as *Saludos Amigos* (1942) and *The Three Caballeros* (1944) featured the popular Disney character travelling and learning about Mexican, Brazilian, and Peruvian culture and history. Half travelogue and half political goodwill propaganda, the films signal a level of direct cooperation

between industry and government interests through the trade organisation operations, studio productions, and Office of the Coordinator of Inter-American Affairs'
activities (Miller and Maxwell, 2007, p. 42; Shaw and Conde, 2005).

More implicit activities or interests reflect industry, trade, and government
investment in a belief of the medium's powerful potential to impact international
audiences' ideas and tastes. This assumes a traditional Sender-Message-Channel-
Receiver communication model where the producer or sender imbeds or uploads
an intended ideological message within the media text. As an audience watches the
film or television show, the theory suggests, viewers read or interpret the intended
message as planned. Significantly, studio executives and producers imagined the
process of international reception through a passive audience; information travels
in a one-way flow with little room for feedback or opposition. According to the
audience model, the power of media rests in the hands of producers.

Studio creatives and policymakers during the classical era were not the only ones
with such a bleak view of all-powerful Hollywood. Max Horkheimer and Theodor
Adorno bemoaned the power of mass media. The Frankfurt School scholars criticised cultural industries such as Hollywood for manipulating audiences and their
view of society. In their foundational essay 'The Culture Industry: Enlightenment
as Mass Deception', Horkheimer and Adorno argue, 'no independent thinking
must be expected from the audience: the product prescribes every reaction …'
(Horkheimer and Adorno, 2006, p. 82). Since the following chapters work to complicate earlier conceptual frameworks of Hollywood and its position within local
markets, I am not advocating for such an extreme view of media reception. Instead,
I aim to show how this view of the cultural industries shaped not only industrial
practices but also academic conversations for decades to follow.

While Hollywood domestic box office hit record highs at the end of World War
II, the late 1940s brought a number of cultural and structural changes for the major
studios that would have international repercussions. Waves of suburbanisation
shifted large populations from urban centres to newly constructed, planned suburban communities. The development of cross-country highway infrastructure and
declining mass transit pushed the middle class, with its individual family car travel,
further away from film theatrical business, which had been historically concentrated
in city centres. Increased mobility, leisure time, and dispersed population impacted
theatrical attendance, which steadily declined in the post-war years. Furthermore,
after a decade-long legal battle, in May 1948 the US Supreme Court decision on
the *Paramount* case ruled against the vertically integrated majors. The case required
the Big Five to divest their theatre chains and to stop certain practices employed to
control their position in the domestic marketplace. As a result, the major studios
forcibly restructured their operations away from a vertically integrated system into
leaner financing and distribution entities (Schatz, 1993, p. 11).

Despite the Paramount Decree forcing the divestment of domestic theatrical holdings, the majors continued to acquire theatres internationally. According to Ross Melnick, MGM, Paramount, Warner Bros., and Fox owned and operated hundreds of cinemas, 'vertically integrated supply chains', across Asia, Africa, Europe, Latin America, and Australia between 1925 and 2013 (Melnick, 2015, p. 154). As individual studio strategies varied, so did regional priorities. For example, Fox acquired the largest pan-African exhibition circuit, African Consolidated Theatres, in 1956. The company consisted of 150 theatres spanning South Africa, Kenya, and colonial Zimbabwe (Southern Rhodesia) (Melnick, 2016, p. 94). Through his detailed archival work on studio international exhibition strategies, Melnick offers a more nuanced view of the majors' integrated global presence in contrast to earlier scholarly conversations. Specifically, he identifies the importance of these theatre circuits as 'cultural embassies'. In addition to reflecting the changing American geopolitical and economic priorities globally during the twentieth century, Melnick asserts that Brazilian MGM and African Fox cinemas operated locally as places 'where local moviegoers mingled amid an atmosphere of hybridized American and indigenous social conventions and theater designs' (Melnick, 2016, p. 94).

Exhibition also changed drastically during this period due to the development and adoption of television domestically. Television as a technology, business model, and viewing experience emerged during the classical Hollywood era. The first regular television broadcast had occurred in the United States by 1939, yet war efforts halted the development of the American television industry. Led by broadcast network pioneers CBS and NBC, regular prime-time programming began in 1948 (Curtin and Shattuc, 2009, p. 8). Unlike popular discourse that paints Hollywood as scrambling to compete with and react to the emergence of television, Christopher Anderson argues that the MPPDA/MPAA and its members were eager to explore investment opportunities as early as the 1930s. However, these efforts were thwarted by Federal Communications Commission (FCC) regulations in the late 1940s. As theatrical attendance declined and the studios lost their domestic exhibition holdings due to the Paramount Decree, television emerged as a new model for potential production and distribution alternatives. Since the government's oversight agency prevented the studios from buying individual stations or forming their own networks, many of the major studios began to back away from their initial interest in controlling the television market and would not actively invest in television production for another decade (Anderson, 1997). Decline in domestic theatrical attendance, suburbanisation, and the loss of theatre chains, alongside the rise of television in the home, punctuated the end of the classical studio system. The regulation of the studio oligopoly largely shaped the domestic market and led to the decline of classical Hollywood.

Not surprisingly, as their control over the American distribution network lessened to some extent, the studios looked to international audiences to expand their activities in other markets.

THE STUDIO SYSTEM'S DECLINE AND THE RISE OF CONGLOMERATES (1950s–70s)

Due to changing industry, cultural, and technological structures, by the early 1950s the studios once again began to refocus their efforts on international markets. As Guback suggests, 'the American film industry was thinking not only in terms of Denver and Boston but was considering the reaction of audiences in other parts of the world' (Guback, 1969, p. 165). During the 1950s and 1960s, international market share became a larger portion of studio business. Overseas theatrical revenue rose from 40 to 53 per cent of overall activities. While 'international operations' remained a purposefully vague area of studio business, activities included distributing and marketing the English-language studio films abroad, acquiring and releasing non-English-language films in the United States, and overseeing international co-productions and theatre circuits. As the studios expanded their activities, they also invested in hiring local personnel for key markets. Many of the studios maintained or opened offices in the largest markets outside North America, including Great Britain, Italy, Germany, France, and Japan, to help manage local operations (Balio, 1987, pp. 222–3; Guback, 1969).

A notable reimagining of production practices followed domestic market changes and an increased emphasis on capturing overseas audiences. Thomas Schatz argues the key to Warner Bros., Fox, Columbia, and the other studios' survival is due to the rise of the blockbuster (Schatz, 1993, p. 8). While this is true for the North American market, the blockbuster should also be understood as central to the increased internationalisation of production and distribution strategies. The studios' gradual reliance on large-scale, expensive blockbusters coincided with growing international co-production practices and an effort to expand overseas market share. As financial and creative alliances with local industry professionals in Europe or Latin America emerged during this period, these international co-productions typically were English-language films intended to travel globally.

Unlike the short-lived MLV practice, and later LLP strategy discussed in Chapters 3 and 4, the co-productions included one-off partnerships for developing and producing an individual film. Some of the majors also established local subsidiaries to gain access to local subsidies or avoid screen quotas. Peter Lev describes an international co-production as 'a film made by companies from two or more nations and governed by specific government to government agreements between the nations' (Lev, 2003, p. 154). In the case of European and Latin American markets, a crucial factor in studio co-production and distribution initiatives during this period involved regulations and quotas introduced as a resistant response to the American film studios. Specifically, in Europe, national industries began to develop and introduce policies to protect local film 'as a vehicle for national culture' by the 1920s (Guback, 1969, p. 17). These measures represented direct actions against Hollywood's position as a dominant distributor in many local industries. Germany introduced a 15 per cent quota on footage produced in the country, whereas the UK implemented a Quota Act requiring theatres to exhibit a minimum of 5 per cent British films (K. Thompson, 1985, p. 211). Additionally, film-makers worked to create broader regional distribution alliances, known as Film Europe, over the course of a series of congresses in the 1920s. These collective efforts to enact strong regulatory policies and regional creative networks to counter Hollywood's presence eventually fizzled out by the following decade (K. Thompson, 1985, p. 114; Higson and Maltby, 1999). All of these attempts reflected shifting local cultural policies and debates prioritising the audiovisual industry's economic and cultural value as well as the objective of chipping away at Hollywood's powerful post-World War I presence. Early protectionist measures would be followed by later regulatory efforts which represented a central part of the dynamics at work in motivating the localisation of Hollywood.

By the early 1950s, the UK, France, and Spain had introduced new protectionist laws to restrict the flow of Hollywood films into their marketplaces and foster development of local productions. As a result, the first wave of co-productions served as a reaction to these protectionist laws and primarily were filmed in Western Europe (Balio, 1987, p. 235; Guback, 1969). Called 'on-location' or 'American-interest' films, many first-wave studio co-productions capitalised on cultural sites or exotic locations, Hollywood stars, cheaper local crews, and a wide-scale blockbuster marketing campaign (Lev, 2003, p. 150). Locations ranged from the UK and Italy to the Caribbean and sub-Saharan Africa in films such as Paramount's *Roman Holiday* (1953), *To Catch a Thief* (1955), and *Funny Face* (1957); MGM's *King Solomon's Mines* (1950), *Valley of the Kings* (1954), and *Ben-Hur* (1959); United Artists' *The African Queen* (1951) and *Summertime* (1955); Fox's *The Sound of Music* (1965) and *Doctor Dolittle* (1967). Also categorised as 'runaway productions', these films mark a decentralisation of studio productions away from Los Angeles-based soundstages in the later part of the twentieth century through a gradual increase in on-location shooting (Scott, 2005). At this time, an average of 40 per cent of Hollywood productions were located and shot outside the United States (Elmer and Gasher, 2005, p. 7). There is a distinction between cultural and economic runaways. Cultural runaways reflect a historic studio practice of looking for 'realistic' on-location sites that also may lower production costs: think of John Ford shooting numerous Westerns in the Navajo Nation's Monument Valley beginning in 1939, and the splashy studio musicals of the 1950s and 1960s, most notably *The Sound of Music*

(Scott, 2005, p. 76). In contrast, the more recent strategy of the so-called economic runaway depends upon inexpensive labour costs and generous local industry incentives for cheaper productions.

By the late 1950s and 1960s, local studio subsidiaries partnered in co-producing economic runaways that could also be classified as local or 'national' films. In reality, as transnational operations merged financing, creative individuals, institutions, and resources, the lines between local, national, and Hollywood products began to blur even more. So, what were the benefits for all players involved? For example, Paramount and Fox created British subsidiaries in order to qualify for financing and to meet screen quotas. Co-producing a local film allowed the studios to circumvent frozen profits by reinvesting these funds and taking earnings out as media products instead of diminished American dollars (Guback, 1969, pp. 164–5). Runaway productions also helped cut studio production costs due to accessible, non-unionised, cheaper labour. For their local British or Spanish partners, these arrangements opened access to financing for projects and a larger integrated distribution network (Guback, 1969, p. 171). However, it is not just about political economic issues. This strategy shift suggested how creative studio management began to rethink big-budget films appealing to audiences beyond the domestic market and reshape their production practices on an international scale (Steinhart, 2013).

It should be noted that the major studios did not expand their activities in all markets, since localisation efforts depended largely on the sustainability of the market size and available production infrastructure (Guback, 1969). Much of this geographical boundary-drawing and decision-making reflected larger institutional priorities that favoured markets with strong filmgoing cultures, extensive theatrical sectors, and established production cultures and resources. As Nolwenn Mingant notes, studio international operations often classify different types of territories – mature, growing, untapped, and closed (Mingant, 2015, p. 75). As discussed throughout this book, the studios continue to develop and maintain bricks-and-mortar operations, from production to exhibition, in more stable and mature markets like Europe, and they continue to prioritise resources for growing or emerging markets in Latin America or East Asia. Setting up business operations in a local market (a more fixed and long-term strategy) follows a markedly different business logic than shooting a one-off runaway production (a temporary, short-term activity).

Furthermore, the move towards on-location operations was not an easy transition for this historically centralised and highly managed studio production culture. In an effort to move from soundstages to shooting in urban or rugged terrain, a number of productions went over budget and over schedule; they also faced harsh weather conditions and unpredictable climates. For example, Fox's infamously troubled *Cleopatra* (1963) production originally started shooting in the UK. Due to massive

Stars Elizabeth Taylor
and Richard Burton
on set of Twentieth
Century-Fox's European
co-production
Cleopatra (1963)
(BFI Stills Collection)

rain and production delays, the filming moved to Italy. Along with an on-set scandal between the two married stars (Elizabeth Taylor and Richard Burton) and the firing and hiring of directors (Rouben Mamoulian out and Joseph L. Mankiewicz in), Twentieth Century-Fox's internationalised ambitions resulted in the negative cost surpassing $40 million and in staggering theatrical losses worldwide. As characterised by Paul Monaco, '*Cleopatra* was not just a movie that had spun out of control; rather, it was emblematic of the breakdown of an entire production process that historically had been well planned, systematic, and accountable' (Monaco, 2001, p. 36). As the studio system eroded, international co-productions were an experiment in mobile production cultures to appeal to global audiences.

In a post-Paramount Decree era, the increased internationalisation of production and distribution efforts paralleled the majors' efforts to restructure their business as financing and distribution companies. Instead of a centralised film-making process controlled by the studios, the majors' role shifted gradually towards negotiating one-off deals with independent producers to financing and distributing their films. Daniel Steinhart characterises the shift from a Fordist to post-Fordist economic model as a 'flexible mode of production' (Steinhart, 2013, p. 135). By the late 1950s, runaway production practices evolved beyond a way of simply accessing block earnings or unremittable funds. In addition to investing in theatre circuits worldwide, Warner Bros., Fox, Columbia, and their peers began to create local corporate subsidiaries to access film funds and production subsidies. Many of these offices were opened in Western Europe. In his work on Paramount's European international productions during the 1950s, Steinhart illustrates the vital role of local studio offices in building infrastructure such as laboratories and equipment or employing local media managers. He identifies such co-productions as a 'transcultural activity' that blended 'language, labor, filmmaking methods, and customs' (Steinhart, 2013, p. 136).

As the studios were rethinking production practices domestically, they aimed to develop and build localised production activities, with uneven success.

The studios also began co-producing and distributing local films in Latin America. For example, Columbia Pictures had established a strong distribution presence in Brazil by 1929. During this period of international expansion, Columbia released a handful of Brazilian films locally, including the internationally acclaimed Cannes Film Festival darling *O Cangaceiro* (*The Bandit of Brazil*, 1953) (R. Johnson, 1987, p. 62). Under a new co-production policy during the tail end of Brazil's neorealist Cinema Novo movement, Columbia Pictures Brazil co-produced the historical drama *Pindorama* (1970) with locally acclaimed film-maker Arnaldo Jabor. One of the key reasons Columbia entered these projects was due to the *cota de tela* or screen quotas, which required that one local feature receive theatrical release for every eight foreign films each year (interview with Saturnino Braga, 2010). However, the co-production plan was short-lived and did not continue with the restructuring of Brazil's nationalised film enterprise in the 1970s. From a local industry perspective, these creative and financial partnerships with local Hollywood offices remained a highly contentious point among a group of critical and politically mobilised Brazilian film-makers. Namely, Cinema Novo co-founder and film-maker Nelson Pereira dos Santos criticised a company like Columbia which 'has in its hands a Brazilian Hollywood that produces films in [Hollywood's] interests, at low cost, and in the country's language, which makes them all the more efficient' (R. Johnson, 1987, p. 68). Dos Santos' condemnation of the Brazilian–Hollywood co-productions of the 1960s and 1970s assumes a process of exploitation and manipulation and reflects historical industry conversations surrounding Hollywood studios' presence in Brazil. The participation by local subsidiaries reveals these partnerships as operating within sites of contested cultural space.

On the one hand, a portion of earlier scholarship explores the economic benefits and financial risks of runaway productions. Most accounts identify the studios' early co-production wave as a reactive business strategy in response to local protectionist laws established across Europe and Latin America. On the other hand, a handful of scholars criticise Hollywood's expansion into local market activities and involvement in co-productions. In his exhaustive study of Hollywood's involvement in Western European markets between the 1940s and 1960s, Thomas Guback suggests this participation 'raises the interesting question of [an international co-production's] ability to transmit local cultural values' (Guback, 1969, p. 176). This statement echoes earlier cultural industry debates and assumes the powerful economic weight and cultural impact of Hollywood films on local industries and audiences. For Guback, these co-produced films are 'not a form of cultural exchange. In reality, they are anti-culture, the anti-thesis of human culture' (Guback, 1969, p. 199).

This extreme logic sets up an unstable binary – European national cinemas signify the authentic and valuable cultural expression, whereas Hollywood represents a calculating business devoid of art or expressing human culture.

Guback was not the only scholar bemoaning the increasingly diversified global presence of Hollywood film companies. In their reaction to Hollywood's post-World War II presence in Latin America, Chilean scholars Ariel Dorfman and Armand Mattelart described the circulation and translation of Disney cartoons and comics for Spanish-speaking audiences as cultural propaganda. Dorfman and Mattelart's provocative account, *How to Read Donald Duck*, credits Disney films and cartoons as well as the creative head Walt Disney himself as interfering with 'our common collection visions' (Dorfman and Mattelart, 2004, p. 145). They criticise the function and position of mass culture as the 'self-colonization of [man's] own imagination' (Dorfman and Mattelart, 2004, p. 149). From this perspective, Mickey and Donald are not benevolent or neutral children's characters but dangerous cultural signifiers carrying loaded ideological baggage.

For Guback, Dorfman and Mattelart, and later Miller *et al.*, the major studios represent Americanisation and carry with them Western, capitalist values that overwhelm a national media culture and identity no matter the strength of the local. In other words, this wave of Hollywood investment beyond North America is aligned with theories of cultural imperialism that emerged in international communication and media studies during the 1960s and 1970s to understand the unequal flow of images, texts, resources, and capital from the United States to the rest of the world. Characterised by a one-way flow, or the West versus the rest critique, cultural imperialism as a theoretical framework shaped scholarly and policy discussions in Europe and Latin America for decades. So many of the accounts and much of our understanding of post-classical Hollywood come from this framework. Yet where are the human agents, production and distribution cultures, and media texts within these debates? Looking at this period through an imperialist lens, focused mostly on financial repercussions or negative impact on imagined local audiences, allows little room to consider the realities of combining production cultures and creative partnerships. Due to the distribution monopoly, Hollywood capital and might are seen as absolute and all-powerful and result in what David Hesmondhalgh (2013) calls economic determinism. As the complex relationship across the production, circulation, and consumption of media texts is reduced and simplified to economic driving forces, a scholarly view of audiences outside the United States – at best passive and at worst naively innocent – unfortunately prevailed in these debates. As the following chapters outline, the financial and creative partnerships are never just a simple case of Western domination or economic might over local culture.

FIRST WAVE OF CONGLOMERATION AND NEW HOLLYWOOD (1960s–70s)

While the major studios pursued production partnerships internationally, the domestic business continued to struggle for a number of reasons. An increased reliance on expensive blockbusters reflected an unstable production climate and resulted in some box-office hits (*The Sound of Music*; *Doctor Zhivago*, 1965) and many bombs (*Doctor Dolittle*; *Hello Dolly!*, 1969). Many of these big-scale, family-friendly musicals that served as a successful formula in the 1950s resulted in massive and detrimental losses the following decade. The baby-boomer generation matured, and studio fare did not reflect changing popular tastes. With the largest moviegoing demographic ignored, much of the runaway blockbuster failures of the early 1960s represented a disconnect between static Hollywood approaches to broader general audiences and trends in American youth cultures (Balio, 1987; Schatz, 1993). The continuing decline in theatrical audiences has also been connected to suburbanisation and fragmentation, with more and more televisions being installed in the home. Along with difficult industry restructuring that led to a reliance on contracting independent producers, the 1960s witnessed the death rattle of the classical studio system.

Significantly, the move towards media conglomeration began during the studio era. Decca Records purchased a controlling stake in Universal Pictures in 1952. Due to Decca's acquisition of the film studio, major talent agency and television production company MCA bought Decca and Universal Pictures in 1962. The newly diversified MCA represented an early sign of the media conglomerates that would emerge in post-1967 New Hollywood (Kunz, 2007, p. 28; Lev, 2003, p. 22). In the midst of a major US economic recession between 1968 and 1972, the studios were reborn or, more precisely, restructured. As Tino Balio suggests, 'the American film industry entered the age of conglomerates during the Sixties' (Balio, 1987, p. 303). In contrast to the earlier classical era, where internal growth built vertically integrated companies, the conglomeration of the film studios created a 'new breed' of media corporations through mergers and acquisitions with larger parent organisations (Balio, 1987, p. 303).

The first major wave of conglomeration began in 1966 when Gulf + Western purchased Paramount Pictures for $125 million. As the editors of *Fortune* reported at the time, 'the increasing tendency of large corporations to diversify, not just horizontally (into related products), or vertically (into products of suppliers and customers) but into many different products that may be quite unrelated to these previously produced' (*Fortune* editors, 1970, p. 3). Gulf + Western, known for its manufacturing divisions, represented this new breed of corporations that, until the Paramount acquisition, did not have holdings in the media industries (Kunz, 2007, pp. 27–8). In the following years, the purchase of films studios continued:

- 1967: multiservice corporation TransAmerica bought United Artists
- 1969: financier Kirk Kerkorian acquired Metro-Goldwyn-Mayer
- 1969–72: Kinney National Services acquired and restructured Warner Bros. into Warner Communications

Why would a company like Gulf + Western, with diversified holdings from zinc to sugar, be interested in a risky global venture such as moviemaking? The studio had a range of assets including undervalued film stocks, real estate, and film libraries (Balio, 1987, p. 303). Decades worth of films were rife for television syndication, and strategically located offices and studio lots were more valuable as rental or sales properties (Monaco, 2001, pp. 32–3). Amid growing pains from a struggling production culture and internationalising business model, the studio business and holdings retained value. In addition to the financial strength and diversification of its parent companies, Paul Monaco argues, 'corporate America saved Hollywood in the late 1960s', particularly steering it through the 1969 to 1971 economic recession (Monaco, 2001, p. 39). Along with an increasing reliance on international audiences and big-budget blockbusters, the first wave of conglomeration set the studios on the path to a transformation that would unfold over the decades to come.

With changing institutional structures came shifts in the studios' production and distribution models. Thomas Schatz identifies this post-studio system period as 'New Hollywood' due to the 'renaissance' of a new generation of film-makers embracing both European and Hollywood film cultures, the introduction of the new ratings system in 1968, and the expansion of distribution windows, or ancillary markets. In particular, the 1970s saw the emergence of the high-concept film and what would become the modern blockbuster release strategy. In his account of post-classical Hollywood cinema, Justin Wyatt defines the high-concept film as a 'form of differentiated product ... [with] an emphasis on style within the films, and through an integration with marketing and merchandising' (Wyatt, 1994, p. 7). He categorises high-concept films – *Jaws* (1975), *Star Wars* (1977), and *Grease* (1978), featuring simplified stock characters and genre conventions easily adapted for marketing materials – as a significant industrial development of this period influenced the contemporary blockbuster. The high-concept blockbuster also helped to reshape the film business with record-breaking theatrical profits by the 1980s. Yet, as David Bordwell argues, the studios and independents released 200 to 500 films annually, many of which were mid-budget genre pictures; in contrast, these years saw only a handful of big-budget blockbusters (Bordwell, 2006, p. 3).

In addition to storytelling, *Jaws* contributed to the transformation of distribution release patterns and marketing strategies. Schatz identifies the film as 'ushering in an era of high-cost, high-tech, high-speed thrillers' (Schatz, 1993, p. 17). Global audiences and the changing distribution landscape due to cable television and home entertainment technology reshaped older studio blockbuster practices: saturated television marketing campaigns, wide theatrical releasing patterns, and the increased importance of opening weekend revenue (Schatz, 1993, pp. 17–19). The expansion and increased dependence on distribution windows beyond theatrical – known as ancillary markets – also characterises the New Hollywood period. First, while the three major television networks began paying more to show studio features, the majors also began co-producing more made-for-TV movies. The rise of cable and satellite television channels during the 1970s and early 1980s transformed the industry and offered another 'window' for studio films to expand audiences and revenue after the traditional theatrical run. Second, the video recorder's introduction to the consumer electronics market in the mid-1970s, and the subsequent resolution to the Betamax and VHS format wars, eventually offered the Hollywood blockbuster an extended life from VHS sale and rentals well into the following two decades (Havens and Lotz, 2012).

While studio priorities began to encompass new ancillary markets through expanded television and home entertainment strategies, the continued importance of international theatrical distribution, particularly in Western Europe, should not be underestimated. Unlike the wave of runaway productions and international co-productions of the late studio era, the high-concept films of the 1970s and into the 1980s represented a move back to big-budget, star-studded blockbusters and away from localised and culturally specific productions as the studios stabilised once again. This blockbuster mentality shaped and drove production and circulation practices into the industry's second wave of conglomeration in the 1990s.

CONCLUSION

How Hollywood evolved structurally and institutionally directly impacted its business practices and approach to domestic audiences, both of which are inextricably linked to its external approach for expanding international operations and markets. Film scholarship historically traces the evolution and transformation of the studio system into Conglomerate Hollywood paying little attention to the dependent relationship between domestic and international markets. In offering an overview of key industrial moments of transformation and the historic connectedness of North American and international business practices, this chapter argues for a transnational approach to historical media industry studies, since the contemporary prioritisation of international audiences is built upon a century-long foundation of some successful studio strategies and many failed ones. The studios' shifting approaches to international production, distribution, and exhibition prior to 1980 reveal these efforts for circulating films globally to be at times flexible and adaptable, and more often short-term and reactionary.

Two important takeaways from this chapter underline the remainder of this book. First, Hollywood, and the film business at large, always operated as a globally focused business. From the early days of the 1900s patent wars to the runaway productions of the 1950s and 1960s, the transnational circulation and exchange of film products laid the foundation for the major film studios. Without the international markets, the Hollywood studio system would never have developed a powerful global media distribution network or grown into one of the most productive and financially lucrative film industries worldwide. Second, the importance of international audiences – or increasingly specific regional markets – is cyclical. Across these various industrial phases – silent films, the coming of sound, the post-Paramount years, and the first wave of conglomeration – refocusing on Western European or Latin American markets typically signals a moment of economic, sociocultural, policy, and technological transformation within the Hollywood business model. Whether institutionally or by an individual division, the film studios scrambled to adapt to the ebb and flow of an ever-changing market. The studios opened local offices in Europe and Latin America by 1915 and began purchasing local cinemas the following decade. These early efforts should be understood not only within the context of the developing studio system but within the larger sociocultural, economic, and political factors that were reshaping these local markets in different ways, as the work of Thomas Guback, Kristin Thompson, and more recently Ross Melnick accomplishes. Furthermore, approaches to local production strategies, or the lack thereof, evolved alongside industrial shifts in technological platforms, narrative storytelling, institutional structures, financing, and labour practices. Even through the growth and decline of talkies or the cycle of international runaway productions, studios returned again and again to the strategy of production and distribution in key local markets, with varied results during the twentieth century.

As the following chapters show, the shifting nature of the major studios' participation within industries beyond the Anglophone market is largely shaped by recent industrial and institutional factors. With the second wave of conglomeration, the studios are nestled inside even more globalised, diverse, and decentralised institutions that have greatly altered their business activities and creative and management cultures. The following chapters explore the new localisation strategies for approaching European, Latin American, and, increasingly, Asian markets, which reveal how the Hollywood studios are reimagining their relationship to local audiences and their position within the transnational media industries.

NOTES

1. Whether a local industry utilises or embraces dubbing or subtitling as its central industrial practices evolved distinctively in various local markets over the next few decades. For further accounts, see, for instance, Gunilla Anderman and Jorge Diaz-Cintas' *Audiovisual Translation: Language Transfer on Screen* and Gilbert Fong's *Dubbing and Subtitling in a World Context*.
2. Chapter 6 discusses the MPA's structure and strategies since the 1990s in more detail.

3

Conglomerate Hollywood and International Operations (1980s–2016)

Sweeping economic and structural changes since the 1980s led to a 'tectonic shift' in the Hollywood film business and global media industries at large. Major transformations across industrial structures, institutional operations, technologies, and audience habits rapidly altered the way the film studios produced and circulated their products for an international market. This chapter explores three driving forces – conglomeration, convergence, and globalisation – that remade the film studios and reshaped their international operations by the twenty-first century. Waves of conglomeration and the increased importance of convergence strategies transformed media ownership structures and platforms. These larger forces also impacted media production and circulation within local territories. As the importance of the international market increased, the majors adapted their approach for localising content. The remainder of the chapter examines how studios adapt the production and circulation of English-language tentpoles and develop local-language production units worldwide. I incorporate fieldwork and interviews with trade coverage and popular press to illustrate how Hollywood studios approach international markets and changing dynamics across Latin American, European, and Asian media industries in increasingly localised and institutionally specific ways.

SECOND WAVE OF CONGLOMERATION (1980s–2000s)
A second major wave of mergers and acquisitions began with News Corp purchasing Twentieth Century-Fox in 1985. Unlike the diversified parent companies of the 1970s, News Corp's acquisition resulted in a new breed of global media giants with holdings spanning film, broadcast and satellite television, music, print, and, later, digital divisions. Known for its consumer electronics products, Sony Corporation purchased Columbia Pictures Entertainment in 1989 as Universal changed hands among four different owners – Matsushita, Seagram, General Electric, Comcast – over the following fifteen years. Significantly, by folding the studios into transnational media companies such as Australia's News Corp and Japan's Sony, and in later periods Japan's Matsushita and Canada's Seagram, international ownership and holdings transformed the scope and scale of Hollywood activities. The American film industry and popular press responded with a protectionist

backlash to what they characterised as a foreign takeover of Hollywood. For example, in reaction to Sony buying Columbia, metaphors abounded, from Japan 'picking off American jewels one by one' to stealing 'a slice of America's precious cultural legacy' (Negus, 1997, pp. 68–9; Reckard, 1992; 'Will Sony Make It in Hollywood?'). The September 1989 issue of *Newsweek* illustrates these anxieties, with the Statue of Liberty depicted wearing a kimono and titled 'Japan Invades Hollywood'. As former CEO Norio Ohga later stated in his memoir, 'the message was unmistakable: Sony was usurping the soul of America' (Ohga, 2008, p. 98). The battlegrounds were drawn between hardware and software, East and West, and Japan and the United States. As documented in earlier scholarly studies, the story of Sony's acquisition is a telling example of anxieties around globalisation and the growing pains involved in expanding a media company's international ownership and operations.[1]

Other sweeping changes followed in the mid-1990s, with the Time Warner merger and Disney's acquisition of Capital Cities/ABC Inc. (Havens and Lotz, 2012; Hesmondhalgh, 2013; Holt, 2011; Kunz, 2007). As illustrated by Table 3.1, a steady wave of conglomeration continued as every major Hollywood film studio was nestled inside larger parent companies alongside other media divisions by the 2000s. However, this wave of mergers and acquisitions did not all result in long-term or permanent unions, in the case of Universal's changing ownership or, most notably, Time Warner's high-profile demerger with AOL in 2009.

Thomas Schatz identifies the Twentieth Century-Fox purchase and subsequent merger and acquisition deals as the moment when New Hollywood morphed into Conglomerate Hollywood (Schatz, 2008). Two key trends differentiate this from earlier periods. First, the conglomeration of US-based media companies led to an increasingly consolidated industry characterised by concentration in ownership. By the 2010s, six media giants owned the vast majority of film studios, broadcast and satellite networks, radio stations, print publications, and so forth. In other words, a handful of massive media corporations produce, distribute, and control the majority

Table 3.1 Key mergers and acquisitions (1985–2013)

1985	News Corp acquires Twentieth Century-Fox Film Corp
1989	Sony Corporation acquires Columbia Pictures Entertainment
1989	Time Inc. and Warner Communications merge
1994	Viacom Inc. acquires Paramount Communications
1995	Walt Disney Pictures acquires ABC/Capital Cities
2001	Time Warner and America Online merge
2004	NBC and Vivendi Universal merge
2009	Time Warner AOL demerge
2013	Comcast acquires 100 per cent of NBC Universal

Sources: Balio, 2013; Kunz, 2007

of the American media landscape. Due to the 'international character' of these new ownership patterns, William Kunz describes the Hollywood studios as 'no longer the show ponies of diversified industrial conglomerates but rather the content pro- ducers for media conglomerates' (Kunz, 2007, p. 30; see also Holt, 2011, pp. 3, 17). The institutional and industrial restructuring into filmed entertainment divisions within parent companies coincides significantly with a refocus on international markets, as addressed in the following chapters.

Second, these industrial changes led to vertically and horizontally integrated companies able to control the production and circulation of their products across multiple platforms. Henry Jenkins characterises this moment of media convergence as 'more than a corporate brand opportunity; it represents a reconfiguration of media power and a reshaping of media aesthetics and economics' (Jenkins, 2004, p. 35). A malleable concept, convergence represents the increasingly merged, inter- connected, and interdependent nature of contemporary media industries across corporate divisions and media platforms. Increased media convergence impacted more than just how the media institutions are organised structurally: what they produce and how they circulate their content are also affected.

The Sony Corporation illustrates the larger industrial forces of conglomeration and convergence. In a 2005 *Newsweek* article, 'Sony Is Not Japan', former CEO Howard Stringer asserts: 'a hardware device is not worth anything without content' (Takayama *et al.*, 2005). Beginning as a Japanese hardware company developing audiovisual products such as Betamax, Walkman, televisions, computers, and PlayStation, Sony was fashioned into a 'total entertainment' model after trans- forming a newly acquired Columbia Pictures Entertainment into Sony Pictures Entertainment (Nathan, 1999, p. 180).[2] By the mid-2010s, the company consisted of a wide variety of subsidiaries from mobile technology, home video, and computer hardware to music and screen entertainment. Sony is the only media conglomerate whose filmed entertainment operation (Sony Pictures Entertainment) is comple- mented by consumer electronics and computing (Sony Electronics).

Sony exemplifies the contemporary industry landscape characterised by deterrito- rialisation – an increased condition of modernity characterised by displacement or delocalisation across time and space – with the increasingly flexible flow of finance, resources, labour, technology, and the media products themselves (Hardt and Negri, 2000). Sony Corporation's participation in producing a vast array of media products across multiple industries resulted in a corporate structure and culture encompass- ing everyone from electrical engineers in Tokyo to film executives in Culver City. Key divisions under the corporate umbrella include Sony Pictures Entertainment, Sony Electronics, Sony Mobile Communication, Sony Music Entertainment, Sony Interactive Entertainment, Sony Digital Audio Disc Corporation, and Sony Biotechnology. Depending on which part of the company is analysed, what sector of the media or entertainment industry is selected, and whether a group is located in Los Angeles or Tokyo, Sony signifies many different meanings for a single-media conglomerate.

However, convergence should be understood beyond issues of ownership and economic structure to include institutional, political, narrative-aesthetic, and technological factors. During the Reagan administration, specific deregulation and policy measures – such as the relaxation of the Paramount Decree in the 1980s – shifted the American political climate. These larger forces had a significant impact on major media institutions in increasingly broad, sweeping ways. Jennifer Holt differentiates these policy and regulatory changes as 'structural convergence' compared to the economic convergence characterised by waves of mergers and acquisitions (Holt, 2011, p. 3).

Franchising, transmedia, and serialised strategies reflect a move towards convergence across studio production cultures. For example, Warner Bros.' *Batman* (1989) franchise encapsulates a new industrial moment. In addition to the wide-released blockbuster strategy, *Batman* extended into multiple soundtracks, animated series, merchandise, and theme park attractions. Due to the success of the film theatrically and its various media iterations, Kimberly A. Owczarski asserts that *Batman* 'functioned as a blueprint for synergy for the newly formed Time Warner' (Owczarski, 2008, p. 101). Significantly, the film ushered in the new Time Warner conglomerate era, reflecting the franchise film practices and cross-division collaborations that would drive the studios in the following decades.

Distribution windows rapidly expanded with the introduction of hardware and software technologies, creating new ancillary markets and extending the shelf life of film titles beyond theatrical and television. Similar to the challenges posed by early television, Universal and Columbia/Sony saw VCR technology as a competing interest and initially fought the introduction of home video in the 1970s. At first, the film studios responded to home video in a way that Paul McDonald identifies as contradictory, particularly due to an effort to protect their copyright while also finding a way to control and monetise the new window (McDonald, 2007, pp. 109, 141). In addition to expanding the circulation of new film products, home entertainment facilitated the monetisation of old studio film libraries through rereleasing and repackaging the 'classics' on home video. Similar to the industrial parent companies in the 1970s, the new media conglomerates saw untapped value in film studio libraries to feed the growing home entertainment sector. Disney re-released a number of their animated films from the 'Disney Vault' to theatre and home entertainment. Along with a new cycle of animated features, many consider the successful exploitation of their older titles through video sales as a strategy that turned Disney around and set it on course to become one of the Big Six.

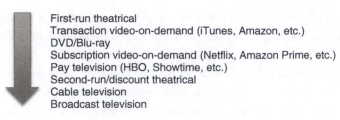

First-run theatrical
Transaction video-on-demand (iTunes, Amazon, etc.)
DVD/Blu-ray
Subscription video-on-demand (Netflix, Amazon Prime, etc.)
Pay television (HBO, Showtime, etc.)
Second-run/discount theatrical
Cable television
Broadcast television

Figure 3.1 Studio distribution windowing

Source: Drake, 2008; Havens and Lotz, 2012

The evolution of home consumer electronics – VHS, DVD, Blu-ray, and, more recently, digital streaming – rapidly transformed ancillary markets for the studios and their parent companies (Balio, 2013, p. 103). All major studios heavily invested in new distribution windows as home entertainment quickly surpassed theatrical revenue, becoming the premiere growth market from the 1980s to 2000s (Wasser, 2008, pp. 122–3). However, each transitional period from VHS to DVD to digital streaming proved challenging and brought format battles, including VHS versus Betamax and HD-DVD versus Blu-ray. As the manufacturers of the new technologies fought for studio support and alignment, the majors responded in a conflicted manner, neither rejecting nor embracing each new platform, particularly in the case of their slow integration of digital streaming (McDonald, 2007; Sebok, 2009). In turn, the expansion of distribution windows alongside conglomeration and digitisation impacted the organisation of the studios and its sibling companies, which were encouraged to develop specific strategies for integration and communication across theatrical and home entertainment divisions. Aided by the increasingly interconnected nature of the conglomerates and new consumer electronic technologies, the multi-pipeline strategy continued to expand with the introduction of new windows as the time between each continued to shrink. For example, Universal gave the sixth instalment in its globally successful franchise, *Fast and Furious 6* (2013), its widest theatrical release – 3,771 screens domestically – for a three- to four-week run, before a drastic decrease in prints exhibited (Box Office Mojo, 2015). The film then moved down different distribution channels – streaming platforms, DVD, pay channels, broadcast television, and so on – in a tightly controlled manner (Figure 3.1).

As the newly formed media conglomerates diversified divisions and distribution windows, they also began expanding international operations by the 1990s. The following section explores how one conglomerate division – Sony Pictures Entertainment – developed their international television business. Sony ventured into satellite television ownership starting in Latin America (and later experimented with production) during the post-acquisition transformative period characterised by new localisation strategies.

SONY TV AND THE LATIN AMERICAN MARKET

Sony actively began to expand international operations through its filmed entertainment divisions in the early 1990s. Shortly after the Columbia acquisition, Sony systematically invested in satellite television channels in Latin America. Significantly, expanding operations reflected massive changes sweeping the region's political, economic, technological, and cultural climate. After decades of nationally focused developmental policies, Latin America's largest nations witnessed a wave of economic liberalisation and democratisation (largely from the pressure of international institutions such as the International Monetary Fund and World Bank).[3] Brazilian, Argentine, and Mexican governments restructured and privatised state-owned communications into broadcasting, telecommunications, and film enterprises to encourage direct foreign investment. As media markets opened and currencies fluctuated, international corporations began to invest aggressively in the region through direct broadcast satellite channels.

The commercial networks CNN, TNT, and HBO International first entered the regional market in 1991, followed by Sony partnering in HBO Olé and HBO Brasil. Time Warner and Venezuela's Omnivision created HBO Olé as a subscription channel available throughout the Spanish-speaking regional market. Initially, the majority of Olé's television programming emerged from deals with Warner Bros., Twentieth Century-Fox, and Columbia TriStar, whereas only 10 per cent of its programming was produced locally (Glenn, 1991). The same year, Sony also partnered with Warner Bros., HBO, Olé Communications, and Televisão Abril (TVA) to create HBO Brasil, a Portuguese-language pay TV network modelled after the success of Olé. HBO Brasil featured movies, sports, and specials twenty-four hours a day with all programming dubbed or subtitled in Portuguese. An early objective for entering the Latin American media market was to find further distribution windows for Sony's English-language television and film content (Duarte, 2001, p. 157; Hettrick, 1994; Stilson, 1994; 'TVA, WB, SPE, etc.', 1994).

In addition to creating Sony Entertainment Television in Latin America, the company launched pay TV channels in Germany, Asia, and the Middle East as part of a larger overseas 'rebuilding strategy', fashioning themselves as a 'global content supplier' (Duarte, 2001, p. 163; Marich, 1995). Sony continued to invest in international television networks and operations such as a Hindi-language channel (1995), a joint venture in HBO Asia (1995), Kuwaiti TV (1996), and a pan-Asian action channel, AXN (1997), a brand which was later expanded across Latin America, Europe, and Asia. At the time, former SPE president and CEO Alan Levine described these strategies as 'an opportunity to leverage assets we already own – namely, our extensive library and the continuing TV and motion picture contributions to that library. We are expanding the marketplace for our own product' (Mermigas, 1995; 'Sept Launched', 1997). It represents a general, one-size-fits-all strategy for exporting American television programmes internationally.

Significantly, the nature of Sony's local investment continued to shift, with specific localisation efforts in key Latin American markets. In 1997, Columbia TriStar International Television ventured beyond broadcast outlets and into the creation of content by co-producing programmes with local producers and broadcasters in Mexico, Brazil, Argentina, and Venezuela. Co-productions ranged from importing and adapting television formats to developing original programming such as sitcoms, game shows, miniseries, and telefilms. Former senior VP and CTIT head of production recalled to *The Hollywood Reporter*, 'the company's drive into the market with local productions is in line with a worldwide move to team with local broadcasters and producers to make local language programming … as a rule, local language programs achieve better ratings than dubbed or subtitled programming' ('Columbia TriStar', 1997). Sony was one of the first filmed entertainment divisions to shift from an earlier strategy of distributing their English-language television library to actively co-producing local television shows.

The Sony executive's 'rule' about local audiences reflects a cultural proximity strategy, which suggests television is more accessible and preferable to local audiences when it incorporates familiar cultural, linguistic, industrial, and geographical elements (Sinclair, 1999; Straubhaar, 1991; 2007). Significantly, this tactic helped to reshape the company's approach to North American, Spanish-speaking audiences. Between 1997 and 2001, Sony jointly owned the North American Spanish-language network, Telemundo, in order to expand into the cultural linguistic region (Pollack, 1997). During this period, Sony financed and co-produced shows for the Spanish-language regional market.

This shift from recycling the English-language media library to co-producing original local programming was not an easy transition within a quickly growing Latin American market. Producing culturally specific media that resonates with local audiences proved to be a challenge when adapting to local industry cultures. In a conversation, one LA-based former Sony television executive described the company as making 'inroads into dramas and telenovelas, but just couldn't effectively build a business to compete with regional players – Globo in Brazil and Televisa in Mexico' (interview with Former International Executive C, 2011). Other accounts from former Sony employees echo this response and suggest the local division's earlier approach of importing programmes worked better from a sales perspective than through involvement with on-the-ground production. As the former Sony VP for Latin America insists,

> you can't go in and produce with television stations that have been doing it the same way for seventy-five years and try to impose another way. We tried and it wasn't the

right model. The right model was what we do with the game shows … we come [to the local territory], we say how it works, we consult, and they do it the way they know how to do. (interview with de Macedo, 2011)

Although for a short period Sony Television offered production services and programme-format sales to local television networks in Latin America, they quickly discovered the political, economic, and cultural problems of trying to sell a different production model to industries with strong, local institutional cultures and production practices. A former Sony VP describes tensions and a 'clash of production cultures' between Sony management and its Latin American partners (interview with Former International Executive B, 2011). According to one of the producers I spoke to, these local partners criticised Sony's production model as inefficient and not specific enough to deal with local market conditions and audiences. In turn, Sony Television scaled their production model back, returned the central business to format and exports sales, and relocated regional offices to the Spanish-language media capital, Miami.

During the 1990s and 2000s, television format sales emerged as a key business model for the international market, where local networks license the rights to make a local-language version of a show (Moran, 2011; Oren and Shahaf, 2011). Sony relied heavily on their television library to sell formats worldwide, including local remakes of *Everybody Loves Raymond* (1996–2005), *Married … with Children* (1987–97), *The Nanny* (1993–9), and *Dawson's Creek* (1998–2003). Sony was involved in the localization of their show *Breaking Bad* into the high-profile Spanish-language 'adaptación', *Metástasis* (2013). Partnering with Colombian Teleset, the show targeted the larger Spanish-speaking geolinguistic region across North America and Latin America with distribution through network Univisión and online platforms like Hulu (Blake, 2014; Hale, 2014; Ramos, 2014). Many criticised Sony's attempts to treat the largely diverse Spanish-speaking market as a singular viewing audience. This series illustrates a new period of international television co-productions, with other companies like Lionsgate and Netflix soon following. Sony's evolving multi-level approach to the Latin American market reflects Timothy Havens' argument about programmes circulating within the international marketplace. In relying on formats and co-productions, media managers are moving away from culturally universal programming for a general audience towards a cultural journey to target specifically niche regional audiences.

Sony's move into overseas television services is significant for the shifting nature of international operations towards a more localised model that began in this period. The strategy established for entering new markets was to partner with knowledgeable transnational or local entities with experience in the regional media industry, an approach that would later shape their local-language film production division. Former executive Luiz Guilherme Duarte describes the 'adaptation curve' Sony adopted to increase local market involvement, experimenting with a variety of models including locally syndicating English-language content, channel development and ownership, and local production units (Duarte, 2001, p. 78). The region served as a testing ground or early experiment for many of the company's local strategies that would be further developed throughout the 2000s and 2010s. Moreover, Sony followed a similar pattern when moving into other key markets throughout East Asia, the Middle East, and Europe in order not only to grasp a foothold in the international television business but also to experiment and lay down roots for further global ventures.

INTERNATIONAL FILM MARKET

The increased importance of international territories marks a significant shift in media production and distribution strategies in the conglomerate era. Efforts to expand globally and adapt locally are not limited to the television business. Three major trends illustrate the reorganisation of domestic and international priorities within the film market. First, as outlined in the opening chapter, industry professionals and scholars point to the shifting importance, since the 1990s, of domestic versus international theatrical box-office performance (Balio, 1998; Mingant, 2007). In a conversation, Anna Kokourina, who served as Fox International Productions' VP of Production between 2010 and 2014, suggests:

> local markets reflect development in the film world in general. If ten years ago, Hollywood box office relied on domestic [audiences], most Hollywood films now live or die by the international market. Also, industries where Hollywood films used to rule, the majority of grossers were English-language films. But many times local films are out-grossing Hollywood. (interview with Kokourina, 2013)

While Hollywood film companies earned on average more than half of their theatrical revenue from markets outside North America since the 1960s, in actuality only since the 1990s have international theatrical receipts out-earned the annual domestic box office two to one.[4] By the 2010s, the North American box office remained stagnant at $10–11 billion, while territories across Europe, Latin America, and Asia grew annually from $22.4 billion in 2011 to $27.2 billion in 2016.

Second, the focus on capturing international markets has impacted how Sony, Universal, Fox, and the other studio flagship film divisions distribute big-budget to mid-sized English-language titles worldwide. As evidenced by the rise of the New Hollywood blockbuster model in previous decades, tentpole projects continue to drive up the average production costs for studio projects. With franchise films like Fox's *Dawn of the Planet of the Apes* (2014) and Sony's *The Amazing Spider-Man 2* (2014) reporting a negative cost of $176 and $255 million, respectively, international

Studio marketing materials displayed outside a São Paulo theatre during summer 2014

markets are a key factor in the cost analysis of producing a film and anticipated prof-itability across various distribution windows (Busch and Tartaglione, 2014). For the two dozen or so English-language titles that an individual studio releases annually worldwide, executives working in international distribution as well as local country managers in each territory have become more involved in the release strategy. As one LA-based international studio executive frustratingly insists, 'It is still an issue for [studio] people to understand the international market. A lot of decisions are being made in the US … it is hard to think outside the US map' (interview with International Studio Executive A, 2014). Therefore, the heads of studio international divisions increasingly rely on their local territory managers, who advise on which release days are best or what genres are most successful in their market. According to this studio executive, his Mexico-based territory manager offers vital input on local moviegoing trends that directly shapes release strategies for individual films. For example, Sunday is the biggest filmgoing day in Mexico, whereas supernatural horror titles perform better at the box office than slasher films in Latin America.

Historically, major studio productions opened first in North America, with a struc-tured delay for international theatrical release. Only after a film's domestic theatrical performance could be assessed would international distribution be planned and a release strategy implemented in more than one hundred international markets. International day-and-date releasing patterns – where the film is released simultaneously or even days

Warner Bros.' local-ised French-language marketing in Paris for *Man of Steel*'s 2013 summer day-and-date release

before the domestic market – have become standard since the 2000s. Universal's Senior Vice President of International Distribution recounts:

> everything used to be US driven. The US [theatrical release] date was more important and everything else fell to three months' delay for international … We were never invited to the table before to decide release dates. Now the international release date is as important or more important than domestic. (interview with Ledwith, 2014)

Rising global piracy rates and increased digitisation of distribution processes directly impacted the circulation of English-language titles worldwide. As the importance of the international box office increased, studios also shifted distribution patterns to deal with increased piracy rates. Simultaneous release became a strategy to combat the leaking of unauthorised content through physical copies or streaming prior to a film's international circulation. Since traditional releasing models began first with North America and later moved into Europe, Asia, and Latin America, these delays actually created demand for unauthorised versions of studio films. The move from staggered to simultaneous distribution illustrates a key reprioritisation of theatrical markets beyond North America, but also an effort to control when and where a studio film circulates.

Localisation efforts in producing content for international territories marks the third trend. In contrast to a universally generic distribution plan for a studio film's worldwide release, international divisions have developed a more multilayered approach tailoring release strategies and the films themselves to key markets. Adapting studio production and distribution models to meet local market conditions varies across individual projects and studio operations. Widely released studio films may be localised as early as the development phase or as late as post-production. For example, changes can be made during the dubbing or subtitling post-production phase for a particular regional market (Mingant, 2011, p. 144). For the international release of the comedy *Ted* (2012), Universal localised various jokes and adapted pop culture references for major cultural linguistic markets, including Spanish, German, and French (interview with Ledwith, 2014). These changes required more resources and time to further localise dubbing or subtitling as well as test the film with local audiences prior to its release. Yet, in the case of *Ted*, the plan to localise elements of the humour for particular markets was an attempt to overcome studio lore that American comedies do not travel.

The majors at times also tailor the development, greenlighting, and production process for big-scale English-language titles to appeal to a broader, global audience. Mary Beltrán identifies Universal's *Fast and Furious* franchise (2001–) as the successful 'Latinization of a mainstream film' to target US Latino and Latin American audiences. Key casting choices – including a number of mixed-race actors of Dominican, Brazilian, and Mexican descent – as well as international location shooting in the Dominican Republic, Brazil, Spain, and the UAE contribute to constructing a 'bilingual aesthetic' and internationalising the franchise for global audiences (Beltrán, 2013, p. 77). Iterations of the *Fast and Furious* films represent the strategic effort by Universal to produce films for the growing Spanish-speaking cultural linguistic market. This series can be classified as an economic runaway due to its transnational production history dependent on tax incentives and cheaper costs. Yet the films exemplify what Nolwenn Mingant identifies as the rise of the 'global-local film' and the calculated construction of a commercial studio franchise from development to release in order to appeal to a culturally specific sector of the international market. She argues this type of film blends

> traditional Hollywood elements such as stars, action-adventure, and special effects (which it terms the strategy of the spectacular) and foreign elements such as foreign themes, locations, actors, and directors (which it terms the strategy of the familiar). (Mingant, 2011, p. 142)

This balance between universal aesthetics as spectacular and cultural specificity as familiar represents a new era of global blockbuster film-making for the studios. Franchises like Warner Bros.' *Ocean*'s trilogy (2001–7) and Disney's *Pirates of the Caribbean* films (2003–) integrate recognisable generic conventions with strategically placed international stars and locations. These films are conceived primarily for large-scale global audiences beyond North America and are expected to travel and play well in a range of diverse markets. In contrast to the widely recognisable global-local blockbuster that determines the foundational production culture, major studios also have developed and experimented with a complementary strategy for small-scale, localised productions since the 1990s: the local-language production.

LOCAL-LANGUAGE PRODUCTIONS

In a 2007 *Wall Street Journal* op-ed, then Sony Pictures Entertainment chairman and CEO Michael Lynton poses the controversial question of whether globalisation has led to an increasingly homogenous global culture and, following from that, whether Hollywood is implicated. As he celebrates the worldwide success of Sony franchises like the Sam Raimi 2000s *Spider-man* trilogy, he contends that local culture is not 'quashed' as a result. Instead, he points to a resurgence of local content and how Sony has adapted its production strategies towards developing local-language content. Lynton argues:

> these are not signs of Hollywood's homogenizing effect on the world. They are signs of the world changing the way Hollywood works. It makes sense to marry our production, marketing and distribution experience with the growing global appetite for entertainment tailor-made by and for a variety of cultures. (Lynton, 2007)

On the one hand, this op-ed illustrates how the major studios engage publicly in globalisation discourses as a way to fashion or reframe their globally prominent position and promote activities in the international marketplace. Beyond evolving strategies for selling English-language studio pictures internationally, on the other hand, this language reflects both an industry-wide and institutional strategy shift in how Sony, Fox, Warner Bros., and their peers began to approach the production and distribution of local films into the twenty-first century.

In addition to developing, marketing, and distributing the latest global blockbuster in culturally specific ways, international divisions are now co-producing, acquiring, and distributing content for locally specialised audiences. This section explores the emergence of the studio local-language production strategy, an aspect of international operations often overlooked by previous media industries scholarship. This localisation practice emerged in the 1990s and evolved on a broader industrial level through three key phases: (1) 1998–2003, (2) 2003–10, and

(3) 2010–16. Local-language projects make up a minor percentage of activities in any given territory – ranging from 10 per cent (Brazil) to over 30 per cent market share (Germany) of total films released theatrically by the majors in an individual market. Yet this practice reveals studio experimentation away from a historically universal approach to include a more localised strategy for key territory offices across Europe, Latin America, and Asia.

Local-language productions (LLPs) are a fairly recent phenomenon of cross-media and cross-company convergence during the Conglomerate Hollywood era (Balio, 1998; Schatz, 2008). Industry-wide notions of a 'biz without borders' that collapses geographical film markets circulate as media conglomerates restructure operations in local markets (Jaafar, 2009). The local-language production represents an experiment in systematic localisation across the global film market (Tartaglione, 2013). This strategy serves as a turning point in studio efforts towards local speciali-sation and global expansion beyond the Anglophone market. Sometimes successful with local audiences, and many times not, Hollywood studios partner with local producers to make local-language films in markets such as Brazil, Germany, China, or Mexico. While co-productions between Hollywood studios and local players are not a new phenomenon, as illustrated by the previous chapter, LLPs reflect a specialised market-by-market and multi-picture slate strategy characteristic of the contemporary global film industry. This current approach is particularly indica-tive of the need and capacity of studios like Sony, Fox, Warner Bros., Universal, Paramount, and Disney to explore what globalisation means for the production, circulation, and reception of media content on a more micro level.

Phase I: WB and Sony (1998–2003)

In the late 1990s, Sony and Warner Bros. launched the first industry-wide local-language strategy. One figure associated with this large-scale initiative for Sony was then SPE chairman John Calley. His period as CEO, from 1996 to 2003, is under-stood within internal corporate memory and industry trade stories as the beginning of Sony's expansive localisation efforts. Madrid-based former Sony executive Iona de Macedo credits Calley with making 'Think Globally, Act Locally' the Sony produc-tion motto and driving force for rethinking the company's international strategies during this period (interview with de Macedo, 2011). Another executive behind developing the wide-scale implementation of Sony's LLP policy was Gareth Wigan, the co-vice chairman of the Columbia TriStar Motion Picture Group from 1997 to 2008. As the head of consolidated international operations, Michael Lynton cred-its Wigan for 'almost single-handedly' building Sony's international film business and 'making him a real pioneer in our industry [since] he recognised early on the power of the global market' (Holson, 2006). Wigan oversaw local production units, greenlit projects, and worked with territory managers (Kroll, 2008).

Not surprisingly, studio involvement in these territories raised criticism from local industry professionals and government officials over whether LLPs are in fact local films or studio films from the beginning. Wigan actively worked to promote, and at times defend, Sony's new strategy. He positioned LLPs as contributing to local economies and producing genuinely local films: 'our goal is to put down roots and become part of the native talent pool and culture' (Leigh, 1999; Pflanner, 2004) He described Sony's creative partnerships through a process of collaborating rather than carpetbagging (Holson, 2006; 'Sony Pictures Creates', 2007). Significantly, the language and logic behind the LLP strategy distinguished it early on from the wide-release, global-local blockbuster model as an approach to cultivating local markets through smaller-scale creative and financial relationships. In response, international studio executives overseeing various local territory units actively defended such criticism by employing globalisation discourses and working to spin these debates. Many studio executives who, like Wigan, oversaw these production units insisted co-productions reflected not only local industry practices and conventions adopted by territory offices but studio investment in developing creative relationships. Other studios continue to employee similar counterspin. In a discussion with Warner Bros.' Richard Fox about the history of WB's strategy, he recounts:

> in the early years, we had a lot of complaints that we were trying to sneak into the back door: cultural imperialism … trying to make the stories more American or making films like we would for US audiences. But we just wanted hits in the country of origin, we don't care about the US [market for circulation]. (interview with Fox, 2013)

During the earliest phase (1998–2001), SPE established LLP operations in what it categorised as three key markets – Hong Kong, Brazil, and Germany. As Wigan argued at the time, 'This is not Hollywood coming to work in Europe … [these] are genuinely European films' (Pflanner, 2004). A local production manager led each operation – Iona de Macedo for Sony/Columbia TriStar Brazil, Andrea Willson for Columbia TriStar Germany, and Barbara Johnson in Hong Kong for Columbia Pictures Film Production Asia. Within six months of launching the German unit, SPE announced the formation of the new Hong Kong-based production company Columbia Pictures Film Production Asia (Hansen and Dunkley, 1998; 'Sony Pictures Unveils', 1998). The production unit resulted in partnership ventures with director Stephen Chow's *Kung Fu Hustle* (2004) and participation in one of Sony's most successful co-productions – *Crouching Tiger, Hidden Dragon* (2000).

Released by Sony Pictures Classics and Columbia Pictures Asia, *Crouching Tiger* grossed over $209 million worldwide and became known as the most lucrative template for LLPs due to the successful widespread release outside its cultural linguistic region. The film's co-writer and executive producer James Schamus is a long-time collaborator with the director Ang Lee. In a *New York Times* piece, Schamus outlines the challenge of transnational co-production partnerships and the disjunctive flow of financing across various institutions they involve:

> Take [*Crouching Tiger's*] financing. Working with a lead partner in Hong Kong and a co-producer in China, a Taiwanese company produced the film in conjunction with a subsidiary in the British Virgin Islands and a limited-liability corporation it created in New York. The deals were handled by our international sales and distribution company and Ang's lawyers, all based in New York – Ang lives there, too – with a bank in Paris providing the cash and a bond company in Los Angeles insuring the production. Separate rights deals were made with a number of distributors in Europe. And New York-based Sony Pictures Classics and its sister company in Hollywood, Columbia Pictures, bought the rights to the rest of the world, allowing the picture to be made. Columbia Pictures Asia, a Hong Kong-based unit of Sony Pictures Entertainment with a brief to help make Chinese-language films, was also in the mix, it being understood that all of these entities are owned by Sony, which is based in Tokyo. Needless to say, even more epic than the film's Gobi Desert fight scenes was the deal making that allowed its finances to be closed in time for production to start. (Schamus, 2000)

The movie is credited with igniting widespread 'ambitions in the world of local-language production' – the idea being that a film could circulate as a glocal blockbuster characteristic of a growing pan-Asian media market and could also perform strongly abroad on the American indie circuit (LaPorte, 2004). Yet, as evidenced by Schamus' account of the film's complexities, this transnational partnership was not reproducible; it came to be considered more an exception than the rule for LLPs. After *Crouching Tiger*, Sony focused more on single-territory productions that circulated specifically in the country of origin.

Described by one former employee as 'the trusted godfather of international', Executive VP of International Richard Fox launched and developed LLP units for Warner Bros. around the same time as Sony (Brown, 2005). Fox studied linguistics in graduate school and began in the Columbia Pictures office in New Zealand before moving to Warner Bros. Japan and later running international distribution from the Burbank office. Fox offers an insightful understanding of the way his experiences abroad shaped how he approaches local productions:

> where I started from gave me the appreciation of how important starting from the ground up is, [how this is] critical for local content or any content approach. You aren't going to do American films that appeal to the diversity of the US from Melbourne or Birmingham. (interview with Fox, 2013)

Similar to Wigan's role at Sony, Richard Fox is credited with developing and championing the studio's local-language strategy internally and externally.

In 1999, Richard Fox proposed and launched a German LLP unit in Hamburg. He recounts:

> I knew I didn't want to get caught in the plan where we do two movies and then we die on one or both of them and then the studio says, 'Hey, you can't do it.' I said the only way we are going to do this, and obviously I had to get a [financing] pool for this, is that we are going to do twenty [films] over five years. (interview Fox, 2013)

Echoed in my conversations with a number of current and former Warner Bros. international executives and local managers, Fox had to convince studio heads of committing to a long-term production strategy as opposed to supporting a few one-off films, as had been the prior industry standard for local productions. Yet a former WB executive frames the origin story differently: 'WB didn't give a shit about local production [in the 1990s]. They made a deal to build the theme park in Germany' and had to build a production office to gain access to subsidies and appease the local film governmental body (interview with Former International Executive A, 2015). While institutionally Warner Bros. initially had different priorities in Germany, Richard Fox managed and aligned the studio's needs in the 1990s in order to build an LLP unit and successful long-term strategy.

Warner Bros. continued to grow their LLP business, adopted the same twenty-picture, five-year financing package, and over the following fifteen years opened units in France, Italy, Japan, Mexico, Brazil, India, and China (interview with Fox, 2013). Several variables are considered before entering a territory and setting up a production unit: as discussed in the following chapter, available tax incentives, theatrical infrastructure, economic growth, and moviegoing trends are all factors. While each studio approaches local production in its own way, overall the LLP strategy operates on a market-by-market basis, with Sony and Warner Bros. focusing on co-producing relationships with local producers for mid-sized-territory, smaller-scale projects for limited local release. LLP budgets and theatrical releases are significantly smaller than those of English-language studio fare. According to Wigan, 'budget ceilings are determined the same way they are [in the American market] – we're looking at what the traffic can bear. If we make a movie in a territory, it has to make back its money in that territory' (Kay, 2007). This is a distinctly different strategy to the one adopted by the English-language studio pictures, which historically have relied on both the domestic and international box office. In contrast, LLPs must recoup their costs within local markets, since the films are not expected to travel (nor do most studios invest resources to distribute them internationally). Richard Fox describes the Warner Bros.' 'measured approach' towards LLPs: 'because we are an American studio, we don't overburden our infrastructure with a lot of local films. We blend it and manage them carefully' (interview with Fox, 2013). Ultimately, a studio's LLP strategy is intended for smaller-scale production and circulation within an individual territory. For example, of the 475 local films WB co-produced between 1999 and 2013, only ten films reportedly were distributed outside their territory.

Similar to Sony's management structure, Warner Bros.' local territory offices – from Hamburg to São Paulo – rely on a country manager system. As discussed in the next chapter, a managing director oversees a single territory, and each reports to Richard Fox. Local managers must balance an annual LLP slate of two to twenty films alongside distributing one to two dozen English-language films in their market. Richard Fox and his local managing directors attest to the importance of the dual strategy, particularly local-language productions for the company's culture. He contends: 'we always have to take care of the Warner [Bros.] films – "studio films". To differentiate ourselves, we are really a local production company. [LLPs] are not just a complementary or supplementary function. Now it has become a core business for us, too' (interview with Fox, 2013). Furthermore, Spain's country manager Pablo Noguerones passionately explains the LLP strategy as part of the institution's overall culture:

> For Warner Bros., local productions are very important. For a number of reasons: (1) It is a philosophy or way of working that WB has always had. We want to be players in every market that we operate. As long as there is enough room for us to be a player, because we see there are more opportunities where there is a return for us. (2) We want to be part of that community, part of that creative community. (interview with Noguerones, 2013)

Significantly, many of the LA-based executives and local managers at Sony and WB with whom I spoke saw LLP units as local companies and the co-productions as representative of local film cultures, such as in Spain, Germany, or Brazil. On the one hand, this raises the issues of how media professionals in international operations imagine themselves differently from the domestic or flagship studio divisions that produce only English-language content. On the other hand, LLPs are differentiated from tentpoles even as they open in the same local theatres or compete for the same audiences. International executives and local managers describe local-language films as ranging from complementary content to distinctive and vital instruments for expansion outside North America.

Phase II: Enter Fox and Studio Friends (2003–10)

As Warner Bros. continued to expand in the 2000s, Sony experienced various changes when restructuring their LLP operations. SPE began an aggressive second phase of growth to expand LLP operations beyond the three early production units.

In 2003, Sony launched Columbia Pictures Producciones Mexico in Mexico City after the success of their acquisition *El crimen del Padre Amaro* (*The Crime of Father Amaro*, 2002) ('Sony Launches', 2003). SPE established production operations across Spain, Italy, France, Mexico, India, Japan, and Russia as Wigan oversaw a dozen Sony LLP operations throughout Europe, Latin America, and Asia. Due to this rapid growth in local units and partnerships, trade coverage characterised Sony's LLP operations as 'the most ambitious worldwide' at the time (Hollinger, 2005; LaPorte, 2004).

As I have argued in other publications, the European LLP units – specifically Spain – illustrated the challenges faced as Sony began to reconceptualise the production model across diverse regional media markets and fluctuating economic conditions (Brannon Donoghue, 2014c). In 2003, Sony closed the Berlin-based production unit after only five years and an inconsistent co-production slate. European LLP operations were restructured and relocated to Madrid under the management of Iona de Macedo, formerly head of production in Brazil. As the LLP strategy spread further, Los Angeles-based executives tried to become more involved in daily operations. This micromanaging led to what one former Sony creative executive in Europe called a 'haphazard approach', because local producers were not given complete creative or financial control (interview with Former International Executive B, 2011). Furthermore, a former international sales executive cites this approach as a source of tension between LA-based executives and local territory managers. He criticised the company for 'trying to control [LLP units] from LA and not giving freedom to work locally' (interview with Former International Sales Executive, 2011).

By 2007, SPE began to scale back and close many of their LLP units, including Spain and China. This move signalled a geographical reimagining of Sony's LLP strategy. First, all existing LLPs units were reorganised and consolidated under a new group, International Motion Picture Production Group, with Deborah Schindler replacing Wigan as president. Within two years, Schindler had resigned – or was pushed out, as several former Sony employees intimated – and LLP operations dwindled. A number of closures followed the consolidation. That autumn, Sony closed Columbia Films Producciones Españolas in Madrid and moved the European production headquarters back to Berlin (Hopewell, 2007). This move stemmed from Germany's booming theatrical attendance and economic climate, in contrast to Spain's declining domestic theatrical market share (averaging between 10 and 13 per cent), dwindling distribution windows, and high rates of piracy (Kay, 2009). Fluctuations in local theatrical attendance and local financing possibilities across Europe led to a shift from Germany towards Spain and back to Germany within the same decade.

On the surface, Sony's LLP strategy appears flexible to the changing industrial climate regionally and locally. In speaking with former Sony local production managers, a major factor in this change was a shift in institutional priorities based on long-term localisation efforts. Some credit the executive shuffle when Calley and later Wigan left Sony, since newer management did not share the duo's wide-scale co-production vision. Former Sony VP Iona de Macedo recalls: '[Sony] had the right instincts, they went in with the right people. John [Calley] retired from that job and the vision began to shift. In the meantime, other studios were saying look what Sony did' (interview with de Macedo, 2011). While SPE successfully co-produced a handful of LLPs in each location, the common perception is that the international production unit had spread its resources and localisation efforts too fast and too far by the late 2000s.[5]

At the same time as SPE shuttered many of its LLP operations, the remaining major studios of the 'Big Six' – Paramount, Universal, Fox, Disney – launched international divisions to handle production and acquisitions for local content (Jaafar, 2009; Graser and McNary, 2010):

- 2007–11: Universal Pictures International (Christian Grass, President)
- 2007–11: Paramount Pictures International (Andrew Crupps, President)
- 2008–15: Fox International Productions (Sanford Panitch, President)
- 2010–11: Walt Disney Studios International Productions (Jason Reed, Executive Vice President)

The new Universal and Paramount divisions resulted from restructuring and breaking up their long-term international distribution joint venture, United International Pictures, in 2007. This reflects a move to a more centralised approach to international for both studios, in contrast to the twenty-four-year shared venture in which domestic and international operations were clearly separate. According to PPI's then president Andrew Crupps, speaking in a trade interview,

> the best way to capitalise on [the international marketplace] is to own and control our own theatrical distribution operations in the major markets. These operations will create increased access to local talent and help us stay on top of local trends and market movements. (Hollinger, 2007)

Compared to Sony and Warner's country manager system, Paramount and Universal relied more on regional executives located in London to oversee local production operations, with some input from territory managers.

Furthermore, UPI relied more on joint alliances with local production companies and less on a general manager choosing and overseeing potential co-productions. Instead of a general manager running an office in Russia or Brazil, division heads at the time, such as Universal's Christian Grass, and regional managers served as contacts for individual film-makers. For example, Universal developed a number of formal alliances in markets where they eventually began co-producing LLPs. Following an earlier $100 million, five-picture agreement with Guillermo del Toro, Alejandro González Iñárritu, and Alfonso Cuarón's Cha Cha Chá Producciones in Mexico, the international division established multi-picture deals with Fernando Meirelles' O2 Filmes in Brazil and Timur Bekmambetov's Bazelevs Productions in Russia (Kay, 2007).

The biggest player to emerge during this phase was Fox International Productions. Led by founder and president Sanford Panitch and a LA-based team, including VP of Production Anna Kokourina, FIP, with twenty employees worldwide, aggressively developed an LLP strategy in a dozen territories including Germany, Brazil, China, Korea, and Russia (interview with Kokourina, 2013, 2014). In contrast to Warner Bros.' decentralised, more expansive country manager system, FIP maintains a more centralised and conservative approach. WB Germany may co-produce and acquire twenty films in a particular local market, whereas Fox aims to co-produce only two to three films per year in an individual territory (interview with de la Tour, 2013). As described by Germany's former head of local production Marco Mehlitz, 'FIP is not interested in having the biggest market share but the right project' (interview with Mehlitz, 2013). This strategy towards local markets reflects Fox's institutional culture, which is both 'conservative fiscally' and tightly managed creatively.

Not unlike peer studios, two factors that drive FIP's local strategy are intellectual property rights and cultivating relationships with creative talent. Any project the studio produces locally can become a 'library title'. The company retains remake rights and increasingly remakes English-language properties or successful local productions (interview with Kokourina, 2013). For FIP and other studios, intellectual property rights constitute a major factor in producing or remaking a film locally. In other words, whether News Corp's divisions Twentieth Century Fox or Fox Searchlight retain rights to a film, FIP can obtain access for a local remake, and vice versa. Former Fox and Warner executive Clifford Werber emphasises the importance of rights in the international market: 'Delivering IP is crucial … the value outside of the local territory has less to do with distribution and more to do with remakeability. The litmus test or "farm leagues" of how to find opportunities outside the US' (interview with Werber, 2015). In fact, one of FIP's first productions was a Japanese remake of the Fox Searchlight release *Sideways* (2004), a buddy road trip story following two friends travelling through California wine country. Fox's local production unit also remade the studio's romantic comedy *Bride Wars* (2009) for the Chinese-language market (Frater, 2014). Significantly, Werber sees the English-language and local-language market not as distinctive or disconnected but as dependent on one another for content. Yet the majors do not always see the value in remaking a successful LLP for another territory. One of Fox's most successful LLPs for Brazil was *Se eu fosse você* (*If I Were You*, 2006) and its

Portuguese-language, or 'National Cinema', DVD section of a Rio de Janeiro department store. A number of these films titles are local-language co-productions with local studio offices

subsequent two sequels. Werber pitched an English remake to Fox, but the studio passed. However, he sold the rights to remake the film in five territories outside the Anglophone market.

In addition to sharing remake rights between Fox Entertainment Group divisions, FIP works to foster local relationships with creative professionals. The production unit may work with the same local film-maker on multiple projects, as they did with Tony Chan, who directed FIP's Chinese-language projects *Xin niang da zuo zhan* (*Bride Wars*, 2015), *Quan qiu re lian* (*Love in Space*, 2011), and *Chuen sing yit luen – yit lat lat* (*Hot Summer Days*, 2010). Furthermore, working with FIP may also allow a director entry into Fox's English-language operations. FIP co-produced *Miss Bala* (2011) with the Mexican Film Board (El Instituto Mexicano de Cinematografía) and the Mexican production company Canana, founded by international stars Diego Luna and Gael García Bernal (Ulaby, 2012). The Spanish-language drama follows a Tijuana beauty queen who is kidnapped by a drug cartel. Both a strikingly violent look at the twenty-first-century Mexican drug war and a breathtaking cinematic depiction of a young woman's struggle to survive, told from her point of view, the film experienced widespread critical success and local box-office success in Mexico after its premiere in the Cannes Film Festival's Un Certain Regard section (Kay,

2011a). The film's director, Gerardo Naranjo, went on to direct the pilot for the FX cable network original series *The Bridge* (2011–), another crime drama involving the murder investigation of a woman found on the Mexico/United States border. Notably, News Corps owns FX, wherein FIP was instrumental in recommending Naranjo to their sister division for the TV pilot job (interview with Kokourina, 2013; Willmore, 2012). The cross-division, cross-territory, and cross-media exchange of IP and creative relationships further emphasises FIP's centralised structure inside Fox Entertainment Group and increased dependence on convergence practices and cross-divisional management.

Phase III: Closings and Openings (2010–16)

The majors' local production units experienced sweeping changes by the early 2010s. While some studios quickly scaled back their newly launched local divisions to focus on other international priorities, others saw massive restructuring due to internal and external forces. As Fox International Productions and Warner Bros. continued to expand their production units across local territories, the industry saw a swift reversal for Paramount and Disney around 2011. As Sony scaled back LLP operations a few years earlier, the two studios shuttered their international production units within months of one another (Goodridge, 2011; Kay, 2011b; Wiseman, 2011a). While Disney froze LLP operations completely, Paramount restructured local production operations and reassigned much of the LA-based employees under a new, more centralised Paramount Pictures International division. This strategy was a striking move by both studios to close or scale back their units, given the short lifespan. Larger forces such as the global economic recession impacted international financing as well as moviegoing audiences, with some local markets experiencing a decline in box office. In the case of Disney, the filmed entertainment group reprioritised its production slate around big global tentpoles and franchises, particularly after the purchase of Marvel Studios in 2009 and Lucasfilm in 2012. Yet some in the industry understand the shift as necessary, since six studios competing in mid-sized markets for a small market share and a handful of co-production opportunities has the effect of flooding the territory with local content and producing an unsustainable model (interview with Werber, 2015).

Universal's international division underwent a rapid series of management changes over a three-year span, including the exit of Christian Grass in 2011. In 2014, Universal restructured its local production and international acquisition unit under Universal Pictures International Productions led by Peter Kujawski, previously EVP of Worldwide Acquisitions. By 2016, UPIP merged with Focus Features, the company's speciality division, and Kujawski was promoted to chairman (Kay, 2014, 2016). At first, shifts in international priorities appeared, due to changing ownership structures, such as Comcast acquiring NBC Universal and moving the focus away from local productions. These changes signalled not only the shifting nature of studio management culture but, more importantly, the increased centralisation of Universal's international production, acquisition, and sales operations under one international division of Comcast. A complex set of political, economic, cultural, and technological factors force studio executives to continually assess and reassess local-language operations on a regular basis. Often, it is not only external industry forces shaping local strategies for each studio but internal factors such as available resources, institutional mandates, and executive priorities.

In another transformative move, Sanford Panitch left FIP for a position at Sony in 2015. Under the newly created Sony Pictures International Film and Television division, he resurrected the company's LLP operations and restructured the approach to co-producing and releasing local content. This was a major blow for FIP, one of the industry's LLP leaders, yet the move signalled Sony's renewed commitment to local content by allocating new resources and hiring management (Frater, 2015). Many credit Tim Rothman, appointed as Sony Pictures Entertainment's new chairperson after Amy Pascal's forced departure in 2014 following the Sony hack. Rothman publicly emphasised the revival and restructuring of SPE's international production unit, which had waned under Pascal's period at Sony (Cieply, 2015; B. Lang and Rainey, 2015).

While decision-making varied from studio to studio, by the 2010s, the LLP model as an industry-wide strategy was in flux, with studio priorities varying widely (Hazelton, 2011). This move reinforced the reactive nature of many local studio production cultures, from closing entire units and divisions to re-establishing them a few years later. Fox and Warner Bros. both continued with lucrative LLP operations across Latin America, Europe, and Asia. By this period, many of the local-language units worked to enter the Chinese film industry. In fact, Warner Bros. reportedly announced a joint venture film company in China in 2014. The partnership between Warner China Film HG Corporation, China Film Group, and Hengdian Group aimed to produce Chinese-language film, television, and animated content (Goodridge, 2004). In May 2015, Sony Pictures announced a co-production partnership with Play Productions and the state-run China Film Co. to remake *My Best Friend's Wedding* (2016) for the Chinese market (Kay, 2015).

Due to past strict audiovisual policies, regulations, and censorship, Hollywood studios historically had a difficult time circulating English-language tentpoles as well as setting up local partnerships in the region. As Michael Curtin argued with earlier United International Pictures and Warner Bros. operations in Taiwan, the Hollywood studios have worked for decades to get a foothold in production, distribution, and exhibition in the Chinese regional market, with varying success (Curtin, 2007). China slowly opened up to foreign investment in the production and distribution of local content in the 1990s, yet the studios struggled with building long-term business foundations. For example, Warner Bros. built a theatre circuit in China beginning with a Shanghai in 2002, yet it sold the properties ten years later (Melnick, 2015, p. 167). To tap into a rapidly expanding middle-class audience, the studios were refocusing efforts in China on adapting English-language content and developing local-language partnerships by the 2010s.

The global expansion of Fox, Warner Bros., Universal, and now Sony reveals how the majors began to prioritise emerging markets (Brazil, Russia, India, China) during the later LLP period and to move away from traditional international territories (Western Europe). The drive towards geographical expansion of the LLP strategy signals that Western Europe is a stable and lucrative international film production market, and an increasingly mature one. As the European economic situation left some of the region's largest film markets (such as Spain and Italy) struggling, film studios are refocusing local production within the BRIC region, as signalled in my conversations with international production heads. The BRIC market has experienced expansion in the number of theatres, screens, and middle-class moviegoers in recent decades, leading to direct foreign investment and ventures not exclusive to the media industries. However, the unpredictable economic climates in both Russia and Brazil have made both markets less attractive and unreliable for local production in recent years, specifically as the latter faced high inflation, unemployment, and political instability in 2016. On the one hand, the studios that have remained committed (Fox and WB) or recommitted (Sony and Universal) to the LLP business reflect how shifting management and divisional structures directly impact institutional production cultures and priorities in the international market. The general health of the movie business in Western Europe and robust growth in key markets across the Global South, on the other hand, undoubtedly influenced whether individual studio units closed or expanded LLP operations.

CONCLUSION

Reflecting on Warner Bros.' mandate driving LLP operations, Richard Fox describes a larger shift in global flows and media cultures: 'the bloom of American culture is starting to go away. Maybe it is because of the local content in each of these countries. People want to see their own football teams, their own music, their own TV shows, their own movies' (interview with Fox, 2013). In dozens of interviews with international studio executives and country managers across various local territories, a central argument emerged again and again – the studios cannot ignore local audience preference for culturally specific media. Whether adapting blockbusters to a broader global-local audience or producing local-language projects for a smaller market, the majors continue to develop new strategies to participate and capitalise upon this realisation. While still a minor area of business compared to the production and circulation of English-language content worldwide, shifts in studio production and distribution cultures signal that business as usual will not suffice for international operations. Particularly in efforts to expand into emerging Global South markets, localisation strategies drive this new period of studio investment and commitment to producing and releasing local content. In turn, whether a short-lived centralised studio practice, in the case of Disney, or long-term mandate for Warner Bros., the emergence of local-language films signifies a larger transformative moment driven by simultaneous globalisation and localisation efforts in Conglomerate Hollywood.

The majors are not the only players in the LLP game. In the 2010s, a number of independents and mini-major studios have entered into co-producing films and television series for local-language markets. In 2016, Lionsgate partnered with Globalgate Entertainment and their local production partners – Belga (Benelux), Gaumont (France), Kadokawa (Japan), Lotte (Korea), Nordisk Film (Scandinavia), Televisa/Videocine (Mexico), TME (Turkey), and Tobis (Germany) (McNary, 2016). Founded by Clifford Werber, William Pfeiffer, and Paul Presurger, the company works with its partners to identify and license remakes of successful local-language productions worldwide. This transnational initiative relates to Lionsgate's partnership with Televisa – Pantelion Films. The distribution venture releases films for the Spanish-language market, including the hit international blockbuster comedy *No se aceptan devoluciones* (*Instructions Not Included*, 2013), which performed strongly in both Mexican and US theatrical releases. Furthermore, as digital platforms like Netflix moved successfully into original television programming, the company announced a slate of local series such as the Spanish-language *Narcos* (2015–) and French-language *Marseille* (2016–) (C. O'Brien, 2016; Villarreal, 2016). It is not enough for Hollywood film studios or digital content providers to circulate their content globally: companies like Lionsgate and Netflix are expanding their efforts to create and release localised media.

This chapter has illustrated, through two central transformations, how Hollywood studios began to reconsider international operations while engaging with larger concepts of globalisation, localisation, and cultural specificity. First, filmed entertainment groups were bought and restructured in waves from the 1980s on, which resulted in significant changes across company structures and cultures. Larger political, economic, technological, and industrial factors directly impacted the transformation of Conglomerate Hollywood and stimulated an investment in convergence across company divisions, media platforms, and international markets. As illustrated by the case of Sony Pictures Entertainment grappling with its newly expanded international television operations, institutional priorities began to shift and strategies were developed to reach broader regional audiences.

Second, as the film studios found themselves positioned inside larger global and more diversified media conglomerates, their approach to international markets shifted from universally global to specifically local. Sometimes a short-term reactionary approach, and other times a long-term consistent strategy, the LLP model signals a markedly different moment and philosophy for studio activities globally. In recent decades, wide experimentation in producing and circulating English-language tentpoles to partnering in local-language projects reflects variable understandings of local territories and audiences and shifting industry narratives about the international market. Most notably, how each filmed entertainment group developed and committed to an LLP strategy (or did not) complicates a macro-level, reductive view of conglomerate operations and priorities as monolithic or static. The differing histories of LLP strategies reflect how institutional cultures and priorities can vary between studios as well as inside a particular company. While larger industrial forces impact a studio's ability to finance, produce, and distribute media in a local market, this broader perspective of international operations offers a limited view that does not account for human agents or on-the-ground factors. In the following chapter, I move from an institutional and industry-wide viewpoint to how individual LLP units operate in local territories from the point of view of local managers, production directors, and their creative partners.

NOTES

1. For further discussion of Sony's Columbia acquisition, see Paul du Gay, Stuart Hall, Linda James, Hugh Mackay, and Keith Negus' seminal work, *Doing Cultural Studies: The Story of the Sony Walkman;* Keith Negus' 'The Production of Culture', in *Production of Culture/Cultures of Production;* and John Nathan's *Sony: The Private Life.*

2. In 1989, Sony Electronics purchased Columbia Pictures Entertainment, a decision that would be questioned, criticised, and eventually lauded in US industrial and academic discourse over the next decade. Widely perceived as an inflated buying price, Sony paid $3.2 billion (and later an additional $1.6 billion of the company's debt) for Columbia Pictures Entertainment. Partially owned by Coca-Cola, Columbia included Columbia Pictures, Columbia Pictures Television, TriStar Films, and Loew Theatres. Within two years of the acquisition, Sony restructured and folded the film and television divisions under the subsidiary umbrella of Sony Pictures Entertainment (SPE).

3. On a large scale, the Brazilian, Argentine, and Mexican governments turned away from previous import substitution industrialisation (ISI) measures that focused on replacing imported products with domestically produced cars, computers, agricultural goods. Instead, this move towards neoliberal reform included privatising state enterprises and encouraging international investment as a method to fix hyperinflation, increase the competitiveness of local industries, and open their economies to global markets.

4. *In Screen Traffic: Movies, Multiplexes, and Global Culture,* Charles Acland points to, in critical terms, a key turning point in industrial discourse, identifying 1993

as 'the first year that international rentals for Hollywood films exceeded domestic'. Acland criticises the 'initial claims of newness' regarding this phase of globalisation, particularly *Variety* calling this process the 'gospel for the 90s' (p. 26). He questions popular and trade publications' short-sighted celebration of global audiences, since the film scholarship of Thomas Guback, Tino Balio, and others raises 'suspicions on the industry sources' claim that the experience of the 1990s was historically unique' (p. 133).

5. For a more detailed account of Sony's shifting LLP strategy, see Courtney Brannon Donoghue's *Cinema Journal* article 'Sony and Local-Language Productions: Conglomerate Hollywood's Strategy of Flexible Localization for the Global Film Market'.

4

Local Studio Operations: Country Managers and the Local-Language Production Process

The studios' expansion of international operations and LLP units since the 1990s signals a foundational shift for their historic approach in local markets. Observing local market conditions from these broader industrial and macro-institutional changes offers a limited perspective on its own. By moving closer to how the individuals and institutions operate on the ground in local markets, particularities and complexities surrounding management cultures and production and distribution practices emerge. How an individual territory office operates provides a mid-level perspective of power, institutional cultures, and decision-making processes across the diverse divisions of global media conglomerates.

Since so little scholarly work has focused on territory offices, and since trade publications offer minimal to inconsistent coverage, much of my research involved parsing the structure of local units and determining how it reflects management activities. When approaching individual operations from Hamburg to São Paulo, I routinely asked the following questions:

- Does the studio have a territory office or a licensee in this market?
- Does the operation include a local production unit, or do they solely distribute and market English-language studio films locally?
- Does the operation integrate theatrical, television, and home entertainment teams? Or are these divisions separate?
- Where is the operation located (which city?) and where is the location of the office (where in the city?)
- What does the physical structure or office space look like? How many employees work in this operation? How does this reflect (or contradict) larger corporate culture?

Whether located in Latin America, Europe, or Asia, local territory offices for Sony, Warner Bros., Fox, and their peers have similar spatial layouts that emphasise studio branding. The corporate logo adorns desks, windows, walls, and so on. Office lobbies often feature posters or promotional materials for upcoming theatrical releases. From the reception area, you move into the main office space, where the hallways are lined with studio film posters, ranging from English-language

Entrance to the
Fox Madrid office
promoting both the
company logo and
upcoming English-
language film release

blockbusters to successful local-language releases. Cubicles divide the central
office area, where marketing, sales, and creative professionals work to release a
studio's big summer release or craft a new local production. The remainder of an
office is typically divided into conference rooms, screening rooms, and executive
offices of the managing director. A territory office exists as a vital hub for the
diverse practices and activities of a film studio operating across a variety of local
and global spaces.

Local studio management structures serve as an illustrative case study for understanding how territory offices operate and how they fit into larger institutional and
industrial dynamics. Therefore, I developed a methodological approach to address
the local studio office as a particular nexus where global and local institutional
priorities intersect. Timothy Havens, Amanda D. Lotz, and Serra Tinic suggest
scholars move beyond a political economic approach that offers only a broad view
of the media industries. Instead they argue that to understand the complexities of
individual power and institutional culture, a new perspective is required. Havens,

Lotz, and Tinic compare political economy methods to a jet-plane approach, in contrast to the 'helicopter' view they propose with critical media industry studies:

> the 'jet plane' vision offers a more expansive view, but many details are obscured. The 'helicopter' view allows us much finer detail, albeit with narrower scope. As per this metaphor, the view of industrial practices and approach to the operations of power particular to critical media industry studies informs us of the complexity and contradiction of power relations that are often obscured at jet-plane heights. (Havens, Lotz, and Tinic, 2009, p. 239)

Because the studio territory office serves as a nexus for specific local operations and broader studio cultures and strategies, it offers an ideal helicopter view of individual and institutional power relations within the contemporary media industries. By hovering in this mid-level industrial space, my approach reveals how individuals in studio management must simultaneously navigate the interactions above and dynamics below. A delicate balance emerges between adhering to transnational corporate cultures and adapting to local industry specificities; a fluid dynamic between flexibility and consistency for creative and economic decision-making.

To expand upon the historical overview of Chapter 2 and the industry-wide focus of Chapter 3, this chapter explores local studio operations from a helicopter view using a handful of studio case studies across Germany, Spain, and Brazil. Covering topics ranging from the country manager system and management cultures to directors of local production for local-language language practices, I explore how territory offices are a dynamic space where global and local business conditions, practices, and priorities intersect. My research is based on extensive fieldwork across a number of markets, and interviews with studio managing directors, directors of production, production partners, and former and current international executives based in LA. What emerges is a more complex picture of the day-to-day creative and financial dynamics of local studio units.

COUNTRY MANAGER MODEL

Local offices of Sony, Warner Bros., Paramount, and other studios have increasingly been organised in recent decades by a country manager system for mid-sized to large markets from Germany to Japan and Spain to Mexico. Entire teams located in Frankfurt, Tokyo, Madrid, or Mexico City run studio activities for an individual market and represent a microcosm of global studio operations and institutional cultures. Local units are positioned inside larger international film divisions and conglomerate cultures with expanding international activities and changing local political, economic, technological, and industrial conditions. Three central areas of each operation include: (1) theatrical distribution and marketing for

English-language studio films; (2) co-production, acquisition and/or distribution of local-language films; and (3) television rights and home entertainment sales for studio and local productions. While the following section focuses on local-language processes, this section explores the country manager system structuring local territory operations and activities of English-language content. I will outline the role of these mid-level country managers – known as managing directors (MDs) or general managers (GMs) – and how they negotiate their positions as intermediaries between local operations and studio priorities.

In their introduction to *Making Media Work*, Derek Johnson, Derek Kompare, and Avi Santo assert that 'management is an unevenly distributed but nonetheless omnipresent dimension of media work in general. Thus, management must be understood as a much wider network of cultural power, negotiated by participants at all levels in institutional hierarchies' (D. Johnson, Kompare, and Santo, 2014, p. 2). They understand management as a discursive category that shifts according to socio-historical and industrial contexts, but also one that is dispositional and tactical (D. Johnson, Kompare, and Santo, 2014, pp. 3, 10). Earlier scholarly perceptions of management often align with popular ideas of '"suits" who oppose the more productive forces of creative talent by shaping productions to meet the needs of advertisers and corporate shareholders' (D. Johnson, Kompare, and Santo, 2014, p. 2). The idea that media management are suits frames discussions of Hollywood executives, distribution pipelines, and their dominant grasp of international markets, yet reductive understandings of management break down when analysing how local offices' structures and operations actually function.

Sony and Fox do not open a local office and maintain a country manager for every territory. While a major international blockbuster like Disney/Marvel's *Avengers: Age of Ultron* (2015) or Universal's *Fast & Furious 7* (2015) will be distributed initially in sixty-five or sixty-six territories worldwide, a studio limits investing in bricks-and-mortar operations to medium-sized markets with a robust theatrical market (Tartaglione, 2015; Tartaglione and Busch, 2015). Typically, the size of the market determines the scale of a studio's local presence. For example, Warner Bros. maintains local operations and country managers in prominent mid-sized markets, including Spain, France, the UK, Germany, Italy, and Japan.

According to the managing director of Fox Spain, 'the value of the market' determines whether there is a team on the ground. He describes the biggest and most central territories – Japan, Germany, China, Brazil – as the billion-dollar markets. Additional mid-sized markets that warrant a local office include Spain, Italy, and Mexico. Smaller markets such as the Netherlands, Switzerland, and Argentina can have an operation on the ground, but it will be one that may oversee multiple territories in the region (interview with Lustau, 2013). For example, it is not uncommon for an office in Belgium to oversee the entire Benelux region (Belgium, the Netherlands, and Luxembourg). Studios do not maintain a territory office in smaller markets, but instead have licensee managers in charge of distributing studio content. A number of smaller markets across the Global South – particularly Africa and the Middle East, categorised as closed or untapped markets – may not have country managers or local operations on the ground. This reflects not only the complex interaction of filmgoing cultures, lack of infrastructure, geopolitical factors, and socio-economic conditions but also how the studios have historically desired audiences in Western Europe and only recently have begun to value economically robust parts of the Global South over others. As Nolwenn Mingant (2015) argues in her work on the decline of studio offices in the Middle East and Northern Africa, economic factors compound political and cultural conditions to determine whether a studio maintains an individual territory, regional offices, or any presence at all.

So, what is the role of manager? Many of my conversations with MDs involved an explanation of their operations' structures, day-to-day responsibilities, and communications. The country manager is a mid-level executive who oversees business operations for an individual territory and leads a team of anywhere from a dozen to more than fifty employees in the local office. Managing directors are responsible for entire theatrical activities and may supervise home media and television in their local markets, as well.

Managers and their teams – creative, sales, marketing, and accounting – release and market English-language pictures for local audiences. A theatrical strategy depends on local market conditions, since average wide-release plans, marketing practices, and release dates vary. A Fox or Warner MD will oversee and schedule the release of a dozen or more tentpole pictures annually. Often, a local unit releases two or more films per month, or on average twenty to twenty-six films per year (Buchala, 2012; interview with Noguerones, 2011, 2013). A theatrical release in a mid-sized market ranges from 200 to more than 1,100 screens and will often be integrated into a larger international day-and-date strategy. Paramount Brazil opened *Transformers: Age of Extinction* (2014) on more than 1,000 screens during the first weekend, which consisted of 40 per cent all of screens in that local market (interview with Silva, 2014).

Territory offices schedule and programme the theatrical slate of studio films supplied by Los Angeles, as well as their local acquisitions or co-productions, against other studio and local releases. For example, if Fox's new *X-Men* instalment is set for a worldwide release between 21 and 23 May, each country manager must negotiate the studio's international roll-out plan with whatever Disney or Warner Bros. are releasing that weekend in the same local territory. This requires a level of flexibility and nimbleness in case a release date is moved up. During summer 2013, most likely anticipating *The Lone Ranger*'s poor performance, Disney moved the film's worldwide release from the last week of May to August (Fleming, 2011). Since Disney had altered their slate, this change allowed more flexibility for other major studio offices in scheduling their releases locally. WB Spain's manager decided to bump up the local theatrical release in their territory for the modestly budgeted horror *The Conjuring*, reworking the film's release for a genre that historically performs well locally (interview with Noguerones, 2013). This illustrates managers balancing micro and macro decision-making to create a local release strategy on a film-by-film basis.

Managers organise and slot major releases in order to best utilise their local teams, resources, and access to local infrastructure. Often these decisions are made to best meet local conditions. Theatrical releases are timed with local holiday weekends or weekdays with higher attendance. For example, a manager may also push back the local premiere date to secure the best theatres or gain access to 3D screens. MDs in Latin America often point to the region as under-screened, therefore programming key theatres is a significant scheduling strategy. In the case of Brazil, the ratio of screens to population size is 1 to 75,000. Therefore, local studio operations must compete for prime screens in urban and suburban theatres (interview with Silva, 2014). Entire summer theatrical slates may be scheduled around access to key theatres with digital or 3D projections in Rio de Janeiro, São Paulo, and other major cities (interview with de la Tour, 2013; interview with Silva, 2014). In fact, one MD kept a giant map of Germany on his office wall using distinctively coloured pushpins to track the growth in local theatres featuring digital projectors.

Once the theatrical cut of a film is delivered to the local office, managers and their teams may have up to four or five months to develop and implement a media plan (interview with Noguerones, 2013). Whether for an English-language studio film or local production, the team constructs a localised media strategy, including print ads, television spots, trailers, and social media marketing. The level of creative control and decision-making over marketing English-language projects varies from studio to studio, as does the specificity of the campaign for the international market. For example, when Paramount launched print ads for the zombie dystopia film *World War Z* (2013), a series of posters circulated worldwide featuring the destruction of major cities from Berlin and Paris to Rio de Janeiro and Mexico City. In the instance of *World War Z*, the destruction of famous landmarks highlighted both the film's international scope and also its localised approach, as Paramount bought space for the Paris poster inside the city's Metro and positioned a Berlin poster in the middle of the bustling Wittenbergplatz.

In general, an LA-based international marketing team designs promotional materials for the English-language titles, which are later sent to the local offices. Trailers or posters may be localised to emphasise a particular actor, theme, or genre that

An example of Paramount France's ad campaign for *World War Z* (2013) in Paris

resonates with local audiences. Paramount Spain's country manager, Montse Gil, described the process of adapting marketing materials:

> depending on what position we want to give to the movie, [the international marketing team in LA] develop spots that we then localise here. We adapt them, we have a Spanish [version] and we give the tone we need for the TV spots. And the visuals we localise or tweak. (interview with Gil, 2013)

In addition to traditional print and media campaigns, local operations maintain websites and social media accounts, including Facebook and Twitter. Paramount Brazil's Twitter feed is mostly promotion for upcoming films, incorporating images that are similar to other territories with taglines translated into Portuguese.

Furthermore, MDs may oversee distribution beyond theatrical, specifically working to set up strategies and ancillary windows for home entertainment and television in their territory. Managers negotiate television rights with local networks and make deals with retailers to release physical and digital media on a film-by-film basis. In the case of shifting home entertainment habits, understanding the local market climate is key. Fluctuations in home entertainment and the steep decline in DVD sales worldwide since the mid-2000s have led local teams to adapt their strategies towards their audiences through more flexible and tailored methods. During the

Paramount Brazil's Twitter account promoting the latest instalment of their *Star Trek* franchise

early 2000s, Sony Brazil localised circulation strategies to capitalise on a large portion of the domestic market without access to first-run theatres. To expand DVD distribution of the religious-themed local-language film *Maria: Mãe do Filho de Deus* (*Maria: Mother of the Son of God*, 2003), the home entertainment division sold DVDs at grocery stores, butcher shops, and pharmacies around the country. Specifically, the head of Sony Brazil's home entertainment targeted northeastern audiences in classes C and D, part of the country's rising lower middle and working classes (Chao, 2014). Breaking DVD sales records, they sold over 300,000 units (interview with Trindade, 2010). Within the local Sony operation, this strategy was understood as a novel approach to reach rural and smaller-town audiences – as opposed to selling pricey DVDs on the shelves of major national retailers Lojas Americanas and Livraria Severo, which are accessible only to upper-middle- and upper-class audiences.

While general distribution and marketing activities do not vary drastically from studio to studio or territory to territory, conversations with MDs reveal how much individualised studio practices impact their operations. Various factors – studio divisions and institutional cultures, local market conditions, individual management experiences – ultimately shape management styles differently for Fox, Warner Bros., and peer studios. Management across a larger filmed entertainment group and relationships between divisions range from more centralised and top-down – as implied by several Disney and Paramount managers – to more flexible, as in the case of Warner Bros. Institutional culture may emphasise certain priorities over others, such as how Fox's notoriously conservative spending habits lead to fewer prints and advertising (P&A) resources or how Warner Bros.' long-term aggressive approach to local-language production allows them to invest in two to six projects per territory.

Furthermore, two or more studios may partner together in a joint venture within individual markets or multiple territories. Joint ventures are a common way for studios to share market expertise, infrastructure, management, and resources. One local managing director may oversee two different studio operations, budgets, and film slates. Most notably, Universal and Paramount formed an international joint venture known as Cinema International Corporation (CIC) in 1970 to co-distribute outside the domestic market. CIC expanded to include MGM's international operations three years later. After MGM's merger with United Artists, the joint venture was reorganised as United International Pictures (UIP). MGM departed UIP in 2001.

Due to the UIP arrangement, several local managing directors oversaw distribution for two studios. A former Paramount VP for Latin America described the UIP arrangement as difficult to manage because of the diverse film slates (interview with Peregrino, 2010). The intricacies of each institution's structures, decision-making processes, and priorities between international and local operations left the joint operation slow to adopt new strategies like local co-productions. Unlike Sony and Warner Bros.' early adoption of the local-language production model in the late 1990s, UIP was not as nimble as its competitors. Neither Paramount nor Universal ventured into developing an LLP strategy until after UIP dissolved and split fifteen mid-size territories between the two studios in 2007 (Hollinger, 2007).

The various individual personalities, industry experiences, and perspectives of local managers are all vital factors that complicate earlier assumptions about studio managers merely toeing the company line. Havens, Lotz, and Tinic emphasise the importance of institutional strategies versus individual tactics when examining corporate cultures and mid-level employees:

> institutional case studies that examine the relationships between *strategies* (here read as the larger economic goals and logics of large-scale cultural industries) and *tactics* (the ways in which cultural workers seek to negotiate, and at times perhaps subvert, the constraints imposed by institutional interests to their own purposes). (Havens, Lotz, and Tinic, 2009, p. 247)

By identifying local management style as a myriad of institutional strategies and dispositional tactics, a more nuanced picture emerges of how mid-level executives negotiate creative, financial, and individual agency in local territories and within their global companies. Beyond day-to-day logistics, a handful of patterns stretch from territory to territory and studio to studio in terms of how MDs understand their roles, offices, and positions in larger company practice. They consider themselves to be more than just suits falling into line with studio priorities. First, local managers are hired with a variety of experience and from areas of the media industries ranging across production, distribution, exhibition, consumer electronics, and retail. While one country manager in Germany started directly after college in studio marketing and gradually moved up through the management ranks, two managers in Brazil began in marketing or sales at the formerly state-run film agency Embrafilme, before being recruited by major studios in the 1980s. Two managing directors in Spain and Brazil both started in exhibition for transnational theatre chains, while a UK country manager came from the scripted programming division at a British television network. Conversations with MDs made it clear that professional experience shaped everything, even one manager's exhibition background that allowed him to easily recite box-office data and theatrical market statistics. Paramount Spain's MD Montse Gil identifies her role in distribution as selling a specific consumer product by utilising her marketing background:

> The marketing business [has] such a short period and the movie has a short lifetime. It is not like launching a different consumer product. You do a launch – short campaign, media campaign, or publicity – for two months and then it is gone ... we don't sell Paramount [as a brand]. There is not a consumer who is going to see a movie because it is a Sony movie or Paramount. That is not the brand. That qualifies that it is by the studios and there is something in that movie already – action, whatever. But the [genre] type itself is the brand. You have to come up with that product which we recreate twelve times per year. (interview with Gil, 2013)

Gil holds a PhD in marketing that shapes her approach, focusing less on particularities and structures of the media industries. Instead, she speaks more to her strengths as a manager in analysing consumer behaviour and applying communication reception theories.

Not surprisingly, there is a direct correlation between a manager's professional background and how they understand their positionality inside the media conglomerate. While some managers see themselves as film distributors with autonomy to shape their slate and the local market, others see themselves as retailers selling entertainment products. This also ranges across industry sectors and geographical boundaries. Warner Bros. Spain MD Noguerones described his position as an in-between place, 'sit[ting] somewhere between the creative side of film-makers and the exhibitors which are the retailers ... being much closer to the source, the origin of the project' (interview with Noguerones, 2013). Another manager made the distinction between the studio home office and their local operation: 'this is not an American operation, it is a Brazilian operation' (interview with Saturnino Braga, 2010). Again and again, MDs emphasised their geographical position and specialised knowledge to locate their agency and authority within the larger studios' institutional organisation.

Second, a distinct discourse emerges between international executives and local employees about the central role and value of the managing director. I often heard studio employees use terms like 'team', 'collaborative', and 'participation' to fashion institutional and industry narratives describing the relationship between local and international executives. Despite these discourses of value and knowledge being bound so tightly within traditional studio operations, a differentiation that divided domestic and international into separate divisions may be eroding. SVP of International Distribution at Universal Pictures Jack Ledwith emphasises that international executives in Universal City 'rely heavily on country managers. We are looking at things from 30,000 feet. [While] we offer direction, they know the people' (interview with Ledwith, 2014). It is this on-the-ground knowledge and fluency that characterises the country manager system, wherein local managers must operate on a scope and scale completely different to the majors' historical approach, where the international market was seen as a homogenous region. As Paramount Brazil's MD Cesar Silva suggests, 'We know what performs well and what doesn't. We know our audiences better [than the LA office].' He cites *Star Trek into Darkness* (2013) as an example, which performed well in English-language markets but was 'never a big blockbuster here in Brazil [which] is a complicated audience with sci-fi'. Silva and his team adapted, tailored, and scaled back P&A for the Brazilian release in anticipation of the film's underperformance with local audiences.

Finally, in one particularly illustrative anecdote, a country manager recounts a dinner where he asserted his value and position through local knowledge to his studio peers and supervisors:

> Many years ago, we were in one of those dinners [with the studio chairman and other MDs] playing a game … on the screen you can see castle[s] from all over the world – Morocco, Germany, Japan, China … They put up a castle and I say that is from Spain! Somebody at the table says [it is from some other place], and that somebody was an American. And I say no, it is from Spain. [Another MD tells the American executive], 'You stupid man, if a local guy tells you something is from his town, he knows!! He knows!!' It is obvious. I didn't participate in any other castles but it was one I knew! It is in *my* country. And you are going to argue with me? Are you joking? I don't argue with you about your movies or any other thing. But if it is something from my hometown, I know better. (interview with Studio Managing Director, 2013)

This quote reveals a striking example of not only how this MD understands his own locality, specialised knowledge, and value as a local manager, but also how he

Exterior signage marking the Paramount Spain territory office

asserts it to upper-level executives. What is most central about managing directors is that they typically are native-born and hired from the local market. There is an aspect of fluency – language, culture, industry – that drives the country manager system. Managers frequently identify the specificities of local audience tastes and habits, financing schemes, audiovisual policies, star systems, commercial production trends, and so on, which are differentiated from US-based studio cultures and unknown to many of their supervisors. In turn, MDs are not mere suits but specialised and localised cultural labour employing management strategies that support translocal operations.

Borrowing from Paul du Gay, Keith Negus, and others, local managing directors should be understood as both 'cultural intermediaries' and a site of intermediation; bound within an institution revealing tensions between local specificity and broader studio cultures. Du Gay and Hall suggest that cultural intermediaries perform 'the symbolic work of making products "meaningful"' (D. Johnson, Kompare, and Santo, 2014, p. 6). So, what meaning or value is being made through these various translocal processes – with the balance between the studio HQ faraway and media content, partnerships, and audiences so close to local managers? I found that their positionalities as local studio executives and tactics for illustrating the value of the local market are key for creating meaning and significance for their roles and territories in general. It benefits them to participate in these discourses about 'the importance of the local market' or 'localising content for our audiences'. MDs must be locally knowledgeable and institutionally savvy to navigate broader studio dynamics with specific individual tactics. As illustrated above, country managers must negotiate this in-betweenness directly and indirectly, making their role meaningful and aligning their professional value with studio priorities publicly, through interviews and trade coverage as well as internally through meetings, pitches, and so forth.

Overall, the country manager system reveals (1) how industry-wide narratives and strategies are changing the way studios approach and understand the international market in the conglomerate era, and (2) how MDs challenge earlier notions of media management and work through their role as active cultural intermediaries. What is significant is how the country manager system has developed and emerged from a moment of transition within studio strategies and priorities towards localisation and cultural specificity since the 1990s. Every manager I spoke with positioned and fashioned his or her role within the larger studio strategies and industry lore about the international marketplace as well as their localisation efforts and specialised knowledge. As Timothy Havens contends, this type of lore functions in the Foucauldian sense as what 'makes the world of the intermediary knowable and manageable, tilling the ground from which dominant media production practices sprout, while simultaneously sowing the seeds of dissidence and change' (Havens, 2014, p. 41). Only through their performance of local power and knowledge do country managers situate and distinguish their role as vital cultural intermediaries within the conglomerate's increasingly diverse global operations.

In addition to understanding the individual tactics of managers, occasional moments of tension emerge in these conversations between international executives' understanding (or lack of understanding) of local markets and how the local managers see themselves. I often asked MDs about the importance of cultural specificity, local knowledge, and value within the larger organisation, wherein the response often resulted in a variation of 'I wish you would tell [LA] that.' At times, there seemed to be a disconnect between the industry lore spanning the trades and general industry discourse about the value and teamwork of the country manager system and the apparent tensions that may arise between local players and their international supervisors. On the one hand, it becomes apparent how the late 1990s to early 2010s were a moment of institutional and industrial transition, with local managers sitting at the cross-sections. On the other hand, how MDs recognise their own power or symbolic value is tied directly to their knowledge of industrial and cultural specificity. The local team's knowledge and investment in a long-term LLP strategy that relies on local networks, relationships, and expertise may be difficult to quantify. In turn, this process is not necessarily something international executives can monetise easily or frame within splashy headlines and box-office discourses that drive the international market. This tension, in turn, makes the flexibility, slipperiness, and adaptability of their roles as managers to various translocal processes even more vital.

In talking to local managers, I discovered a more complicated picture than even I anticipated: their work is at once dislocated from and challenging Hollywood's traditional approach to the local market but still bound within studio products, cultures, and priorities. They must think through cultural geographies, industrial conditions, production cultures, formal/informal circulation, and changing consumption patterns. MDs serve as cultural intermediaries navigating content, culture, and strategies of the studio but also adapting business tactics to policies and trends in their local markets. This in-betweenness of the local unit is demonstrated in participation and partnerships with local-language productions – the topic of the following section.

DIRECTOR OF PRODUCTION AND LOCAL-LANGUAGE UNITS

While local studio operations dedicate a significant portion of their distribution slate and resources to releasing English-language studio titles, many MDs in mid-level markets also oversee local-language production units. The process for producing and distributing these co-productions involves a number of studio and independent players (who see their contributions and collaborations from varying perspectives) partnering on the local and international level. This section builds upon the previous chapter's industry-wide history of the LLP strategy to explore how managers and creative teams develop, greenlight, co-produce, and distribute these projects in the local marketplace as well as negotiate with studio home offices in LA. In addition to interviewing managing directors, I spoke with several local directors of production about this strategy, as well as local production companies partnering with these units. The process for developing, packaging, producing, and releasing LLPs involves the need both to follow studio-structured decision-making and to adapt to local production cultures. Since I had the opportunity to interview international executives, managing directors, local production directors, and other studio employees for Sony, Fox, and Warner Bros., I focus on three territory offices – Sony Brazil, Fox Germany, WB Spain – in order to trace this process.

The local-language film, as outlined in Chapter 3, is a strategy for co-producing and distributing content on a specialised and limited scale for a particular market. As opposed to large-scale, big-budget, English-language studio tentpoles intended

for worldwide release, country managers and their teams partner with local producers in their market – in this case Brazil, Germany, or Spain – to produce content
specifically for local audiences. The local studio units distribute an LLP theatrically
and often release it through home entertainment. LLPs are not solely owned by
the studio but are collaborative partnerships between local management and their
co-producers. Not strictly a studio film or a local independent film, an LLP exists
somewhere in between, as a translocal product shaped by various institutional
and industrial factors. Notably, the former VP of Production at Fox International
Productions highlights that local production units and films differ from massive
studio operations in that 'big operations are designed for certain things. The studios
are not as nimble as the local guys … and we have to quickly learn to adapt to stay
[in a local market].' She also adds that the typical studio infrastructure and overhead
that supports years of development and months of production and post-production
is too expensive and not sustainable for local films (interview with Kokourina,
2013). The larger filmed entertainment groups are not willing to invest in a massive
local operation, nor will the theatrical audience, which drives most LLPs, sustain
it. Local-language productions are a model drastically different in scope, scale, and
practice than the average studio English-language fare.

In general, LLPs are developed and produced quickly, usually spanning one to
two years from a script or treatment entering the local office to the distribution
of a theatrical cut.[1] The negative costs for an English-language film budget may
range from $180 to $250 million for a tentpole blockbuster to $22 to $40 million
for comedies, horror, or other genre projects. LLPs are produced with significantly
smaller budgets (Busch and Tartaglione, 2014). Budgets vary from market to market, and may be anywhere from $1 to $10 million for above-the-line costs. Yet local
Sony or Warner Bros. units will not be the sole producers or investors. In partnering
with a local production company, country managers and their teams typically enter
as minority producers and invest less than 50 per cent of a film's budget, usually
10 to 30 per cent. LLPs are limited not only in financial scope but also in terms of
how far the films will circulate. The films are distributed within the local territory,
typically nationally or some cases regionally, on an average of 200 to 400 screens
(interview with Geike, 2013; interview with Noguerones, 2013; interview with
Uriol, 2011).

LLPs allow territory units to expand their activities in the local market and
diversify and grow their annual film slate. The projects reflect topical local trends,
production cultures, and blockbuster cycles. Genre cycles, from romantic comedies
to historical dramas, may shape LLP trends in an individual territory. For example,
during the late 2000s and early 2010s, a cycle of successful religious or spiritual dramas were made in Brazil. *Chico Xavier* (2010) and *Nosso lar* (*Astral City: A Spiritual
Journey*, 2010), co-produced by Sony and acquired by Fox respectively, became two

of the highest-grossing titles in Brazilian film history. While the former was based on the life and memoirs of the nation's most famous and controversial medium, the latter was an adaptation of Xavier's novelised conversations with spirits from the 'other side'. Rooted in particular Brazilian *nordeste* (northeastern) and religious cultures, the films touched on the *espiritismo* (Spiritism) movement as well as larger aspects of regional geographic and class distinctions. This production trend bound within regional culture translated to a successful cycle of Brazilian LLPs during this period.

While the country manager oversees all local operations for English-language and local-language projects, each unit has a director of production who manages LLP activities, shepherds the script from development through final cut, and reports to the MD. A director of production's duties reflect the work of a typical studio creative executive, which include:

- reading scripts or treatments for potential projects
- meeting with local producers for project pitches
- attending committee meetings to discuss and select projects to pursue
- advising producers on script, cast, above-the-line talent, etc.
- assembling a package (cast, synopsis, director, comprehensive market numbers based on similar projects) for international executive approval and/or greenlight
- serving as liaison during production and offering 'notes' as needed
- reviewing early and final cuts and offering feedback

While the director of production manages the process, a handful of players from the local unit typically collaborate on selecting projects and offering feedback to their producing partners. One model – WB Spain – involves the managing director, director of production, marketing analyst, and sales analyst reviewing scripts and making a collective decision whether to pursue a local project (interview with Robles, 2013). For local units where theatrical, home entertainment, and television are integrated in the same operation, each of these division heads also will be in the room. This alternative model reflects Sony Brazil's structure, which involves the managing director, production director, television head, and home entertainment head reviewing and voting on projects together (interview with de Macedo, 2011).

After an LLP package is assembled, the MD sends it to the regional supervisor and/or international executive in the Los Angeles home office. For Fox International Productions, this would be the President (formerly Sanford Panitch) and VP of Productions (formerly Anna Kokourina), whereas for Warner Bros., the Executive VP of International (Richard Fox) receives it after the regional supervisor. On the one hand, greenlight approval is necessary to move forward, so there is a level of reliance on decision-making from LA. On the other hand, the review and packaging process that originates from the local level is thorough and, according to conversations with a number of production directors and MDs, will almost always guarantee approval. One director asserted that, for as long as they had held the MD position, LA had never gone against the recommendation of the 'local guys'. In fact, this was a central discourse surrounding LLPs and emerging from both the local units and the international division at the home office: local expertise is valued and recommendations are followed.

While most local units for Fox, Warner Bros., or Sony aim to co-produce at least two to three titles per year, MDs and their local teams may also acquire or pick up distribution rights for finished local productions. Through acquisition and distribution deals, the slate of local films can increase anywhere from six to twelve in order to complement the English-language slate, averaging around twenty films per year. Whether a co-production or just a pickup, a local unit develops the marketing and distribution plan. Unlike the English-language studio films that arrive with a media package that will be localised, LLPs require the creation of trailers, TV spots, print and social media campaigns, and so on, from the ground up. Managing directors and their teams often describe the process as more demanding and expensive but creatively rewarding. As opposed to marketing for English-language titles, LLP marketing is differentiated as locally grown, which begins during the development phase. The local marketing division is involved from the start with the script and typically produces a trailer and teasers as the final theatrical cut is completed (interview with Robles, 2013; interview with Winther, 2014).

As argued throughout this chapter, the way Fox, Sony, Warner Bros., and other studios approach local operations and strategies reflects different institutional cultures and priorities. A local production unit's relationship with the international division, known as the home office, varies from studio to studio and directly impacts local-language units. Significantly, a local Sony or Fox director of production, like their managing directors, must negotiate between larger institutional strategies and local tactics adapted to industrial conditions, partnerships, and production cultures. Some local directors have less oversight from LA and more autonomy than others. Fox International Productions oversees all LLP operations for the Fox Entertainment Group. According to Kokourina, FIP has twenty local production directors worldwide. While the directors are located under country managers in local territory offices, Fox notoriously has a centralised operation and strategy, with everything reporting back directly to FIP main US office.[2] Yet Fox's director of production in Germany describes the relationship as a huge team: 'Fox is different from other studios; other studios will be entirely independent from LA and operate separately. We are very close' (interview with Mehlitz, 2013). This translates to email communications, phone and in-person meetings, and a smaller production slate worldwide, managed by FIP's VP of Production and LA team. Development flows in both directions, since the FIP office in LA may propose a project to a local office or spearhead the remake of a Fox property for another market, as happened with the Chinese remake of *Bride Wars* (Shackleton, 2014).

FIP typically maintains a conservative slate with an average of two films annually in each market, whereas Warner Bros. units may have a more expansive production strategy based on the market's potential. Local WB production units across Germany, Spain, France, and Italy co-produce anywhere from two to eight films per year. While Richard Fox oversees the Warner Bros. country manager system and local production directors, these production units also reportedly have more flexibility and support than other studios. WB Spain manager Noguerones describes the process of sending an LLP package to the regional supervisor based in London before it moves on to Richard Fox's desk. He asserts, 'at the end of the day, the decision is mine. I make the final decision ... it is just the greenlight stamp of approval comes from LA' (interview with Noguerones, 2011, 2013). WB is known for an aggressive LLP strategy working to capture the largest market share of any of the major studios. Each WB managing director I spoke with proudly cited his or her unit's dominant position in LLP theatrical market share. The lack of micromanagement from LA may be a practicality, since the EVP and his team logistically cannot be deeply entrenched with every LLP in each market worldwide. But, from speaking with Richard Fox, it also appears to be part of his management style and the institutionally specific production culture for Warner Bros.

Understanding the relationship between local and international managers with respect to a studio's changing LLP strategy reveals a more complicated dynamic between studio priorities and local market conditions. A studio's LLP strategy involving both international executives in LA and local managers and directors in a territory office reveals how priorities and interests are not static. Instead, this dynamic often represents challenges for a studio's flexible localisation strategy, a concept I introduced in an earlier publication to describe how studio LLP strategies are envisioned and change over time (Brannon Donoghue, 2014c). When I first spoke with Sony Brazil in 2010, the managing director asserted the unit's creative and financial autonomy from the home office when co-producing and releasing LLPs. Rodrigo Saturnino Braga contended at the time, 'LA does not interfere [with LLPs]. They leave us alone because Brazil is complicated.' Most notably, he cited a disconnect between the extensive legal paperwork common to studio contracts and the more informal Brazilian partnership dynamics and production culture. Local Sony management and their Brazilian producing partners insinuate that the bureaucracy of studio legal and financial arrangements have to be simplified and adapted for local-language arrangements (interview with Saturnino Braga, 2010). Therefore, it is not *studio structure* or *practices* that must be locally flexible to achieve LLP arrangements, but the *production directors* and their colleagues.

In conversations spanning 2010 to 2014, shifting corporate interests and structures directly impacted Sony Brazil's methods for investing in local-language films. Director of production Eloisa Winther argues,

> nothing has changed here but [the changes are] with the home office. Sometimes they are interested in [LLPs] and sometimes they are not ... the [local unit's] interest in LLPs has not changed since the *retomada* [Brazilian rebirth of the 1990s]. But the structure of Sony's home office and process changed ... changes with executives because some know the local business and some don't. (interview with Winther, 2014)

Furthermore, it is not just the home office's priorities which impact LLP practices but also the fact that financing is directly bound by local tax incentives and box-office performance, an aspect which has become clearer in years when Sony's film slate did not perform well in Brazil. Notably, the Brazilian tax incentive introduced during the 1990s ushered in a production boom for local cinema: Article 3 allows international film companies to reinvest a portion of their taxed income back into local co-productions.

Since the late 1990s, many LLP units from Sony to Warner Bros. built their strategies on this funding mechanism. Winther makes the connection between declining box office, Article 3 funds, and LLP investment: 'When Sony's line-up is weak for international [English-language] productions, we have little generation of Article 3 and so the following year is difficult for local productions.' For many years, Sony's globally focused English-language tentpoles, such as *The Da Vinci Code* (2006) and *The Amazing Spider-Man* (2012), performed well in local theatrical releases – with average local box-office receipts totalling $18 to $30 million (Box Office Mojo, 2015). When the major studios' box-office returns in Brazil are strong, then the taxed income available through Article 3 from these films provides a more generous pool for local-language investment. In 2011, Sony's international box-office receipts dropped the distributor from second-highest-grossing studio, with 12.33 per cent of the global market share, to fifth place, with 6.73 per cent (Wiseman, 2011b). When Sony had another weak theatrical year in 2013, with underperforming films like *White House Down* (2013) and *After Earth* (2013) earning around $3 and $6 million, respectively, local-language investment in the Brazilian market was directly impacted (Box Office Mojo, 2015; Szalai, 2013).

LLPs are film co-productions with prominent independent producers and talent. When deciding on a partner, country managers and production directors typically look at the script, market conditions, and the producer's track record. MDs and their production directors emphasise the importance of a strong story concept, yet developing and maintaining long-lasting partnerships is a central part of a studio's LLP strategy. Desirable partners may mean an internationally recognised film-maker or star (Juan A. Bayona in Spain, Til Schweiger in Germany), prominent companies (X Films in Germany, Lereby Produções in Brazil), or television networks (Globo in Brazil, Telecinco in Spain). Fox Germany's Marco Mehlitz describes the local producing relationships as an 'investment' (interview with Mehlitz, 2013). A local unit may sign a formal multiple picture deal with a producer or have a more informal first-look agreement. As will be discussed in Chapter 7, WB Germany signed a multi-picture deal with director-producer-actor Til Schweiger. As noted by the diversity of a country manager's industry experience, MDs and their production directors bring a creative network of contacts to the local studio operation, which may in turn become a lucrative creative partnership for their LLP business.

Local co-productions are financial and creative collaborations. As discussed above, the local studio unit invests in a portion of the production budget and may cover P&A and distribution costs, as well. How much a studio invests varies with the market's average budget, available subsidies, and where they enter in the process (during development versus final cut). In addition to offering notes on scripts and suggestions for casting, the director of production serves as the liaison between their studio and production-company partners. As FIP's former VP Kokourina emphasises, 'I don't speak Korean or Chinese. It is easier for local producers to get notes, communicate with local executives. No translation involved and no language barrier' (interview with Kokourina, 2013, 2014). While they do not visit the set every day or watch dailies, the studio will offer feedback on a particular scene or a film's ending. According to Begoñia Robles, Warner Bros. Spain's director of production, 'we give [our producing partners] a different perspective ... we are not the producers, we are not the directors. We want to sell the film and make people go and see the film. We give them some comments that are more commercial' (interview with Robles, 2013). The issue of 'commercial viability' arises in every conversation about LLPs with studio employees, yet the concept remains a slippery, flexible one. What directors imply by 'commercial' in Germany (family films and romantic comedies with a prominent male star lead) is not the same in Brazil (ensemble comedies or television adaptations featuring Globo television stars) (interview with Winther, 2014).

Chico Xavier proved to be a massive theatrical success for Sony's Brazil unit and their partners. The production partnership on the film involved negotiations with a mix of translocal companies:

- Sony Brazil (local division of transnational media company)
- Lereby Produções (Rio-based independent production company)
- Downtown Filmes (Rio-based independent distribution company)
- Globo Filmes (Brazilian transnational media conglomerate)
- Estação da Luz (non-profit civil enterprise based in the state of Ceará)

In addition to creative and financial partnerships with independent producers, Sony and other Brazilian studio operations may partner with a local independent distributor to share P&A costs and distribution resources. A prominent producer and head of Downtown Filmes, Bruno Wainer, originally acquired the rights to the biographical source material for the film. Downtown is one of the only independent distributors in Brazil dealing solely in *cinema nacional* (Brazilian cinema). After an initial development phase, Wainer offered a *parceria* (partnership) to Sony Brazil, including investment through Article 3 and co-distribution rights. Significantly, part of the deal included an exchange of participation in one local film project for another. Downtown leveraged the *Chico Xavier* partnership for a deal based on Sony giving up their participation in the lucrative project *Meu nome não é Johnny* (*My Name Isn't Johnny*), which went on to become one of the top-grossing Brazilian films in 2008. Wainer and Downtown Filmes negotiated Sony Brazil's participation, and together they took the project to director Daniel Filho's production company, Lereby (Filho, 2010).

Prominent independent producers like Lereby or distributors like Downtown hold a position of power in the Brazilian industry. They are often involved in the most successful local releases, work with the most bankable stars and film-makers, and have relationships with local financiers and policymakers that span decades. Therefore, the relationship between local studio managers, production directors, and their partners should not be understood in simple or reductive terms – the big powerful studio versus the little local guy. Sony Brazil has a formal working relationship with Downtown, yet it reflects a more complicated scenario of how creative and financial power operates on the local level. Wainer understands the partnership as a 'mutually beneficial relationship'. Sony has financing to invest because of local tax incentives and studio resources to produce marketing materials, to conduct audience research, and to release through an expansive distribution pipeline. Within the Brazilian context, independent distributors like Downtown Filmes and Paris Filmes emerged as major players partnering, and at times competing, with Sony, Fox, and Warner Bros. for local projects. In 2012, Paris and Downtown, alongside their partners Globo Filmes (film division of Brazil's Rede Globo) and RioFilme (Rio-based private-public municipal film financier and distributor), collectively distributed six of the seven top-grossing local theatrical releases (Hopewell, 2013b).

According to Wainer, 'RioFilme has given us the power to battle the studios for the best projects ... We're a kind of local major, a powerhouse, with a long-term project for the future' (interview with Wainer, 2010). Significantly, local distributors are starting to understand their own industrial position, which in turn is becoming a strategy they leverage in working with *os majors*. As Sony Brazil's director of production argues, partnering with Downtown or other strong local distributors is a way to continue the LLP strategy during a period of weak box office when LLPs receive waning support from a particular studio. There is a level of mutual dependency. For example, Sony Brazil distributed the biopic of globally popular Brazilian author Paulo Coelho, *Não pare na pista: a melhor história de Paulo Coelho* (*Paulo Coelho's Best Story*, 2014). The biopic shows Sony Brazil moving away from their earlier strategy based on investing in production, providing P&A, and distributing the film locally. Instead, around 2014, the local unit entered a period when participation in an LLP project depended heavily on whether the producer or co-distributor could cover the P&A costs, since the international home office was less inclined to provide those resources (interview with Winther, 2014). From 2010 to 2014, Winther and her colleagues adapted a financial and creative strategy to circumvent the lack of local resources and home office support to continue participating in LLPs.

Not surprisingly, independent producers and distributors also criticise local studios and their co-production activities. A well-known Brazilian commercial producer also describes the relationship with *os majors* as 'friction with cooperation'. The friction emerges from institutional and industrial differences between studio practices and local production cultures. He asserts:

> in reality, when a major invests, they consider themselves the 'don' of the film. Here [in Brazil] they are not the 'don' but a co-producer. The 'don' of the film is the producer. Many times they are shocked ... they have [provided] 30 per cent of the film's cost, the other 70 per cent is mine. I have to give them a realisation ... That is not how it works here. This also reflects a [different] relationship of power. We are partners, we are not [Sony's] employees. I brought most of the resources, so I am a partner with you. (interview with Independent Producer A, 2010)

This quote is a significant articulation of industrial, cultural, and financial power. The producer and other prominent local players are recognising their increasingly strong position in their home market and local studio divisions' reliance on their experience, labour, and resources. Local producers and distributors gain market share, financial resources, and increased networks to share with their local studio partners, wherein these assets translate as tactics for negotiation. Furthermore, it is common for the independent production company to retain film theatrical cut with most studios. Whereas the director of production, MD, and their team will give feedback on a project, the director and his team most often have decision-making power over the final film. The majority (independent) producers versus the minority (studio) producer results in real-world financial and creative power differences.

The former president of RioFilme, the Rio de Janeiro-based major financing and distribution company, describes the challenge of partnering with local studio operations: 'they are super slow, bureaucratic, and have no autonomy. Everything goes through LA. Independent [partners] are more flexible, reliant ... more specific [when handling a local co-production]' (interview with Sá Leitão, 2013). In fact, a prominent Brazilian producer recounts how he chose to informally pitch his latest project to FIP's VP of Production during the Marché du Filme (Film Market) at the Cannes Film Festival instead of going through routine formal channels with the Brazilian MD and local unit. This producer has partnered on local-language projects in the past and found the process to be slow and cumbersome. Due to FIP's centralised decision-making process, he decided to circumvent the local studio team and go directly to the international executives in order to save time and move the project along more quickly (interview with Independent Producer B, 2013).

One Spanish producer describes partnering with a major studio as co-producer and distributor on local-language production:

> You will find excellent professionals, money, P&A investment but [the studios] are not used to creating a marketing campaign out of the blue. What they do is basically adapt the American campaigns to Spain ... So when you bring them a local film, you force them to do something they are not used to ... and they don't have the time or they don't have the patience to really think about how to milk a P&A budget. They have an industrial [sized] big-scale marketing campaigns. They do genre ... they are used to selling very identifiable product. (interview with Uriol, 2011)

The producer explained how even local studio strategies and production cultures are incompatible with the creative flexibility needed for producing independent projects and marketing films to a more specialised audience. He argued LLPs are still bound by large-scale investment logic and marketing formulaic genres.

On the one hand, the local-language process still relies heavily on studio decision-making culture, commercial logic, and studio priorities as part of a push to expand international operations. On the other hand, the LLP landscape is firmly grounded in and shaped by local market conditions, studio employees, and independent partners. The director of production's role illustrates how the development to distribution process is mostly locally managed and controlled. Beyond studio mandates and priorities, individual experience, taste, and industry practices factor heavily into a local unit's involvement. One director of production discussed her role in shepherding a local franchise from production to release: 'it is true if you don't live in a place where the film is going to be made, you might not understand what is really local. I don't like this franchise but I understand why people do' (interview with Robles, 2013). How a managing director understands his or her own role as a studio employee and creative professional in the local industry demonstrates what Timothy Havens and Amanda D. Lotz describe as circumscribed agency, where 'executives work within routines, expectations, and environment that allow them agency that is not unfettered ... but which remains meaningful nonetheless' (Havens and Lotz,

2012, p. 136). The development and greenlighting process does not reflect top-down decision-making, with the studio international executives dictating to local executives. Instead, local directors of production understand, articulate, and exercise this agency in visible ways and must negotiate the wider studio LLP strategy with their local producing partners and changing market conditions.

CONCLUSION

While local-language production is an industry-wide strategy, it is by no means standardised or homogenous. Instead, LLP practices and processes vary widely from studio to studio, unit to unit, and market to market. So much of this variation is bound within institutional culture, whether LLPs are a priority for expanding international operations or merely a small-scale practice in a few mid-sized markets. How a local co-production is managed and circulated involves a number factors – not least, local market conditions, trends, and policies. Partnerships with independent producers, finally, are a vital factor in local-language production and these relationships reveal the complicated layers of local management cultures and media work. As illustrated in various conversations with studio executives and their partners, financial and creative power operates through fluid and multifaceted channels that are not top-down, nor solely studio driven. A local production operation may have a strong foothold in an individual market one year but as local conditions change and studio priorities shift, they may be at a disadvantage and rely even more on their powerful local producing partners. When working with local studio units, production and distribution partners often articulate their position and also leverage projects, networks, and resources to their advantage.

Local studio offices offer a unique perspective on the diversified operations of filmed entertainment groups during the Conglomerate Hollywood era. Primarily, managing directors must market and release studio content from English-language to local-language for audiences in their territories. Managing directors function as cultural intermediaries between the international studio and local market. They must balance and negotiate their own experiences and management cultures with institutional structures and industrial conditions. Most revealing is how these mid-level executives understand their value and make meaning of this in-between position, how these studio mid-level employees leverage and negotiate their positions within the local industry and overall studio structure. MDs are not merely suits or company women or men, but remarkable examples of corporate media workers performing value and circulating industry lore, which is subtle and relies heavily on access to localised knowledge and cultural specificity.

Beyond distribution and marketing of English-language content, the local-language production process reflects how many individuals and institutions are involved in development, greenlighting, co-production, and distribution. Whether by studio strategy or co-production practice, a variety of players with vastly different experiences and priorities work to develop and circulate these translocal products for increasingly localised audiences. The local director of production maintains a specific role shepherding new projects across local decision-making, studio channels, and partnerships. Since most of the process occurs on the local level, production directors maintain a level of circumscribed agency from studio oversight for creative decision-making. Yet, as minority partners, studios must also give way to their independent partners, who often maintain prominent and powerful positions in the local industries. In conclusion, territory offices and local-language productions reveal a view of local operations and management culture that relies on negotiation, collaboration, and changing localisation practices that vary across studios and local markets.

NOTES

1. The average speed of developing and producing LLPs is an issue for a few managing directors and production partners. As compared to studio prestige pictures, which can benefit from development deals and may be in development for years before going into production, the LLP process allows for less time to workshop and develop the script before principal photography starts. According to one MD, a few of their film projects would have benefited from more time in script development but lacked the financial resources to do so.

2. My experience communicating with FIP professionals confirmed the existence of more centralised and tightly managed operations and communications. In fact, after numerous conversations with FIP, I asked to be placed in contact with the Brazilian managing director and director of local production. The LA operation responded by letting me know they would be happy to answer any questions about the Brazilian market and strategy.

5

International Media Hubs: Studio Production Cultures and Local Infrastructure

The central focus of this chapter emerged from fieldwork observations gathered from visits to over a dozen studio offices across five territories. I realised, despite the common production strategies and distribution patterns outlined earlier, how territory operations are at once physically distinct from their home offices and also structurally similar across these various local markets. Unlike the splashy, expansive, and iconic division headquarters located in the Los Angeles area, local territory offices often house production and distribution operations on streamlined floors of multistorey office buildings in a major city's business or corporate sector, where they operate discreetly with little to no signage marking a studio's presence. The everyday operational ordinariness tucked away in business parks or nondescript high-rise buildings symbolises international studio operations' invisibility, or at least their historically decentralised position. As implied by many country managers I spoke with, these territory offices are a distant, if not misunderstood and overshadowed, member of the Hollywood studio family tree. Unlike the iconic gates of Paramount Studios or Sony Pictures in California, local studio offices are not featured in any tourist guidebooks or captured in popular cultural memory. These local unit operations and activities exist largely beyond their bricks-and-mortar offices and are integrated into local industries in increasingly complicated and expansive ways. While previous chapters considered the question of what these local operations do, I now pose a different set of questions: what is the operational footprint of local studio operations, and how do they intersect with international media networks and the industry centres in which they are located? How can we map and understand a studio's physical and geographical presence on the local level, from long-term infrastructure development to short-term co-production strategies, and what does that entail?

Building upon the discussion of how the country manager system and local production units operate internally, this chapter examines the complex dynamics of Hollywood production sites, offices, and business operations navigating particular industry spaces/places. An important aspect of Hollywood's presence and positionality within local media centres is a reliance on specific locational factors, everything from the material to the symbolic resources available. The majors locate these units strategically in cities that serve as sites of transnational flow for international commerce, finance, technology, tourism, promotional activities, and labour as well as established creative and artistic centres. Often, studio infrastructure and activities help to support, and can be dependent upon, local industries by contributing to this flow. I expand upon scholarly debates surrounding international media hubs as merely temporary sites for runaway productions. Instead, how do Hollywood production activities intersect local media sectors as part of a larger industry network of global production and circulation?

After outlining previous theoretical discussions regarding Hollywood international operations in major media centres, from runaway productions to media capitals, the first section briefly explores efforts to transform Rio de Janeiro into an international production centre alongside recent Hollywood production activities. The remaining sections explore specific studio business activities through two distinct locational studies: (1) Germany's regionalised media sectors, growing support services including the VFX industry, and major studio participation in English-language and local-language co-productions; and (2) Warner Bros. UK Leavesden Studios, and 'The Making of *Harry Potter*' experience. It is in analysing the specific industrial, political, economic, and cultural contexts that Hollywood's international production activities emerge as simultaneously globally focused across a network of media hubs and locally adapted for individual markets. Overall, this chapter examines the physical presence, or geographical footprint, of local studio operations and how they intersect with evolving media industry centres.

INTERNATIONAL MEDIA HUBS

Global media and communication studies in recent decades has explored the way post-Fordist decentralisation has led to a global media economy characterised by flexible labour and mobile operations (Appadurai, 1990; Hoskins, McFadyen, and Finn, 1997; Miller *et al.*, 2005; Mosco, 1996; Wasko and Erickson, 2008; Goldsmith, O'Regan, and Ward, 2010). A central conversation regarding Hollywood's globalised operations involves runaway productions. As discussed in Chapter 2, economic and creative runaways emerged as a key strategy during an unstable period of the mid-twentieth-century studio system. The latest wave of international productions since the 1990s represents the deterritorialisation of a particular sector of studio production processes and company operations in the conglomerate era, and the global economy at large. Whereas the factory assembly-line bound and centralised the studio business historically to Los Angeles in the twentieth century, the rapid expansion of film projects geographically in scope and scale during the late capitalist era represents a distinct period of increasingly 'globally dispersed production' practices in the twenty-first century (Goldsmith and O'Regan, 2005, pp. 19–20). A recent shift occurred between Hollywood's presence in local territories and the emergence of a network of media clusters with specialised infrastructure, professionals, financing, and resources.

Earlier scholarly accounts trace decentralised production cultures, or the mobility of runaway productions, and a reliance on deterritorialised operations to larger global political economic forces (Goldsmith and O'Regan, 2005; Miller *et al.*, 2005; Wasko and Erickson, 2008). Toby Miller identifies the New International Division of Cultural Labour as a form of flexible specialisation resulting in temporary, exploitative labour practices for local industry workers driven by neoliberal policies. In other words, Miller and his *Global Hollywood 2* co-authors argue that Hollywood outsourcing negatively and disproportionately impacts local professionals and the media industries at large. Whether framing these creative and financial collaborations as 'runaway productions' or 'cross-border cultural production', media studies scholars continue to debate the cultural, political, and economic impacts of these projects through exchanges of dominance, dependence, or exploitation (Elmer and Gasher, 2005; Miller *et al.*, 2005; Wasko and Erickson, 2008).

Many of Hollywood's activities in the international marketplace are understood through individual projects or co-productions that are temporary and impermanent. Local co-productions, especially involving Hollywood studio divisions, may be understood as capitalising from unstable local conditions ranging from fluctuations in currency and attractive incentive systems to shifting labour and technological services. Yet this scholarly conversation does not address the material and symbolic infrastructure and increasingly complex relationships of Hollywood studios with local industry networks, instead focusing more on the short-term activities or temporary, mobile nature of film co-productions. In moving beyond sites of temporary production and short-term objectives of the English-language blockbuster as primary activity, how can we understand long-term studio presence in local industries, particularly in a moment when the prioritisation of international markets has led Hollywood to become increasingly dependent upon and integrated within these media centres? How do we understand the dynamic of Hollywood studios operating inside these local industry clusters?

Whether in Tokyo, Berlin, Rio de Janeiro, or London, the local business operations that Hollywood establishes strategically in major cities serve not only as centres for national and regional media industries but spaces that operate as part of a larger network of international media hubs. These urban cosmopolitan cities function as clusters, or sites of concentrated business, linked not only by competition but also by 'commonalities and complementaries' (Porter, 2000, p. 16). The transnational concentration of media professionals, capital, technology, and culture contribute to these spaces/places operating as multilayered sites of media production, circulation, and consumption. Historically, Hollywood studios had established offices in London, Paris, Tokyo, and Rio de Janeiro by the early twentieth century in order to distribute English-language films; later, they were sites from which to launch regional theatre circuits. International operations slowly evolved alongside significant geopolitical and economic shifts since the 1980s – namely, larger forces of globalisation and localisation. The studio's presence in local markets – whether understood as a core or peripheral part of their business – came to reflect the complex flow of global cultural goods and finance at the turn of the twenty-first century.

Beyond traditional media hubs, new opportunities also have come from emerging markets across the Global South, particularly as complex flows of media increasingly include reverse and lateral exchanges. The diversification of media technologies and delivery platforms – cable, satellite, home entertainment, online – has allowed for the expansion of peripheral media centres in recent decades (Curtin, 2011; Thussu, 2007). From the development of India's Hindi film industry into the Bollywood powerhouse based in Mumbai, to the slow opening and relaxation of state-run Chinese film policies to increased direct foreign investment, Hollywood operations and partnerships migrated alongside the state of shifting global media capital(s).

Yet Hollywood cannot, or chooses not to, operate in all media hubs, whether because geopolitical upheaval bars studios from the historical Arab media centre of Cairo or how the commercially prolific Nigerian film industry, Nollywood, exists separately from Global North industrial structures. Both of those regional media centres operate on a global level – Nollywood's video films appear in the UK and South Asian markets, and Arab satellite networks extend into North America and Europe. Media content emerging from the Global South circulates transnationally due to increased technological access, migration patterns, and shifting audience habits (Curtin, 2011, pp. 541–4). Hollywood studio business activities, or the lack thereof, reflect larger and dynamic flows in global, regional, national, and local industries as a result of cooperation, competition, or closure.

Michael Curtin describes these new industry city centres as media capitals, whether historic or emerging, and as 'a nexus or switching point, rather than a container' for the complex flow of economic, social, and cultural patterns (Curtin, 2003, p. 204). He argues,

> we should understand [media capitals] in the manner that geographers like Doreen Massey [1992] and Kevin Robins [1991] understand cities, as meeting places where local specificity arises out of migration, interaction and exchange. As such, media capital is a relational concept, not simply an acknowledgement of dominance. (Curtin, 2003, p. 205)

The notion of media capitals as meeting places is one I want to expand upon. I aim to complicate the relationship of international Hollywood practices with local market forces beyond one-way. As vital as it is to recognise the decentralisation and flexible nature of studio production cultures in recent decades, focusing only on this area of international operations ignores other significant facets of local business against larger dynamic media capitals. The relational, alongside the locational, is useful in understanding the way studio activities are integrated into local industry dynamics. It is through this relational dynamic that I am most interested in exploring the varied relationships between Hollywood local operations and specific international media hubs. How do studios adapt to and develop physical infrastructure and unit-based business activities inside and across international media hubs? And, in turn, what part does Hollywood play in forming or maintaining these 'switching points'?

One point of entry for understanding the connection of established or emerging media hubs to international studio activities involves local production, financing, and industry support services. Ben Goldsmith and Tom O'Regan identify a shift in policy and support towards the 'film services approach' across local industries in recent decades (Goldsmith and O'Regan, 2005, p. 55). From Australia's Gold Coast to Germany's regional media centres, local industries invest in infrastructure and services to support a mix of local, regional, and international productions. In my conversations with film commissioners and funding boards across Latin America and Europe, local film institutions fashion their role as facilitators and offer a handful of services – location support, creative professionals, equipment, financing schemes, and promotional campaigns – intended to attract local and international production partnerships. In order to participate in international media circuits of production, local film institutions must navigate intra-industry priorities alongside continued transformations in the local economic, political, labour, and technological climate. It is important to understand the varied relational and locational dynamics that must be negotiated simultaneously between local players and Hollywood partners within international media hubs.

Rio de Janeiro

During the 1990s, the Brazilian industry introduced a new series of tax incentives and subsidies in order to encourage international investment and partnerships and to transform local financing and commercial production cultures. Measures to stimulate private financing, co-productions, and foreign investment – such as the Article 3 tax incentive allowing the reinvestment of taxed income by foreign companies like the Hollywood majors – worked to reimagine the local film industry from a traditionally state-supported enterprise to a more commercial, soft-money system open to transnational partnerships. The new incentives ignited a significant boom in Brazilian film-making, from fewer than nine films in 1993 to over one hundred annually by the 2010s. In turn, as the new system gave way to a wave of Brazilian blockbusters, local Hollywood operations systematically began to invest in commercial Portuguese-language co-production and distribution deals (Brannon Donoghue, 2014b; Rêgo, 2005).

Historically known as the media capital housing Brazil's most powerful media conglomerate and broadcast network, Globo, the city of Rio de Janeiro benefited from the industry's rebirth and served as the location for a handful of Hollywood productions in the 2010s. Federal (ANCINE), regional (Rio Film Commission), and municipal (RioFilme) film institutions have been key in structuring, facilitating, and financing Portuguese-language and English-language co-productions between independent players and local and international studio offices, as discussed in Chapter 3. Most notably, the mixed public-private enterprise RioFilme, under the leadership of Sergio Sá Leitão from 2009 to 2014, increased investment in the local sector from R$1.1 million in 2008 to R$51.4 million by 2013. The institution participated in over 480 projects between 2009 and 2014 (Hopewell, 2013a; interview with Sá Leitão, 2010, 2013). Film projects during this period ranged from *Tropa de Elite 2: o inimigo agora é outro* (*Elite Squad: The Enemy Within*, 2010), the most successful Brazilian theatrical release of all time, to the young-adult book series turned hit film franchise *Twilight: Breaking Dawn, Part 1* (2011).

RioFilme is housed in a large, historic colonial house in the Laranjeiras neighbourhood of Rio. Tall ceilings and dark woodwork mix with brightly painted spaces and wall-to-wall posters featuring successful local comedies, dramas, and biopics that received RioFilme support. The building also houses the Rio Film Commission, which offers general location support services, and is routinely a site of policy discussions, creative development, and event planning. The location serves as a municipal institutional centre for financing and shooting films in Rio de Janeiro. The majority of RioFilme's financing originates from the Rio municipal budget and recouped profits from participation in commercially lucrative audiovisual projects. When acting as a co-producer or co-distributor on an approved project, the institution offers two types of financing – reimbursable (maintaining an equity share on the returns) and non-reimbursable (with no financial expectations to be returned).

RioFilme maintained and promoted a broadly commercial and market-driven model during the early 2010s, greenlighting investments only after a process of comparing a project's specs to the profitability of similar films. The institution supported a range of local and international film production and distribution through this soft-money system. Whether from his office in Rio or at a major international film market in Cannes, Sá Leitão worked to promote the city as an audiovisual production centre not only for Brazil but for Latin America as a region (Brannon Donoghue, 2014b). In conversations with Sá Leitão during his early tenure at RioFilme, it became clear that his commercial approach was accompanied by a pragmatic scepticism of Hollywood's involvement with local-language and English-language projects and what that involvement contributed to the overall Brazilian market. Sá Leitão argued:

> In Brazil, we already have today, in addition to the [Hollywood] majors, national independents that are active, competent, have capacity. I think that the distribution system today is very mature. The line of capital for national distributors [allows them to] compete with a major [Hollywood studio] with the best Brazilian content … I don't want to villainise the majors … It is good for the country that they are here. It is good that American cinema is available … [but] we are competitive … It needs to be free, democratic. What people want to see, the control of the consumers. (interview with Sá Leitão, 2010)

He passionately supported financing local productions to strengthen the local industry; he also understood and articulated the benefits of Hollywood's value in the market.

Significantly, and revealing of the complicated dynamic between Hollywood local activities and Brazilian industry players, RioFilme was a key force in attracting a handful of major Hollywood productions to the city during in the early 2010s. Lionsgate/Summit shot a pivotal sequence of the *Twilight* film, *Breaking Dawn, Part 1*, in Rio and Paraty. The production benefited from RioFilme financing and location services, which directly invested around $500,000. As an example of a creative runaway, the Brazilian financing covered only part of the $3.5 million in costs spent during the one-week on location (Hopewell, 2010; Mueller, 2011). Only a small portion of filming took place in Brazil, while the majority of the film was shot in British Columbia and Louisiana, two regions offering competitive incentive systems. At the same time, Universal Pictures shot portions of *Fast Five* (2011) in Rio. Unlike *Twilight*, the *Fast and Furious* instalment did not receive financing from RioFilme, reportedly due to the film's negative representations of local crime and poverty. That RioFilme invested in Lionsgate/Summit's production and not Universal's reflects fluid priorities and an institution strategically, and not universally, aligning themselves financially with Hollywood players.

Project-by-project decision-making and local industry priorities are part of the Rio-based film institution's work to rebrand the city as an attractive international media production centre and promotional site for tourism. Whether RioFilme directly participated in a blockbuster production shoot or not, the city's media sector still gained global coverage and buzz due to the presence of two high-profile franchises in 2010. Studio production presence translates to long-term symbolic capital, or what Sá Leitão described as promoting a 'picture-postcard' view, towards expanding a regional media capital into a global centre.[1] The Rio-based studio projects also illustrate two different models for local production activities and partnerships. Whether directly or indirectly supported by Brazilian industry incentives, Hollywood's production presence relies on the visible resources of the media hub itself (Rio's favela communities, beaches, historic colonial neighbourhoods, trade press coverage, and celebrity gossip) and the invisible resources of industry services

View of Rio de Janeiro's iconic Pão de Açucar (Sugarloaf Mountain) often featured in local and international film productions

(policymaker and institutional support, location guidance, incentives and subsidies, trained crews, hotels, restaurants, etc.).

Utilising a different local production strategy, Universal Pictures co-produced the English- and Portuguese-language film *Trash* (2014), which also received support from both the Rio Film Commission and Brazil's largest film festival, Festival do Rio (interview with Santiago, 2014). The film represents a particular global-local dynamic Universal actively cultivated domestically and internationally during this period, most notably with the *Fast & Furious* franchise. Shot in Rio de Janeiro and more than two-thirds in Portuguese, the crime thriller follows a group of children living in a favela who find a wallet full of cash at a trash dump. *Trash* features American actors Martin Sheen and Rooney Mara as well as Brazilian stars Selton Mello and Wagner Moura, known for an array of local blockbusters and Globo television roles.

Significantly, *Trash* represents a specific translocal co-production approach for Universal that differs from the international blockbuster or the industry-wide LLP model, particularly since the major did not maintain a local production unit in Brazil during that time. Universal Pictures paired key players and long-standing partnerships across local territories to assemble the official UK–Brazil–Germany co-production (Hopewell, 2013c). O2 Filmes is one of Brazil's most prominent production companies and home to internationally acclaimed director Fernando Meirelles, known for *Cidade de Deus* (*City of God*, 2002) and *The Constant Gardener* (2005). In the mid-2000s, Meirelles was working in multiple industries across Brazil, Europe, and North America, and signed a three-picture first-look deal with Universal Pictures (Mohr, 2006). The film involved the UK's Working Title Films. Since 1999, Universal has maintained a major production deal with Working Title, known for prestige pictures, romances, comedies, and dramas that travel widely across the Anglophone region and internationally (McNary, 2015b).

Much like *Fast Five*, *Trash* did not receive funding from RioFilme but did receive significant location support from the Rio Film Commission. The co-production served as a 'triangular' financial and creative partnership, with Working Title, O2 Filmes, and Universal Pictures Germany splitting the $12 million budget 50-25-25, respectively. To access the specific federal subsidy and tax incentive, *Fondo Sectorial Audiovisual*, *Trash* needed to qualify as an international co-production under an official treaty agreement. While Brazil and the UK negotiated a co-production agreement in 2012, as of 2016 it still has not been ratified ('Film Co-Production', 2012). Therefore, Universal Pictures' German territory office, not Universal Brazil or domestic operations, served as the official partner, since the two countries have maintained a co-production treaty since 2005 (Blaney, 2005, 2013). While multilayered transnational partners and forces shaped the production process, the film operated as a globally packaged project and circulated largely as a locally focused and culturally specific feature. *Trash* premiered to awards at the Festival do Rio in 2014 and earned $1.2 million in 252 screens at the Brazilian box office, as compared to its limited seventeen-screen US release the following year (Box Office Mojo, 2015). Rio served as an important hub, or switching point, for arranging the financial agreement and creative partnerships, yet the co-production also required Universal's transnational network of local territory offices. Significantly, the major studio leveraged locational dynamics of two European territories in order to produce and distribute the Brazilian-produced film.

STUDIO COMPLEXES AND INFRASTRUCTURE: GERMANY

Following the Eastern Communist bloc's dissolution, previously separate German industries had to reconcile and organise after a long-term split between Western and Eastern media centres, infrastructure, and film-making cultures beginning in the 1990s. Wide-sweeping privatisation, deregulation, and commercialisation across Europe directly impacted these separate media systems. Reunification led to national and regional cultural policy shifts towards market-driven incentive systems intended to develop commercial projects and partnerships, not unlike the neoliberal wave happening across Latin American media systems (Goldsmith and O'Regan, 2005; Halle, 2006, p. 251). A transformation in institutional and industrial logic surrounding local production and international co-production support led to increasingly commercially bound industry forces tied to market-driven logic and box-office per-formance, as discussed further in Chapter 7. In this industrial climate, Hollywood studios worked to integrate evolving international production strategies – both English-language and local-language – into Germany's specific geographical spaces and institutional structures.[2] While many of these partnerships qualify as creative or financial runaways for the majors, I want to move beyond looking at these films as merely one-off outsourcing of production. Instead, I consider the post-1990s wave of international co-productions as a multifaceted process for the German film industry's transformation into a new era international media hub, which also complicates previ-ous understandings of contemporary blockbuster production cultures across global media networks. Significantly, Hollywood co-productions with German players illustrate how the majors, and increasingly mini-majors like Lionsgate/Summit, are becoming integrated into local industries through financial, geographical, physical, and labour channels. In this section, I explore how Hollywood production cultures intersect a specific German media complex, media sector, and media geography with varied long-term and short-term success.

Studio Babelsberg

The German film market encompasses a strong, regionally diverse market with multilayered production and circulation practices from small-scale local projects to big-budget international co-productions. A unique regional dynamic organises film-making practices, which are at once dispersed across four key cities – Munich, Hamburg, Cologne, and Berlin – and transnationally connected across Europe, Hollywood, and other international markets. Due to the industry's local, regional, and global dynamics, Randall Halle argues the German film business challenges traditional notions of a 'national' cinema that can be understood as a centralised and unified industry (Halle, 2006, p. 252). A range of regional institutions, film com-missions, and funding bodies – from the municipal to the federal level – financially structure and drive regionalised production activities.

The Berlin-Brandenburg region reflects the shifting nature of the global media economy and ongoing efforts to transform a media hub into a commercial produc-tion centre for local and international projects. Encompassing two German states, the Berlin-Brandenburg region serves as the country's film-making centre and is home to a diverse array of media institutions. A centrepiece of the regional creative cluster is the historic Studio Babelsberg.[3] Known as Germany's oldest film studio, Studio Babelsberg was privatised and sold by the federal government in 1992, and subsequently underwent massive state-supported renovations to update the soundstages, offices, equipment, and so on to transform the studio into an inter-national production outfit. By the mid-2000s, the studio had changed ownership from French media company Vivendi to a German investment group including

Charlie Woebcken and Christoph Fisser, respectively studio president/CEO and vice president/COO. The studio, whose official tagline is 'Act Global, Spend Local', seeks international partners and may operate as a co-producer and equity partner investing $250,000 to $2 million on average for half of the films shot there (Meza, 2012a; Studio Babelsberg, 2015). The studio advertises itself as a 'one-stop-shop', including production spaces (twenty soundstages and extensive backlots), production services, art design, and production design on the 39-acre lot. Despite past financial struggles due to high overhead costs and rumoured mismanagement, the complex emerged as one of Europe's most prominent production complexes in the mid-2010s, particularly as competitor complex Ciudad de la Luz in Spain filed for bankruptcy in 2012 (K. O'Brien, 2004; Studio Babelsberg, 2015).

Studio Babelsberg operates at the intersection of shifting German cultural policies and practices with Hollywood's increasingly flexible, prioritised international operations. During the 2010s, Babelsberg partnered with a wave of Hollywood majors and independents to co-produce English-language films, from prestige festival features to blockbuster sequels. In addition to available on-site location services, many of these films also qualified for German Federal Film Board (FFA) rebates, returning up to 20 to 25 per cent of local costs. In addition to accessing the German Film Fund (Deutsche Filmförderfond/DFFF), many of the nation's sixteen states house regional film commissions that offer additional support and subsidies for film-making efforts, from script development to production support, intended to aid and stimulate German cinema (German Film Commission, 2014). Federal funding is eligible to be combined with regional funding from Berlin-Brandenburg, Bavaria, and other states. Federal and regional funds remain flexible enough to support, and intentionally target, international co-productions involving partners ranging from Hollywood studios to prominent European independents.

This incentivised financing structure relies on studio complexes and local infrastructure like Babelsberg, which serves as an official German co-producer for Hollywood films shot at the complex. Studio Babelsberg co-produced English-language historical dramas *The Monuments Men* (2014), starring an ensemble cast led by actor-director George Clooney, and *Bridge of Spies* (2015), starring Tom Hanks and directed by Steven Spielberg. The two projects represent prestige vehicles for these major actors and directors, who maintain significant leverage and power within studio structures that allow them to secure financing and international location shoots for the mid-budget adult dramas (the films reported production costs of $70 million and $40 million, respectively). Both films utilised studio services and on-location shooting around Germany as well as qualifying for Medienboard Berlin-Brandenburg funds. On the one hand, the German location served a prominent creative role contributing to *The Monuments Men*'s World War II and *Bridge of Spies'* cold war-era settings. On the other hand, by partnering with

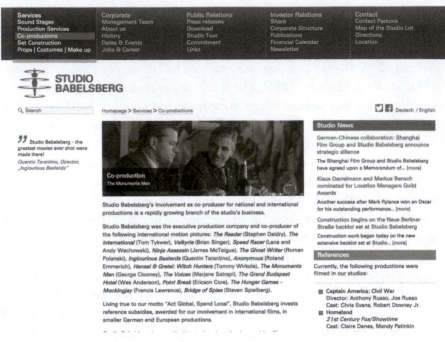

Studio Babelsberg's website prominently promotes their co-producing partnerships with Hollywood films

Babelsberg, the two prestige productions utilised available financial and physical resources, which in turn the German complex highlighted in promotional materials marketing the studio's services and regional incentives.

In addition to star-driven prestige dramas, Studio Babelsberg also co-produced franchise instalments of Lionsgate/Summit's *Hunger Games: Mockingjay – Part 2* (2015) and Disney/Marvel's *Captain America: Civil War* (2016). The *Hunger Games* and *Captain America* series represent the financial studio model, cobbling together a variety of local funding from different media hubs to subsidise the estimated $160 to 250 million production budgets. In addition to Germany and other international locations, Lionsgate/Summit and Disney/Marvels' franchise instalments shot significant portions in Atlanta, Georgia, which offers competitive tax incentives, studio facilities, and production crew. Studio blockbuster franchises serve as an expensive and expansive production model for Conglomerate Hollywood, since they are increasingly co-produced across a network of local industries and institutions. These films are a product of media hubs from Germany and Australia to London and Atlanta. Studios often utilise resources across these production centres for individual films. Babelsberg's development and operations are part of a larger international network of studio complexes and production centres housing vast studio lots, hundreds of skilled production and post-production professionals, and other location services.[4]

The growth and development of local media sectors, from below-the-line crews to digital post-production facilities, also connect sites across the international network of media hubs. For example, the globalisation of studio blockbuster production cultures shaped the growth and concentration of the visual effects, or VFX, industry into a transnational business. Visual spectacle through digitised characters, settings, and story worlds built for action, sci-fi, and fantasy blockbusters has come to characterise most big-budget Hollywood tentpole projects since the 1990s. Key media hubs such as the UK, Germany, New Zealand, France, and Canada develop and invest in local VFX facilities and training schools for local media professionals as part of a film services model to attract high-profile international partners (Salisbury, 2016). In turn, the VFX industry's development and decentralisation connects to an international network of production companies, local studio complexes, film funds, and key location services.

Babelsberg–Hollywood co-productions utilise the growing regional VFX sector. Germany's VFX industry emerged in the 1990s and 2000s with three key players – Munich-based ScalineVFX and Trixter, and Frankfurt-based Pixomondo. All three companies work on high-profile English-language and international projects as well as commercials and animation. For example, Pixomondo collaborated on the mid-range *Bridge of Spies* as well as the bigger-budget *Hugo* (2011) and *Star Trek into Darkness* (Meza, 2009). The company maintains offices across a variety of international industry sites, including Los Angeles, Toronto, Frankfurt, Beijing, and Shanghai. Similar to Hollywood globalised production strategies and localised practices, industry sectors like VFX also have expanded to map onto and integrate themselves into the same network of media capitals.

In 2015, the German government launched a subsidy programme to support the post-production sector. Marvel's *Captain American: Civil War* qualified for the Munich regional film fund to support and facilitate partnerships between international co-productions and local VFX professionals. The Bavarian-based company Trixter qualified for close to $500,000 to supply VFX work on the production. The post-production company already had an established relationship with Marvel, having working on a number of their comic book franchises, including *Ant-Man* (2015), *Iron Man 3* (2013), and *Avengers: Age of Ultron* (Blaney, 2015).

There is an important connection among big-budget English-language co-productions, VFX professionals, and training programmes. The Hochschule für Fernsehen und Film München (HFF Munich) is one of Germany's prominent film schools and offers courses on visual effects and digital production. Considering the geographical proximity to Trixter and ScalineVFX, the Munich programme is inevitably a training school for professionals who want to be hired by the VFX houses and work on the next wave of co-productions; at the same time, investment, infrastructure, training, and support are reinvested in the region. The German VFX industry can be understood as part of a translocal circuit of post-production, represented in Figure 5.1:

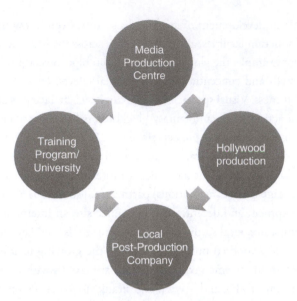

Figure 5.1 Hollywood co-productions intersecting local industry infrastructure

Goldsmith and O'Regan (2005) contend that access to European Commission funds transformed key Germany facilities into particular media cities, like Babelsberg and Munich, including television and broadcasting centres, VFX houses, and film and television colleges. Initiatives to build training schools and support local post-production companies reflect regional and national cultural policies set on economic development through reimagining German creative clusters.

This wider view of local post-production networks offers a mid-level understanding of industry-wide forces, but not of how they impact individual workers or companies on the ground. Labour conditions for creative professionals often are an invisible side effect of increased flexibility and mobility in global film work, and a conversation that did not arise in my fieldwork or in direct studio communication, since I was not looking at individual productions. While creative below-the-line labour is not the focus of this book, it presents a significant dynamic in English-language international productions operating and employing local professionals across an increasingly interconnected network of media hubs. By looking beyond the industrial and institutional viewpoint, larger conversations around the precarious labour of the VFX industry emerged in the 2000s, notably after the bankruptcy of the US-based Oscar-winning studio Rhythm & Hues. Alongside the decentralisation of studio post-production work that has followed the rise of the big-budget English-language international co-production comes a mobile, flexible creative professional force working across international media hubs with uneven employment, regulations, and labour conditions (Curtin and Sanson, 2016).[5]

Sony Berlin

In addition to Hollywood's international blockbuster co-production activities, Studio Babelsberg served as the operational site of Sony's first attempt to co-produce German local-language productions from 1998 to 2003. As discussed in Chapter 3, studio LLP units present a strategy intended to participate in and adapt to local production cultures. Sony's initial experiment failed not because of available facilities or financing. Instead, Sony parted ways with Babelsberg due to the incompatibility of conglomerate management cultures and priorities with German production cultures and market conditions in this period.

On 1 January 1998, Sony Pictures Entertainment launched its first German production unit, Deutsche Columbia TriStar Film Production GmbH, with Andrea Willson serving as the managing director. Based on a five-year plan similar to Sony LLP operations in Hong Kong and Brazil at the time, the unit planned to invest an estimated $55 million to produce German-language films. Initially, Willson's office planned to release one to two films per year and eventually to expand into four to five films annually (Hils, 1998). Significantly, SPE housed their unit at Studio Babelsberg reportedly due to the production facilities and resources concentrated in the area as well as the access to growing regional subsidies. At the same time, Warner Bros. also developed a multi-year investment plan for co-producing and distributing LLPs based out of their Hamburg office.

The following year, the German production unit had three films in production and twelve in development. Deutsche Columbia TriStar's initial release, *Anatomie* (*Anatomy*, 2000), starred German actress Franka Potente, who had reached international fame from her role in the successful local thriller *Lola rennt* (*Run, Lola, Run*, 1998) (Elley, 2000; Hils, 1999). The Sony horror thriller follows a group of German medical students investigating the mysterious circumstances of a dead body found in their anatomy lab. *Anatomie* found box-office success in the German market and, in a rare move for LLPs, Sony gave the film a limited distribution on eight screens in US theatres, to small returns. Deutsche Columbia TriStar's additional LLP attempts, including a sequel to *Anatomie*, largely were considered box-office flops and the unit had a hard time repeating the first film's success with subsequent LLPs. Instead of taking a long-term approach for developing relationships and a slate of local projects, as its peer Warner Bros. Germany had done, SPE international executives reacted swiftly and closed the Babelsberg office in 2003 due to the string of failed LLPs, rising overhead costs, and general uncertainty in the local market. According to a European-based former Sony executive I interviewed, closing the Germany office after a few successful films was a '[knee-]jerk reaction', especially as WB and Fox established and continued to build long-term LLP strategies during this period.

A central problem for the German LLP unit's long-term sustainability was that the operation's location at Babelsberg separated it geographically from other Sony offices, including home entertainment and television. While officially Sony cited changing conditions in the German film market for closing the local production unit, the studio unit reportedly had difficulties integrating its own institutional structure into the specifically regionalised nature of the local industry. The former executive recounts that when the office was closed, Sony consolidated European operations in the Madrid office under a newly appointed production executive, who oversaw production and managed the scaled-down German activities remotely. However, they contend that, even with a full-sized production unit on the ground,

> Germany [was at the time] a very complicated territory for Sony because home entertainment is in Munich, television is in Cologne, and the film group is in Berlin. So there is no geographical unity. It is very complicated. If you want to have a meeting with the three German GMs, you have to take three days to go to three different places. (interview with International Studio Executive B, 2013)

The decentralised nature of the German market proved to be a major challenge for Sony conducting business, especially considering the collaborative efforts necessary across theatrical, TV, and home entertainment to co-produce and release a local-language project, as well as the studio's overall waning interest in expanding this sector of international operations. This is in direct contrast to Warner Bros., which built and has maintained a local-language unit in Hamburg integrated with its other operations for over two decades. Sony's decision-making, management, and divisional structure was in direct conflict with the realities of producing and releasing a film from multiple offices scattered across Germany. Significantly, SPE did not stay out of the German market long and ended up re-opening an LLP unit in 2008 under new management in Berlin with a smaller scale production strategy.

LEAVESDEN STUDIOS

As one of the world's financial and cultural capitals, London is situated at a prominent position and intersection of national, regional, and global economic activities. Saskia Sassen identifies London as an example of the new global city, a specialised centre concentrating industry, finance, and the marketplace. She characterises a post-1990s landscape: 'cities [London, New York, Tokyo] concentrate over vast resources, while finance and specialised service industries have restructured the urban social and economic order. Thus a new type of city has appeared' (Sassen, 2001, p. 4). In Sassen's focus on financial corporate sectors, she positions major cities like London as a central node for the world economy.

In connection to its space/place as the British media capital, the city historically has existed as one of a handful of 'creative and operational centres of the international media economy' (Curtin, 2011, p. 541). London serves as an important site of media production and distribution for the larger Anglophone and European regional markets as well as diverse diasporic audiences, including South Asian and sub-Saharan African. Depending on which facet of the British media industries is observed in this global city centre, a nexus of constantly shifting and evolving capital, migration, labour, cultural trends, technologies, and ideologies exists. Based on on-site observations and trade press coverage, this section explores how one particular site reflects the intersection of national and international media activities and priorities – Leavesden Studios. On the one hand, Warner Bros.' acquisition and renovation of the UK's historic Leavesden Studios into a production studio serves as a strategic promotional vehicle for its lucrative *Harry Potter* franchise. On the other hand, the studio complex's evolution reveals how the Hollywood player's strategy for the local studio infrastructure is invested in mobilising metro London's local industry specificity and prominence as a media hub.

London serves as the main creative cluster for UK media business. In the mid-2000s, around 80 per cent of UK film production was based in and around London. UK and international studio-based film productions are concentrated in the 'western-wedge' region and rely heavily on media professionals who live and work in this area (Goldsmith and O'Regan, 2005, p. 135). Located along this region are a number of studio complexes, ranging from larger facilities at Pinewood and Shepperton to smaller locations at Ealing. Similar to Studio Babelsberg's activities and priorities, many of these historic sites of production for UK-based and international projects reflect a wave of investment in production infrastructure and training of creative professionals to support and attract domestic and international projects.

Hans Mommaas (2009) suggests that 'a broader *cultural turn* in both urban planning and regional development strategies' emerged across Northern and Western Europe during this period in order to build major European cities into creative clusters for entertainment, media, technology, and business. Specifically, studio complexes benefited from British policies with a cultural-creative clustering agenda that David Hesmondhalgh explains linked arts and cultural policy to social regeneration and economic growth (Hesmondhalgh, 2013, p. 176). These economic and public policy initiatives included a series of tax incentives put in place to encourage investment, not only in building infrastructure for media production but also for 'cultural-creative clusters' to attract productions that train and develop a regional core of media professionals.

The US–UK industries are integrated and intertwined through a relationship of collaboration, reliance, and reaction (McDonald, 2008, p. 220). The British film industry has maintained a historic relationship with Hollywood as a site for the majors' international business activities since the 1910s (K. Thompson, 1985). For example, cultural policies historically fluctuate between economic protectionism and stimulating international investment and partnerships in part due to Hollywood studios' long-term presence. As discussed in Chapter 2, the UK emerged as an important market for international expansion and later as a site of production and post-production for a number of major studio projects. McDonald suggests, 'London represents in microcosm the intricate array of interactions that pertain between Britain and Hollywood. In the international film market, the city has remained an operational and creative cluster for the studios to work through' (McDonald, 2008, p. 226). Metro London continues to be a central global cluster for studio production and distribution activities in the conglomerate era, including Disney/Lucasfilm's latest iterations of the *Star Wars* franchise. Furthermore, a number of studios have their European and EMEA (Europe, Middle East, and Africa) regional headquarters situated in the city.

One of the largest studio complexes operating in the western-wedge production cluster is Leavesden Studios. Originally, the facility served as an airfield and aircraft manufacturing plant run by the Ministry of Defence during World War II. In 1967, Rolls-Royce took over the manufacturing site to produce their line of luxury vehicles. The automotive operation closed in 1992. The studio was converted into a film production site built to attract a diverse slate of big-budget international productions, such as the temporary housing of *GoldenEye* (1994) and *Stars Wars: Episode I – The Phantom Menace* (Goldsmith and O'Regan, 2005, p. 144; 'History of Leavesden Studios', 2014). Ben Goldsmith and Tom O'Regan distinguish Leavesden from other studio facilities in the western wedge as a 'blank canvas' during this transitional period in the film industry, which allowed one-off productions to build sets, crew, and support services from scratch. This strategy relied on rental relationships with Hollywood and short-term contractual work, whereas Leavesden offered a more fixed local presence for the studio (Goldsmith and O'Regan, 2005, p. 135).

In 2001, Warner Bros. leased Leavesden and shot the first instalment in the *Harry Potter* franchise. All eight instalments were filmed at Leavesden, with WB taking long-term rental of the facilities for over a decade. As one of the most massively successful tentpole franchises of the conglomerate era, *Harry Potter* production budgets ranged from $125 million for the first film to $250 million for the last two. President of Warner Bros. in the UK, Ireland, and Spain, Josh Berger, credited the decision to shoot the franchise in the UK due to London's concentration of media professionals, resources, and a generous tax credit that offered up to a 25 per cent cash rebate. Berger contends: 'film production is a global service industry right now and the productions find the places that combine tax credits with skills and facilities and a location where people want to go for three months to make a movie' (Goodridge, 2012). The tax incentive and studio facilities kept Warner at Leavesden and, over the course of eight films, the franchise hired more than 4,000 creative professionals from the local industry, which offered longer-term, stable employment for the British-based crew.

After principal photography for the eighth and final instalment ended in 2010, Warner Bros. bought the studio facilities and invested $186 million in renovations. Warner Bros.' acquisition of Leavesden coincides with a period of increased prioritisation for international operations. The Leavesden purchase serves two key purposes for Warner Bros. filmed entertainment division. First, Leavesden became the first Hollywood studio facility in the UK since MGM London in the 1940s (Lodderhose, 2012). After the completion of the *Harry Potter* franchise, studio facilities expanded into over a dozen soundstages, a backlot, offices, and post-production facilities. Warner Bros. utilises the studio to shoot their own productions such as *Pan* (2015) and *Tarzan* (2016); it also rents out the site to other production companies (Tartaglione, 2014). Berger, who in addition to running the regional office now oversees Leavesden Studios, contends:

> [Buying Leavesden] was about putting down a flag in a country outside the U.S., which would be the first time we've done that, and actually own the land and develop it and keep it busy … The broader message for us is that we are by far the biggest investor in British cinema in terms of production activity and spend … in addition to our TV production and video-games business here. We will continue to build on that and Leavesden is a critical part of that. (Goodridge, 2012)

Warner Bros.' ownership contributes and extends the long history of London as a relational site – financial and creative – for Hollywood studios to collaborate with British companies, invest in the local industry sector, and diversify their international activities.

Second, Warner Bros. transformed a handful of soundstages into 'The Making of *Harry Potter*' studio tour. The tour opened to much fanfare and press in 2012, notably as the Duke and Duchess of Cambridge and Prince Harry attended the inauguration (English, 2013). Set on two cavernous soundstages and a backlot on one side of the studio complex, the interactive tourist attraction features an array of props, costumes, sets, and stories from the franchise's creative and technical production process. A large plaque sits at the entrance of the site, which reads:

> dedicated to the 4,000 people of the British film industry who brought their passion, skill, and creativity to interpreting the seven *Harry Potter* novels into eight compelling films and to the Harry Potter fans all over the world whose enthusiasm and support made the films the most successful motion picture series in history.

As my on-site observations reveal, 'The Making of *Harry Potter*' operates on multiple levels: a behind-the-scenes fan experience, a love letter to the media professionals who created the films, a promotional vehicle for Warner Bros.' operations in the

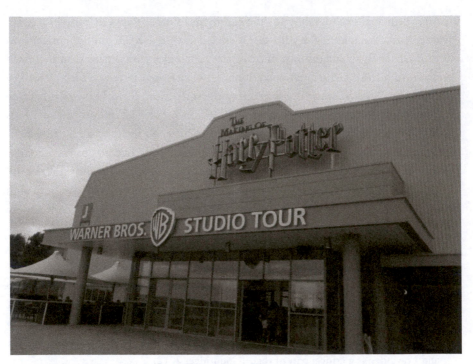

Public entrance to Warner Bros.' 'The Making of *Harry Potter*' tour at Leavesden Studios

UK, and an investment in the local industry. Bound within an interactive fan experience, the tour works to make visible the often invisible nature of film production and celebrates media workers, creative labour, and collaborative decision-making.

Access to the tour reflects a controlled process characteristic of how major studios operate. After a short train ride from London to Watford Junction, visitors arrive at the studio via Warner Bros.' shuttle. Tour tickets must be booked online in advance for an 'appointment' to tour the site. After picking up tickets at a box-office window, a visitor must queue inside a lobby waiting area before entering the site. An entry system controls access, since only a handful of people with the same appointment are admitted at a time. The waiting area begins to shape a specific narrative, 'from pen to production', around the tour experience. Along with Harry's cupboard under the stairs set piece for visitors to observe, large signs offer a tidy chronology of J. K. Rowling's initial idea from book to film series. This origin narrative carries into the first two rooms, which are the initial stops prior to entering the main soundstages. These two spaces seem to be the most controlled experience, since visitors must watch two short films, and photography is only prohibited at this point of the tour. The first room is dark and lined with digital posters of the films. Visitors stand and watch the screens transition from the posters to a projected short film that recounts how the film's producers discovered the books and their subsequent massive global fandom.

The second room is a large theatre screening of another short film narrated by the franchise's lead actors, Daniel Radcliffe, Emma Watson, and Rupert Grint. The footage of the actors describing their experiences of working at Leavesden with a cast and crew for eight productions is interspersed with a montage highlighting behind-the-scenes moments and technical 'secrets'. The promotional strategy of these introductory films manufactures a level of intimacy directed at fans, both through the celebratory tone and personal address by the three narrators. For example, Radcliffe directly addresses visitors, warning 'you may never look at Quidditch the same again'. A particular mythology of *Harry Potter* emerges at this point, a place where fandom, discourses characterising blockbuster scope and scale, and studio promotion intersect. Recognising this reflexive world-building as myth-building is central to understanding how a studio production space like Leavesden operates simultaneously as a site of promotion for the media property and functional studio.

As the short film ends, the screen lifts and reveals entry doors into the Great Hall, a central gathering space in the Hogwarts School of Witchcraft and Wizardry where students and their professors eat meals, attend assemblies, and gather for events. The reassembled Great Hall set features long tables staged for a school meal, as well as mannequins dressed as students in school uniforms and other key characters in costume. Most striking is the disconnect between spaces where the immersive experience begins and the film props end. Unlike the Great Hall's picturesque night-time sky featured in the films, the walls reveal an open movie set with scaffolding, lights, and wires. This is an excellent example of where the celebratory and promotional tension lies, between recreating the *Harry Potter* story world as an immersive experience while deconstructing and revealing the 'secrets' behind it.

After a brief look around, visitors are then allowed to wander the tour at their own pace. The first soundstage (J) houses dozens of interior sets and props ranging from the Gryffindor common room to Headmaster Albus Dumbledore's study. Interspersed throughout the soundstage are signs highlighting above-the-line individuals such as screenwriters, directors, and key department heads for production design, makeup, graphic artists, and visual effects throughout the film series. A visitor can actively participate in learning about special effects and green-screen technology with an opportunity to simulate flying on a broom during a Quidditch match. Executive producer David Barron credits the film franchise for investing and strengthening the British VFX industry:

> *Harry Potter* created the UK effects industry as we know it. On the first film, all the complicated visual effects were done on the [US] west coast. But on the second, we took a leap of faith and gave much of what would normally be given to Californian vendors to UK ones. (Gilbey, 2011)

Costume and makeup design featured in the *Harry Potter* films

UK-based Double Negative, which is highlighted in the tour, worked on all eight films and now is considered one of the leading and most successful VFX houses in the global network. Not only is the tour an education in the process of creating the *Harry Potter* films but it also shows the scope and scale of labour and individual roles required to maintain the studio's blockbuster production culture and the local industry's part in it.

At the exit of the first soundstage is a backlot. In addition to a concession stand featuring food and drinks from the film, a number of recognisable sets include Harry's childhood homes on Privet Drive and his parents' cottage at Godric's Hollow, as well as various vehicles and larger outdoor set pieces. The second soundstage (K) houses an array of creatures, characters, and makeup design as well as building blueprints and models, including a scaled-down model of Hogwarts and the set of the magical commercial district called Diagon Alley. Strikingly, the emphasis on the creative artistry and detailed design of the sets, props, and characters highlights the extensive labour involved in this franchise. The process for designing, building, and creating the physical *Harry Potter* world involved hundreds of technicians and artisans from the local UK industry. At one point, a large sign displays a quote from production designer Stuart Craig describing how concept artists created the visual looks of the films: 'the process is magical. Artists turn pencil doodles into beautiful classical paintings with a digital brush.' Perpetuating the myth of movie-making as a magical art is key to the tour's narrative. The celebratory tone and continuation of the franchise's magical motif highlights the

Production and art design blueprints for locations in the *Harry Potter* films

creative and technical process of film-making, simultaneously revealing and disguis-
ing the below-the-line local labour. In this instance, creative labour is employed
for symbolic and promotional purposes. Highlighting professionals who designed
and constructed the *Harry Potter* cinematic universe becomes less about exploring
actual labour practices and industry working cultures and more a part of a larger,
institutional tactic for selling the franchise as an experience.

At the end of the tour, visitors are dropped into a large gift shop featuring an
array of *Harry Potter* merchandise. After learning about the HP universe, the final
participatory act could be purchasing Hermione's wand, Gryffindor T-shirts, or
other pieces of memorabilia that serve to reinforce the fan experience at Leavesden,
to locate or authenticate this experience inside the production space, and to extend
studio promotional activities beyond the studio gates. Significantly, where Warner
Bros.' operations at Leavesden intersect the *Harry Potter* franchise represents the
transformation of this production space into fan tourism around the 'making of'
narrative. While Universal Studios and Walt Disney theme parks have utilised this
behind-the-scenes strategy for decades, Warner Bros. constructs the experience
simultaneously to be locally detailed and globally universal around this UK location.
The tour operates as a promotional space, 'remaking' and localising the narrative
of Hollywood studio activities. Studio production culture and franchising history

is transformed into local experience of labour, physical infrastructure, and industry accessed via immersive fandom.

On the one hand, 'The Making of *Harry Potter*' represents the extension and continuation of Conglomerate Hollywood's transmedia strategies for franchising. Derek Johnson suggests 'transmedia storytelling results in the production and maintenance of fictional "worlds", like those of *The Matrix* or *Harry Potter*, that consumers experience in collaboration with one another by piecing together narrative materials professional producers have strewn across media platforms' (D. Johnson, 2013, p. 30). For Warner Bros., the tour extends the franchise's lifespan within a controlled local studio space and fan experience. Visitors can gather deeper understanding and personal engagement in the franchise through close-up experiences with props, sets, and production histories despite the completion of the eight-film series. From the introductory short films to merchandising, the experience celebrates and privileges insider fan knowledge as continuing the *Harry Potter* lifespan.

On the other hand, in addition to this hyper-localised expansion of the transmedia story world, the tour transforms a global franchise into a behind-the-scenes narrative as contained and captured on Leavesden's soundstages. This tour distinctively reflects Hesmondhalgh's discussion of creative clusters through a 'celebratory nature concerning the insertion of local sites of cultural production into the global circulation of cultural products' (Hesmondhalgh, 2013, p. 173). The tour operates as a promotional space around the local scope and scale of this global blockbuster series and the studio's presence in the London media hub. In observing the tour and visitors, I was struck mostly by the promotional dance between revealing secrets – the 'magic' of studio production processes – and constructing a cohesive narrative around the franchise's creation and local Warner Bros. activities supportive of and dependent upon the UK film industry. The global franchise is grounded in local production cultures and infrastructure, which in turn reinforces, promotes, and spins WB's presence in the UK. Yet it also emphasises an investment in developing and building this sector of the creative cluster beyond a cycle of big-budget productions. The relationship between Warner Bros. and the London-based industry only deepens, particularly as Warner Bros. UK's Berger was named chairman of the British Film Institute in December 2015 (Pulver and Brown, 2015).

Warner Bros. UK continues to invest heavily in the *Harry Potter* business. Based on a spin-off book written by J. K. Rowling, the studio shot *Fantastic Beasts and Where to Find Them* (2016) at Leavesden Studios and around London. Helmed by David Yates, who directed the last four *Harry Potter* films, the studio plans to launch two sequels after *Fantastic Beasts* and shoot them at the studio complex. Furthermore, Warner Bros. launched the London-based *Harry Potter* Global Franchise Development Team in 2014 to manage the studio's related properties and growth of the brand (Rosser, 2014). This initiative reflects the studio's commitment to maintaining and growing iterations of one of their most successful media properties located largely in the UK unit. Warner Bros.' long-term strategy within the British film industry appears to be based not only on the successful development of the *Harry Potter* film franchise and subsequent related projects but also on an investment in physical infrastructure and institutions which will continue to actively shape both international operations and London as an international media hub.

CONCLUSION

This chapter explored how local infrastructure and institutional relationships intersect broad studio activities in three distinct media capitals – London, Berlin-Brandenburg, and Rio de Janeiro. Each local context has its own histories, dynamics, and challenges. What emerges from these three cases are the complexities of studio operations on the ground, how physical and symbolic infrastructure is built, the varying interests and priorities from player to player, and where studio complexes and partnerships intersect from market to market. Moving beyond specific institutional cultures into larger industry-wide dynamics offers a different understanding of how Hollywood studios navigate and adapt to local market forces and the broader global film industry. In particular, as the UK anticipates the impact of the 2016 Brexit vote to leave the European Union and Brazil grapples with managing its image on the world stage amid political, economic, and health crises, institutions, infrastructure, professionals, and film projects in London and Rio de Janeiro inevitably will be affected in complex ways.

Studio involvement, investments, and locational factors within these creative clusters, whether emerging or mature, range from supporting physical studio complexes to opening local production units. In general, these case studies illustrate how the varied nature and complex history of studio local operations map onto globalising cultural industries and prominent media centres. Producing an English-language blockbuster or setting up a local production unit relies on a relational exchange among local film funds, cultural policies, film commissions, trained creative professionals, and physical production space. Because local studio activities are positioned in media hubs as part of a larger international network, they increasingly intersect with policy initiatives, financing schemes, and infrastructure development with far-reaching implications locally, regionally, and globally. In other words, how studio units participate in local production and distribution activities directly and indirectly intersects with the development or support of broader cultural industries.

How Hollywood mobilises local studio complexes and services cannot be understood separately from how local studio complexes and industry sectors in turn mobilise partnerships with the major studios. This complex, albeit at times uneven, dynamic reveals the ever-changing conditions within local media industries and the shifting footprint of the studios globally. In the following chapter, I explore one historically powerful institution representing the major studios outside of the United States – the Motion Picture Association. As the Motion Picture Association of America's international arm, the MPA manages and negotiates the local audio-visual climate outside domestic operations in order to promote and support studio priorities globally.

NOTES

1. RioFilme has been criticised for its investment in Hollywood runaway productions. Local industry professionals and academics claimed the film institution funnelled most of their resources into big-budget Brazilian commercial films involving the majors during the early 2010s, while ignoring small to medium independent productions that did not reflect the commercial blockbuster model. During the 2014 Festival do Rio, a protest movement picketed the event and RioFilme's participation. Known as 'Rio: mais cinema. Menos cénario' (Rio: More Cinema, Less Scenery), the group included industry professionals and students who saw RioFilme as reproducing a singular model of investment that privileged international players and a handful of prominent local producers. After the announcement that the institution's reimbursable line of investment possibly could be dissolved, the group of 'professionals, curators, exhibitors, distributors, film club members, researchers, teachers' began to protest in person and through social media. In a Facebook mission statement, the group criticised RioFilme's intention to build a Cinema Carioca to 'sell a finished image of the city' ('Rio: mais cinema, menos cénario', 2015). RioFilme witnessed major structural changes in leadership and financing support with Sá Leitão's departure as president in early 2015.

2. The Hollywood majors have maintained a long, and ever-changing, relationship with the German film industry. US film companies had begun to set up local branches in Berlin by the early 1920s, while Paramount and MGM developed a short-lived distribution partnership with the state-run film company Universum Film AG (Ufa) in 1925. Furthermore, during World War II, a wave of German film-makers emigrated to Hollywood and continued to work in the studio system with varied success. Following the division of the national film industry into East and West German sectors, the relationship between the Hollywood studios shifted dramatically after the country's reunification and democratisation in the 1990s. For a historical account of Hollywood's relationship to the German film industry, see Jan-Christopher Horak's *Film History* article 'Rin-Tin-Tin in Berlin or American Cinema in Weimar', and Kristin Thompson's book *Exporting Entertainment: America in the World Film Market, 1907–34*.

3. For a more extensive history of Studio Babelsberg prior to 2005, see Goldsmith and O'Regan's *The Film Studio: Film Production in the Global Economy*.

4. Recent scholarship explores the role of specific studio complexes in developing local media capitals. Ben Goldsmith, Tom O'Regan, and Susan Ward's *Local Hollywood: Global Film Production and the Gold Coast* explores the transformation of Australia's Gold Coast into an international production centre and the challenges around sustaining the local creative cluster. Additionally, Kristin Thompson's *The Frodo Franchise: The Lord of the Rings and Modern Hollywood* examines the *Lord of the Rings* trilogy and its role in transforming Wellington, New Zealand, into Wellywood.

5. For a more detailed discussion of precarious labour in the global media industries, particularly the VFX industry, see Michael Curtin and Kevin Sanson's edited collection *Precarious Creativity: Global Media, Local Labor.*

6

The Motion Picture Association and its Member Studios: Policy, Piracy, and Promotion

Alongside broader studio operations and specific local industry cultures, Warner Bros., Sony, and peer companies navigate an array of audiovisual policies to produce and distribute local content from French to Chinese markets. By exploring how a range of regional, national, and local policies and strategic partnerships encourage or prohibit local studio participation in specific markets, this chapter complements earlier chapters that offered an on-the-ground view of management practices and production cultures inside local units. A powerful and expansive organisation – the Motion Picture Association – represents the six major studios internationally to negotiate and, at times, battle local audiovisual policy and protect how their content travels. Through two arms – domestic (Motion Picture Association of America) and international (Motion Picture Association) – Hollywood's lobbyist and trade alliance works to expand studio member activities worldwide.

The following chapter explores the role of MPA regional offices in representing local studio interests vis-à-vis changing industry conditions and internal restructurings. I outline the MPA's institutional activities, culture, and changing strategies in local territories since the 1990s. After a brief discussion of the international's history and structure, I organise the discussion of the MPA around three priorities – policy and market regulation, piracy, and promotional activities. As studio territory units and their international divisions increasingly partner and collaborate with various local players from production companies to industry guilds, the MPA must react to a shifting audiovisual climate. At times, these partnerships reflect mutually beneficial priorities for local players and at other times competing interests.

A historically massive distribution infrastructure and content supply serve as the foundation for the major studios' powerful global position. Media and communication studies have widely reported and analysed how the MPA supports, champions, and operates as a powerful arm of the Hollywood studios. Scholars have a long history of exploring the MPAA/MPA's influence, particularly from a political-economic approach, to understand Hollywood's international presence (Guback, 1969; Kunz, 2007; Miller *et al.*, 2005; Pendakur, 2008; K. Thompson, 1985; Trumpbour, 2002; Wasko, 2003). Questions of ownership and protection of local content are viewed largely from a macro level, where economic motivations drive media policies and little attention is given to complex dynamics among diverse media organisations and the industry cultures in which they operate. This body of work analyses widely reported trade negotiations and the hard-line approach adopted by Jack Valenti during his controversial tenure as head of the MPAA/MPA from 1966 to 2004 – a scholarly perspective limited to the interdependent relation-ship between the MPAA and US government under his administration.

While not overlooking or dismissing the organisation's unprecedented promi-nence and political position internationally, my objective is to offer a different perspective on the MPA. By focusing on MPA regional offices, professionals, and activities, this chapter explores major structural and strategic shifts since the mid-1990s amid an increasingly digitised and globalised media landscape. In recent decades, the international branch offices expanded personnel, reassessed resources, and refocused efforts to build partnerships in local territories to address the chang-ing priorities of member studios. I highlight how, with the rise of Conglomerate Hollywood, digital piracy, and increased importance of the international box office, the MPA began a new phase by reimagining an internal structure and approach towards what former President of International Chris Marcich describes as 'a softer form of cooperation' (interview with Marcich, 2016).

One of the challenges in analysing the MPAA/MPA is how the organisa-tion historically has been closed off to the public, especially scholarly research. As Manjunath Pendakur argues in his essay on their domestic operations, 'the meet-ings and documents of both the MPAA and MPA are not accessible to the public, except for what they themselves decide to reveal. In fact, only representatives of the member companies are invited to attend their meetings' (Pendakur, 2008, p. 186). Previous research relied heavily on public documents, trade press coverage, and MPAA press releases. Through industry fieldwork, my method aims to shift the conversations from a bird's-eye view to one closer to the ground.[1]

This chapter explores the MPA's global priorities, current structure, and local partnerships based on interviews with current and former MPA executives and managers in the Latin American and European offices. A significant contribution of this chapter is my methodological approach, due to the unprecedented access I gained to MPA regional offices. I argue this is part and parcel of a larger strategic shift in the organisation's public relations strategy. This approach raised a number of questions: How has the prioritisation of international operations impacted the MPA's regional structures and localised activities? In particular, as studio filmed entertainment divisions integrate localised production and distribution strate-gies in key markets, what part has the MPA played? What is the role of regional MPA offices in negotiating favourable local incentives or tax policies that facilitate local studio business? For two regional MPA offices (Latin America and EMEA), local operations and lobbying activities directly intersect the rise of international co-productions and local-language production activities.

Speaking with MPA employees illustrates a somewhat mixed or ambivalent relationship to local audiovisual policies that support and encourage local-language partnerships and practices. My concern here is not whether the MPA's lobbying initiatives are effective or represent American economic might, all of which has already been well documented. Instead, I am interested in how the MPA defines market barriers, who internally and externally is involved in battling them, and how they understand this process as part of a new era for the organisation. Regional offices and individual managers rely upon a network of communication that requires negotiating studio priorities in increasingly flexible and constantly shifting ways. In looking beyond trade headlines, which often treat the MPA as a monolithic organisation, I argue that what initiatives against market barriers make visible is the extent to which MPA professionals operate on the ground through industry alliances, boards, and so forth as part of an institutional cooperative turn.

ORGANISATIONAL HISTORY

The Motion Picture Association of America has undergone a variety of institutional objectives and activities since its formation in 1922. Known as the Motion Pictures Producers and Distributors Association (MPPDA) until its 1945 renaming, the trade association represents major Hollywood studios both domestically and internationally. The MPAA and its international division, the Motion Picture Association (MPA), make up an 'export cartel' working to influence audiovisual policy and trade barriers that do not benefit the majors' North American and global business. When established in the 1920s, the MPPDA's domestic agenda aimed to avoid external censorship of studio movies and focused on self-regulation, particularly in the light of a handful of PR disasters that damaged the studios. The early organisation intended 'to restore a more favorable public image for the motion picture business' (Wasko, 2003, p. 181), most notably after a violent sex scandal and public court case irrevocably damaged the career of silent star Roscoe 'Fatty' Arbuckle (Petersen, 2014). After decades of self-regulating content through the Production Code, in 1968 the MPAA adopted and has continued to oversee the Ratings and Classification System (Wasko, 2003, p. 212).

In addition to steps taken to avoid outside cultural and government institutions regulating studio content, the MPAA has been actively involved in US and international audiovisual policy, or what Nolwenn Mingant calls 'cartel diplomacy' (Mingant, 2010). Historically, the MPAA has maintained a 'deep-rooted industry/ State [Department] relationship' (Trumpbour, 2002). From the first director, former Postmaster General Will H. Hays, to the most recent chairman, former

1945 *Film Daily* cover story about the MPEAA activities and international trade (Media History Digital Library)

Senator Christopher Dodd, the trade association maintains strong ties with US Departments of State and Commerce. According to John Trumpbour, 'the US State department, as overseas negotiator for the film industry, and the US Commerce department, in carrying out annual market research and relaying business intelligence, gave the corporatist leadership assistance in consolidating Hollywood's global supremacy' (Trumpbour, 2002, p. 4). Earlier scholarly work maps larger ideological and nationalistic forces driving the MPAA's aggressive international export activities. During his term as the association's first head, Hays famously remarked, 'we are going to sell America to the world with American motion pictures' (Trumpbour, 2002, p. 17). The MPAA is seen widely in the international film community as supporting not only the uninhibited flow of American products but also free-market capitalist values that underlie ideologies of the American dream and exceptionalism. A key example discussed in Chapter 2 is a series of World War II Disney animated films – *Saludos Amigos* and *The Three Caballeros* – embracing the Good Neighbor Policy and friendly foreign relations with Latin American governments (Miller and Maxwell, 2007, pp. 42–3). Positioned as family-friendly travelogues, Donald Duck's visits to various Latin American countries to learn about their cultures and forge friendships parallel the films' international distribution and circulation ambitions.

On the international side, the organisation historically championed trade policies and opposed local government intervention regulating industry activities on
behalf of member studios. Nicknamed the 'little State Department', the MPAA
understood its role as not only selling film content but also acting as a proponent
for the American free-market capitalist system. As a distinct international division,
the Motion Picture Export Association of America (MPEAA) was formed in 1945.
It was later renamed MPA in 1994, a change prompting Toby Miller *et al.* to note
how 'excising the territorial moniker "America" points more to the priority of the
international market' (Miller *et al.*, 2005, p. 213).

STRUCTURE AND OPERATIONS

The MPAA headquarters sits in the American political hub, Washington,
DC, whereas the other domestic office is located in the historic media centre,
Los Angeles. The MPA maintains offices in Toronto, São Paulo, Brussels, and
Singapore. While one office may be responsible for an individual industry
(Toronto), most offices oversee entire regions. The São Paulo office covers Latin
America and the Caribbean, Singapore oversees all of Asia Pacific, and Brussels'
territories include all of Europe, the Middle East, and Africa. Located in a central
business district of Brussels, the MPA's Europe, Middle East and Africa (EMEA)
office occupies an expansive penthouse floor overlooking the European Union's
capital city. The office's proximity to the EU's governing body, as well as to the
media capitals of London and Paris, allows for ease of access to government
officials, communications, and other concentrated resources flowing through the
European economic hub.

Chairman Christopher Dodd and his team oversee all MPAA and MPA offices
worldwide, while each regional office houses executives and territory managers
who specialise in individual markets. Press coverage often focuses on the organisation's chairman or broader institutional activities, with little focus on the dozens
of professionals in local offices. In reality, an executive oversees administration for
each regional office and dozens of employees, many of whom serve as territory
managers. All regional presidents report to the President of International, who
oversees all international offices and reports to Chairman Dodd. Former President
of International Chris Marcich describes the position as coordinating activities and
communication among regional offices: 'Each office was aware of what the other
was doing. Same issues and similar challenges. Headquarters knew what was going
on … international heads were up to date with US [operations]' (interview with
Marcich, 2016).

The association describes their position within the industry via a 'Meet the
MPAA' section of their website: 'We are the voice of one of the country's strong-
est and most vibrant industries – the American motion picture, home video and

television industry. We aspire to advance the business and the art of filmmaking and celebrate its enjoyment around the world' (MPAA website, 2015). In representing the six major studios, the MPAA is indeed the powerful voice for their members' political, economic, and cultural interests globally. The organisation supports the wave of liberalisation, privatisation, and deregulation that swept media industries in recent decades and opened up markets for Hollywood studio investment and participation.

Cultural policy debates are often historicised through a commercial-versus-culture dichotomy that does not reflect the complex state of studio and industry-wide practices. Miller describes contemporary policy debates as 'one justifying monopolistic competition on the grounds of the fabled sovereign consumers, the other justifying state support in the name of the fabled sovereign citizen' (Miller, 1996, p. 79). He highlights the Uruguay GATT talks during the early 1990s, most notably, and how the trade discussions focused on whether media content should be protected under cultural exception policies as public goods (European argument) or a free-market product that should be able to flow without restriction (US argument). However, more than two decades later, many in the MPA argue the lines of media policy cannot be drawn so neatly between either cultural protectionism or free-market proponents: 'The situation is not as polarised as it was twenty years ago. People would like it to be' (interview with Former MPA Executive, 2013). Perhaps this viewpoint reflects the MPA and studio opinions, but, as will be discussed later in this chapter, some local players still do maintain the same perspective.

Significantly, the name change from MPEAA to MPA occurred during a period in the 1990s when international box office increased in importance for the majors' overall business operations. Chris Marcich, who served as president of the EMEA office from 1995 to 2015 and as President of International until 2016, witnessed what he calls 'structural changes' inside the organisation. When he started at the MPA, international operations were small and concentrated in regional headquarters with one to three offices in key countries. Within the following decade, Marcich points to a period of expansion, where the Asia Pacific and EMEA office staff increased and US domestic staff decreased to handle the rise of global piracy and extend outreach activities in local markets. He describes how the MPA drastically reimagined its approach as 'a shift away from confrontation to identifying areas of mutual interest with local professionals, organisations, etc., in Russia, China, France'. In particular, he characterises this new period of MPA relations and policy efforts as moving 'away from confrontational to more cooperative' (interview with Marcich, 2016). It is this self-aware logic grounded in cooperative and collaborative initiatives that many MPA professionals foregrounded in our conversations.

The international division, like the filmed entertainment companies it represents, employs an array of individuals working within, and at times negotiating against, the confines of this globally expansive trade group. While this global media organisation may have overarching priorities and objectives, an on-the-ground perspective offers a more nuanced view of institutional dynamics, individual roles, and their relationship to local industries. A pivotal, yet largely invisible, role in regional operations is undertaken by the territory manager. In conversations with Olivier Dock, the territory manager for Spain and France, he describes EMEA office activities as representing the interests of their six member studios – Disney, Fox, Paramount, Sony, Universal, and Warner Bros. He identifies territory managers as a 'point of contact' for local studio operations, partnering organisations, and local officials.

Specifically, Dock cites two key objectives for regional operations. First, the MPA works towards content protection, since piracy is the 'biggest challenge' for the studios. Digital piracy has transformed MPA strategies, since there is 'no comparison to what the MPA was doing in the '90s with disc piracy' (interview with Dock, 2013). Executives and territory managers lobby for legislation for copyright, treaties, and so forth, relating to piracy in individual territories. Second, a regional office is concerned with 'commercial' or regulatory issues such as customs, dubbing, or any restrictions on studio commercial activities. Many MPA and studio professionals I spoke with assert the importance of the territory manager's role in representing and negotiating studios' interests and priorities locally.

POLICY AND MARKET REGULATION

David Hesmondhalgh defines media policy as governmental intervention in cultural markets through three areas: (1) *legislation* – creation of laws, (2) *regulation* – agencies and institutions monitoring industry activities, and (3) *subsidy* – direct or indirect supplemental funds (Hesmondhalgh, 2013, p. 123). He identifies the largely neoliberal ideologies – privatisation, deregulation, commercialisation – shaping media policies across Europe, Latin America, and Asia since the 1980s. He describes how the 'marketisation' of telecommunications led to more open audiovisual industries with fewer regulations driven by commercial imperatives, as well as increased private media companies concentrated in the hands of fewer owners (Hesmondhalgh, 2013, p. 125).

On a broad level, the MPA's activities represent these larger shifts in the global film economy. Manjunath Pendakur characterises the MPA's efforts 'to keep the markets open for Hollywood cinema, lower tariffs, eliminate censorship, and oppose any attempt by national governments to create national cinemas as a competitive force vis-à-vis Hollywood' (Pendakur, 2008, p. 185). The association historically has worked to negotiate better terms in local markets for the unrestricted flow of Hollywood films onto local screens. These interests include flexible trade deals with local territories but also favourable policies and incentives to participate in local production, distribution, and exhibition. In conversation, current and former MPA professionals quickly identify 'market barriers' against studio member content as a central priority, including the strict screen quotas in China or limited film financing support for local-language partnerships in France. MPA professionals often not only describe the global media industries by what regions they cover but also categorise markets by levels of access from closed to open. Yet, as I argue throughout this book, within industry practice, a competitive, commercial local cinema and local Hollywood studio activities are not necessarily mutually exclusive.

In light of this new phase in MPA 'cooperative' relations, one regional executive describes how, when faced with 'potential market access barriers', his initial approach is to 'look for more market-friendly solutions' by building alliances with local players who have similar interests (interview with Former MPA Executive, 2013). Territory managers, who are directly involved in their assigned local market and regulatory climate, rely upon a vast network of studio and local contacts for media policy updates:

> If there is something that happens in one territory, we sometimes hear it in the press. Sometimes it is from a content protection organisation or a contact consultant ... it might also be a studio or subsidiary in those major markets or a licensee that informs the regional London office. We then take over, assess, and see if it is important, a problem, is there anything that can or should be done. (interview with Dock, 2013)

Despite the MPA's global presence and its international expansion in recent decades, the organisation should not be understood as ubiquitous or immediately reactive in local markets. So much of the work they do relies on established relationships, alliances, and industry networks, at once intangible and difficult to value by market logic. A territory manager may sit on a local distribution organisation or belong to a content protection agency. In Spain, the Federación de Cines de España (FEDICINE) is a Spanish organisation that represents local distributor interests including the major studios and Spanish independents. Along with FEDICINE's president, Estela Artacho, MPA territory manager Dock works to challenge regulatory measures which they identify as impacting both member studios and independent distributors. For example, in 2012 the Spanish government passed a 13 per cent value-added tax (VAT) on theatrical tickets, the highest in Europe, during a particularly weak moment in the national film industry and overall economy when theatrical attendance was at an all-time low and independent distributors began to close operations (Sarda, 2012). Both Artacho and Dock recount the beneficial partnership between these two organisations, as they worked together to meet with Spanish officials to propose changes to the VAT increase and other audiovisual policies (interview with Artacho, 2013; interview with Dock, 2013).

In the northeastern Spanish state of Catalunya, the regional parliament passed a measure in 2010 requiring all film distributors to dub half of their theatrical prints into the local Catalan language by 2018 (Hopewell and Mayorga, 2009). Dubbing studio films costs anywhere from $30,000 to $40,000 for each title (Adler, 2010). Dock argues this issue impacts European independents more than local studio offices: the 'legislation discriminates against European works and gives an advantage to non-European Spanish-language works' from Latin America (interview with Dock, 2013). He emphasises Spanish efforts where MPA and independent priorities align over mutual interests. In the digital era, the MPA operates on the industry logic that digital piracy has flattened the playing field and that 'we are all in this together' on policy protection. It is from this perspective that the organisation responds against piracy.

In addition to market barriers, the MPA may work on behalf of its members for audiovisual policies that encourage local productions, particularly alongside the emergence of the local-language strategy. In Brazil, the MPA has had a level of involvement since the 1990s in film financing measures, despite the initial ambivalence of studio members early on to invest in local films. Part of their lobbying strategies aimed at procuring subsidies and tax incentives to benefit local studio units. For example, one Brazilian local studio manager argues the Article 3 tax incentive responsible for the rebirth of the national industry was actually designed to encourage local Hollywood investment. He suggests that the studios had little interest in Brazilian LLPs and were hesitant to invest at first. The trajectory of an industry-wide strategy based on this incentive, as outlined in Chapter 3, supports his claim. Sony and Warner Bros. began to invest in film co-production using Article 3 financing four years after the policy went into effect. Slow to follow, the other studios – Disney, Fox, Universal, and Paramount – only began investing on a small scale by the early to mid-2000s. As this country manager contends, 'the majors saw investing in Brazilian films as "a kind of tax", since it never generated the same type of money as their English-language projects' (interview with Local Studio Manager, 2010). Significantly, this anecdote illustrates a disconnect, or a contradictory viewpoints, between local MPA and studio managers with LA-based studio home offices. Yet a handful of Brazilian LLPs achieved box-office success in the 2000s, and the view of MPA member studios began to change as market share and theatrical attendance for these local blockbusters increased.

MPA territory managers may work for studio co-productions to be classified as local to gain access to incentives and subsidies. In a widely reported case in France, the battle over the French-language co-production *Un long dimanche de fiançailles (A Very Long Engagement, 2004)* led to years of legal limbo. The controversy began when Warner Bros. France, along with the local studio unit's head, Francis Boespflug, launched a production company called 2003 Productions. WB France owned 32 per cent, Boespflug maintained 16 per cent, and the rest belonged to company employees. The new venture, and their subsequent French-language co-productions, ignited industry debates over whether 2003 was owned by a Hollywood studio or considered a French company. 2003 Productions acted as majority co-producer for the French-language drama alongside minority French partners TFI Film Productions and Tapioca. Directed by French film-maker Jean-Pierre Jeunet, led by French star Audrey Tautou, and based on a best-selling French novel, *Un long dimanche de fiançailles* had a $50 million production budget, making it one of the most expensive projects ever produced locally. In 2003, France's National Cinema Centre (CNC) categorised the co-production as a local film under its points classification system determined by language, cast, crew, locations, etc. Whereas a film must meet at least 76 out of the 100 points on the scale to qualify as locally French, the CNC awarded *Un long dimanche de fiançailles* 99 points (Frater, 2004; Tartaglione, 2003a, 2003b).

With national classification, a film gains access to a French film subsidy, *compte de soutien*, that operates as a revolving fund giving the producers future access to a percentage of the film's box-office, television, and home entertainment sales to invest in a new project. The state support fund is open only to French producers. While the CNC supported the film's access to the revolving fund, and later proposed allowing the US majors direct access as well, the French Independent Producers' Association and Independent Producers' Union filed a complaint in court claiming 2003 Productions did not classify as an independent company and should not be entitled to state film support. Even after the film's production wrapped in 2003, between November 2004 and June 2005, the Administrative Court of Paris heard a series of lawsuits and appeals over the nationality of Jeunet's film. The Parisian court also banned another 2003 Production, *L'Ex femme de ma vie* (*The Ex-Wife of My Life*, 2004), from accessing the revolving fund, although this ruling was later overturned at appeal (Tartaglione, 2003c, 2004a, 2004b). At the height of the legal battle, 2003 Productions released a statement pressing for the production's nationality as French:

> all of the auspices in front of and behind the camera are French, starting with noted French filmmaker Jean-Pierre Jeunet, and his movie tells a French saga, is adapted from a French novel, was filmed completely in France and in the French language. It provided work for over 2,000 French extras, over 500 technicians as well as 30 French comedians, for over 18 months. It also saved from bankruptcy the French special effects company Dubois. (Frater, 2004)

Even as the Minister of Culture, Renaud Donnedieu de Vabres, condemned the French court's final decision as 'contrary to aiding employment', ultimately *Un long dimanche de fiançailles* was unable to access the funds in 2005, which was seen by many in the European audiovisual sector as a win for cultural protectionism (Tartaglione, 2005). Governmental and industry institutions inside France, from federal to municipal levels, maintained competing, and at times contradictory, views of what constitutes a French production in the Warner Bros./2003 Production case. This case exemplifies the slippery nature of trying to locate a film's origin within a nationally defined system that does not reflect the transnational nature of contemporary film financing and production, and how the studios' local operations work to be flexible enough to blur those lines.

Disputes over what counts as a local or Hollywood co-production reflect larger conversations occurring across local territories in recent years. The former director of the EU's MEDIA programme, Aviva Silver, describes the objectives of regional, national, and local subsidies as 'corrective measures' necessary for independent production companies to balance their inequality of resources with respect to well-established international studios and conglomerates like Sony and Warner Bros. (interview with Silver, 2011, 2013). For Silver, funding mechanisms protect local film in Europe, providing smaller countries with funding they would not other-wise have access to, a sentiment echoed by several MPA managers I interviewed. Yet eligibility for film subsidies varies from industry to industry: the majors can access Brazil's tax incentive Article 3, but not France's stricter *compte de soutien*. Many major studios argue 'their films are local', as outlined in earlier chapters. However, Silver and many of her European contemporaries classify local-language productions as definably studio projects, and not 'local', particularly considering the vast financial power and historical presence of Hollywood. On the one hand, the inability of *Un long dimanche de fiançailles* to secure French nationality represents a long legacy of protecting national cinema in response to Hollywood's presence, or what initiated the revolving support fund's creation in the first place. On the other hand, as studio territory offices become more involved and integrated in local audiovisual sectors aided by MPA efforts, the battle over what is 'local cinema' will continue to be fought along the contentious lines of aesthetic and creative factors versus financing, employment, and geographical location.

PIRACY

The unauthorised sale, copying, and circulation of film content – what the film industry refers to as piracy – occurred first in the form of stolen prints during Hollywood's nickelodeon era. As studio distribution windows diversified across home video, DVDs, and digital streaming, and as monetary dependency on these platforms increased, the circulation of unauthorised content evolved to include print theft, camcorder piracy, disc piracy, and digital internet piracy. By the 2010s, Ramon Lobato would describe an 'online distribution ecology' and the deterritorialised exchange of content through linking sites, video-hosting sites, and cyberlockers (Lobato, 2012, p. 100). The Hollywood studio system historically developed an economic model based on monetising exclusive rights of their products. With quickly evolving software and hardware technologies and wider global flow of their products, the major studios increasingly focus on protecting their intellectual property from copyright infringement.

The MPAA established the Film Security Office and organised an aggressive assault on piracy worldwide beginning in the 1970s. Then association head Jack Valenti famously took a polemically brash stance, calling the piracy of member studios' content 'a cancer in the belly of the film industry' and describing the MPAA/MPA's action as 'our own terrorist war' (McDonald, 2007, p. 189; 2015, p. 69). Valenti's rhetoric reflects the organisation's continued stance, which aims to transform the most powerful players in the film industry into what Paul McDonald describes as 'a living and vulnerable being – the body of Hollywood – an organism attacked both internally and externally by malignant or malevolent forces' (McDonald, 2015, p. 69). This narrative spins the studios as victims and users as perpetrators.

Furthermore, Lobato describes US-based debates on 'copyright wars' as 'focusing on questions of revenue leakage and financial losses to cultural products' (Lobato, 2012, p. 69). For example, the MPA widely circulates policy reports and social media statistics estimating revenue loss of its members. He complicates understandings of copyright infringement beyond Western commercial studio definitions through six categories of piracies: theft, free enterprise, free speech, authorship, resistance, and access (Lobato, 2012, p. 70). Despite this chapter's focus on how the MPA characterises and approaches piracy as theft, this is an important distinction to make, because the flow of unauthorised content moves differently across formal and informal markets, from Nigeria to Brazil. My discussion of the MPA and piracy is less concerned with an extensive history of institutional strategies or expansive global analysis of user activities. Instead, I focus on how the MPA manages a large-scale global policy, legal, promotion, and partnerships campaign to protect member interests, issues which are addressed in this section.

Amid the internal structural changes that have occurred since the 1990s, the rise of digital technologies transforming the production and circulation of media content globally has shifted the MPAA/MPA's policy focus towards protecting digital copyright and securing the intellectual property of its member studios. Dock contends:

the MPA has evolved over time since 1922 and what it has become now ... [content protection] is a big chunk because that is perceived by the studios as the biggest challenge. Digital piracy on the internet has no comparison with what the MPA was doing in the 1990s ... disc piracy limited to street peddlers and large-scale operations in some territories, Russia at the time and Southern Europe, Asia. Now piracy is everywhere. (interview with Dock, 2013)

In my conversations with MPA representatives and studio managers, piracy inevitably arises, typically in connection with the organisation's priorities and strategies in representing its members. Battling digital piracy has become such a core part of studio activities that a former MPA executive based outside North America derisively criticised contemporary operations as 'basically [an] anti-piracy enforcement agency' (interview with Former MPA Executive, 2013). How the organisation battles piracy on the ground in individual markets represents larger priorities and an increasingly collaborative approach across legislative, policy, and promotional efforts.

Legal activities initiated by regional MPA offices vary from market to market. One Brussels-based MPA manager contends, 'the certainty is that the movie will make it to the internet. The challenge is to reduce the time it will take to appear on the internet. Sometimes it is a matter of days … to protect each window from theatrical on' (interview with MPA Territory Manager, 2013). In a highly publicised UK case, the MPA won a 2010 lawsuit in London's High Court of Justice against Usenet to shut down the decentralised message board's indexing site Newzbin. The site had evolved into a way to share unauthorised audiovisual files through a sophisticated automation tool. Users downloaded movies and television shows automatically, in contrast to sharing files directly or through cyberlockers. As a result, the UK-based Newzbin was shut down, ordered to remove copyrighted materials, and required to pay damages to the major studios. However, at the time, the now defunct Newzbin2 launched in the former site's place, hosted briefly in Sweden and registered in the US. The following year, the MPA returned to the High Court and was successful in forcing the British internet service provider BT to block access to the new site under the UK's Copyright, Design, and Patents Act (Halliday, 2011; Healey, 2010; Lindvall, 2010; Sweney and Halliday, 2011).

Regional MPA offices also lobby local governments to enact stricter laws against piracy, or what the organisation calls addressing 'market access barriers'. Spain notoriously is one of the audiovisual markets with some of the highest rates of unauthorised streaming and P2P sharing worldwide despite a series of laws enacted by Parliament. An earlier legislative initiative known as La Ley Sinde, or the Sinde Law, named after Minister of Culture Ángeles González-Sinde, failed to be signed into law, and was followed up by the passing of the stricter 2014 Intellectual Property Law (Rolfe, 2014; Rucinski and Reinlein, 2011).

The MPA frames the pressure they apply for stricter anti-piracy policy as an industry-wide effort involving their competitors. These initiatives more often happen in local institutions and alliances behind the scene. The MPA maintains a majority membership in the Federal Association of Spanish Audiovisual Producers (FAPAE), a group made up of the majors' local units and independent producers. Dock describes the benefits of FAPAE as 'an alliance with local players who understand the risks and impacts of piracy' (interview with Dock, 2013). One central Spanish alliance exists between FAPAE, EGEDA, and the MPA. Spain's division of Audiovisual Producers Rights' Management Entity (EGEDA) manages collective rights for local audiovisual producers, particularly those that cannot be negotiated or closed individually. MPA partners with the non-profit organisation globally to protect content producers. In the Spanish market, EGEDA helped to develop two streaming platforms to limit unauthorised content leaking online. While the VOD platform Filmoteca operates similarly to Netflix, the Veomac (Video Experience Online) platform offers access for Spanish Academy members to individually watermarked films in lieu of more expensive DVD screeners. Significantly, EGEDA is developing similar protected platforms for film academies, festivals, and institutes globally (interview with Antón, 2013).

As both Lobato and McDonald argue, an illuminating aspect of the MPA's stance on piracy is the striking rhetoric and PR spin. McDonald identifies the 'two lines of argument [against piracy]: one moral, the other economic' (McDonald, 2015, p. 69). I quickly discovered how MPA professionals and their studio partners circulate these two narratives widely from the global to local level. First, a long-term argument for the organisation's anti-piracy activities rests on the harm incurred by member studios and their loss of revenue. As part of MPA comments in the 2016 National Trade Estimate Report on Foreign Trade Barriers, EVP of Global Policy and External Affairs Joanna McIntosh connects profit loss to damaging creative industry innovation: 'content theft, particularly in the form of illegal camcording in theatres and the expanding scourge of rogue websites can devastate the creation and innovation of new works, and in turn the nation's economic growth' (McIntosh, 2015). Many Spanish country managers and independent producers echo these sentiments by bemoaning the impact that piracy has on theatregoing attendance and the almost non-existent home entertainment market for all players in the market. Moreover, local Spanish-language films have a limited lifespan beyond theatrical and depend almost entirely on box-office gross. In turn, regional MPA professionals work to identify precisely how 'piracy is bad for everyone' and point to the value of local partnerships and alliances with organisations like FAPAE and EGEDA. The 'all together' narrative supports a similar sentiment made by so many local studio managers regarding 'what is best for all of us' in the fight for content protection. The MPA and member studios' promotion of strength through collaboration serves as a direct counter-narrative to earlier debates about European cinema culture versus American commerce, which worked to position the studios as solely opportunistic and profit-minded corporations.

Second, the MPA and its member studios also reframe the discussion about piracy as an ethical or moral dilemma. In conversations with studio country managers across Brazil and Europe, a similar narrative emerges around the need to 'educate' audiences about piracy. One Spanish country manager argues:

> it is hurting the culture … how do I get those kids to understand that pirating content is stealing from someone. They don't see it like that. They see it as cool. To be a pirate sounds like a cool thing. In Spanish, being a *pirata* is like a compliment instead [of] you are a thief … that is the educational part that we have to care about and the government should do something about that habit … it needs to be taught in school. (interview with Studio Managing Director, 2013)

Similar to the 'victimless crime' arguments driving MPAA domestic campaigns, regional MPA professionals and their studio members frame sharing unauthorised content as a 'deviant' cultural behaviour in need of correction. The MPA's anti-piracy efforts reflect what Lobato calls a 'public relations exercise' that happens simultaneously in a number of local markets (Lobato, 2012, pp. 70–1, 73–4). This exercise works to redirect the focus onto respectability (of audiences and users) and ethics (of consumers) and away from the organisation, its member studios, and Hollywood's powerful presence globally.

PROMOTION

In addition to a global campaign against piracy directed increasingly at changing audience behaviour and enacting policy protection, a significant part of the MPA's new strategy since the 1990s involves promotional activities. One of the organisation's main functions is to control, manage, and increasingly rewrite industry spin about themselves, member studios, and the industry at large. A new approach to public relations and outreach includes extending and promoting local activities through social media campaigns in order to reimagine their own image within the international film market. With efforts to protect studio members' interests and businesses internationally, the organisation not only deals in promotional strategies and rebranding efforts but also actively invests in local relationships and cultivates a long-term presence in local industries.

Beyond the MPAA home office, regional managers and executives are quick to acknowledge the organisation's controversial image globally, particularly the view of Hollywood studios as a cartel. MPA representatives' understandings of this reputation reveal an astute awareness and sensitivity to their villain image and close relationship to the US government. In conversations about Hollywood's presence internationally, one manager responds in frustration:

> such a mix of sentiments [regarding cultural imperialism claims] that you really have to be careful … very quickly people pull a sort of trump card of Hollywood dominance

and you wanting to crush everyone. No, no, no, no. We are just saying that whatever you come up with, a regulation, law ... has an impact on the business and sharing our views ... you have points of pressure, things that are easy for the other guys to illustrate at the multiplex of twenty screens where fifteen go to *Harry Potter*. (interview with MPA Territory Manager, 2013)

And it is this complex dynamic that emerges in discussions of local audiovisual policy and Hollywood international activities: one that is bound up in a long history of economic, political, and cultural weight but also complicated by institutional relationships and interpersonal exchanges. Warner Bros. may produce and circulate *Harry Potter* worldwide, but at the same time audiovisual policies facilitate the studio's investment and partnerships with UK institutions.

As part of the organisation's shifting approach – since the 1990s – towards 'collaboration', regional offices experiment in cultivating relationships with local creative professionals through awards programmes and training initiatives. Jack Valenti helped to create the Prix Michel D'Ornano Award in 1991, renamed D'Ornano-Valenti twenty-four years later. The Franco-American Cultural Fund (FACF) took over financial support for the award in 2007, granting a cash prize to the chosen French film's director-writer, producer, and distributor. Founded by the Directors Guild of America, Writers Guild of America, and French Société des Auteurs, Compositeurs et Éditeurs de Musique, the FACF works to protect intellectual property rights and claims 'to promote French cinema, develop ties with American distributors and facilitate access to the North American market for many French film-makers and producers' (FACF website). In the early 1990s, in the midst of tense trade negotiations and protectionist policy backlash, the French film industry maintained a difficult relationship with the Hollywood studios. Marcich sees the FACF and the film-making award as part of a larger effort by the MPA to 'build bridges between the US and France ... you have to build relationships and trust each other' (interview with Marcich, 2016). What it also reveals is the integral connection between Hollywood's position in the local market, alliances with content-protection organisations, and the long-term labour involved in producing positive public relations spin.

For over twenty years, Steve Solot worked as the senior VP of MPA Latin America and ran the Rio de Janeiro office until its move to São Paulo in the late 2000s. The American ex-pat describes his former position as overseeing regional operations, lobbying on behalf of the majors for commercial legislative measures including copyright and intellectual property protection. While Solot contends the MPA aimed at competitive distribution practices and were most concerned with the studios' 'bottom line', he understood the importance of cultivating relationships in the Brazilian and other Latin American markets. In addition to specific policy matters, so much of the work of regional offices is fostering connections between studio members and local professionals, long-term efforts not necessarily character-istic of studio presence internationally until that point. In 1990, he began offering production workshops in partnership with film agencies in Mexico, Argentina, Chile, Colombia, and Brazil. These workshops developed into the Latin American Training Center (LATC), an initiative which Solot still runs. Much of the early training involved script development and technical training; he proudly notes that the screenwriter of *Cidade de Deus* – one of Brazil's most commercially successful films – participated in one of these workshops with an early draft.

Solot contends that training a new generation of writers, cinematographers, and other media specialists made Brazilian films and professionals more competitive in a global business during a transitional period. Solot started the LATC as a bridge between Brazilian film professionals, MPA, and major studios, later extending that work as the president of the Rio Film Commission. This strategy represents a long-term investment in industry infrastructure as opposed to a one-off, short-term investment in co-production. The programme also coincides with a period in Brazilian cinema of increased industry incentives for international companies when Sony and Warner Bros. began developing their early LLP strategies. Furthermore, where the MPA member studios initially saw little short-term value at the time, Solot's investment and championing of these workshops became 'important to reduce opposition (both political and cultural) against the US and its domination over [local theatrical] market share' (interview with Solot, 2010). He understood workshop and creative relationships with local partners not just as a financial invest-ment, but as a 'pro-active strategy' for long-term studio involvement. On the one hand, this strategy helps to rebrand the position of the MPA and its member studios as contributing to the industry instead of merely dominating the market share. On the other hand, this represents a new long game for the MPA, which Marcich says reflects the international activities of studios which increasingly are 'in it for the long haul' (interview with Marcich, 2016).

In addition to on-the-ground partnerships, MPA promotional strategies operate through industry event visibility and social media presence. One of current MPAA head Christopher Dodd's key roles is to be spokesperson and figurehead for the organisation. Dodd often appears at industry trade shows: he has given speeches at the National Association of Theater Owners' CinemaCon, introduced Sony Corporation's president and CEO Kazuo Hirai at the Annual Technology and Engineering Emmy Awards, and cut a ceremonial ribbon at the American Pavilion during the Cannes Film Festival (MPAA, 2015). Dodd has a different media pres-ence to that of his predecessor, Valenti, partially due to their different political careers (one behind the scenes in the Lyndon B. Johnson administration and the other as an elected US senator). The state of the organisation and larger audiovisual industry also shifted drastically from Valenti's era, when domestic box office was the studios' central business, to the more globalised and digitally decentralised industrial climate of Dodd's. In a *Vanity Fair* profile, Dodd compares the twenty-first-century industry to the more straightforward climate of Valenti's period: 'when Jack took this job, there were three networks, I think thirteen freestanding studios, and [MCA/Universal's] Lew Wasserman ran the world' (Purdum, 2012). During Dodd's first five years, the MPAA unsuccessfully lobbied to pass the Stop Online Piracy Act (SOPA) in 2012 before the US Congress and had to manage the broad sweeping fallout after the 2014 Sony hack.

MPAA and MPA offices aim to control or rewrite the industry spin surrounding studio films, professionals, and activities across local industries, with social media and blogging as a key method of communication. In addition to annual online statistical reports highlighting studio theatrical performance worldwide, the MPAA/MPA participate in trade shows, film markets, workshops, press conferences, and social media promotion on behalf of their member studios. These alliances are featured prominently through their social media accounts. The current administration has embraced and developed a widespread social media presence, a notable strategic shift in institutional PR efforts.

The MPAA launched a Twitter account in 2011; three years later, the MPA EMEA office followed suit. The MPAA Twitter account often live-tweets speeches and press conferences, meaning that excerpts and commentary are posted in real time. During the 2015 CinemaCon trade show, the Twitter feed served as a backchannel for Dodd's speech. The social media platform offers a way to further extend the association's heavy promotion of labour and trade issues, specifically Dodd's highlighting of the 1.9 million film professionals working in the film and TV industries. The association releases this data through infographics, including the 2015 'What Does Trade Have to Do with Your Favorite Movie?', which promotes global trade to film audiences. Namely, the infographic claims, 'As an industry, we had a bigger services trade surplus than telecom, computer services, or advertising.' Promotional materials work to frame the conversation around mobile production and international studio activities as creating jobs domestically and producing export revenue globally.

The social media presence often takes a celebratory and congratulatory tone. Beyond official news and industry reports, the MPAA website features a blog offering an overview of activities and events, with headlines such as 'Thousands of New Yorkers Brought HBO's *Vinyl* to Life' and 'City of Lights, City of Angels: Milestones in Franco-American Cooperation' (MPAA, 2015). The organisation's culture and management understand an active online presence as a tool for advocacy and a way to circulate central talking points promoting studio interests as well as overall industry health, employment numbers, and content protection. According to one former manager, 'the studios are in the business of media. When it comes to their own interests, they are really bad at it. They sometimes are their own worst enemy ... [they] have a problem getting the message across. We live in a time where usually the loudest wins' (interview with Former MPA Executive, 2013). As illustrated by this new phase of social media communication, the MPA may still be one of the loudest voices in the international film industry; however, in recent decades the organisation has expanded promotional efforts in order to retool and soften that message through various channels.

CONCLUSION

Hollywood's international activities ultimately raise the question of local audiovisual policies and industry priorities: not only who benefits but who is involved in decision-making processes and what this mean for studio operations and their partners in local markets. A consistently powerful voice for the six major studios worldwide is the Motion Picture Association. As this chapter illustrates, various institutional strategies and factors shape how the MPA represents member interests and priorities. In an industrial climate of global and digital connectivity, the organisation has entered a new strategic phase to address constantly shifting market barriers, unauthorised content, and promotional and communication needs. The significance of this chapter arises from the access that made conducting fieldwork possible. Due to communication with MPA executives and mid-level managers, as well as introductions to local studio units, I was given an unprecedented view into how the organisation and its employees understand operations and activities. Even as my attempts to secure interviews and subsequent conversations were filtered and managed as part of an overall PR strategy, I am interested in what it reveals about how the MPA understands this new era of 'cooperation' and their position in the local markets and regional media industries.

As an organisation, the Motion Picture Association has witnessed a number of sweeping changes internally and externally in recent decades. Internally, the twenty-first century brought leadership changes alongside changing studio member needs and the increased importance of international operations. Most revealing in my research is how the organisation developed, and now understands, a new institutional culture – one that moves away from hard-line confrontational tactics in local markets and towards collaborative initiatives and softer strategies. I witnessed this approach in my own interactions with their executives and communications director: a calculated willingness to discuss larger institutional history and objectives that undoubtedly reflects these rebranding efforts. Externally, methods of digital communications – how MPA representatives speak to other industry actors and the public at large – continue to evolve as the organisation strategically embraces social media platforms. This network of communication, based on regional offices and individual managers, complicates understandings of the MPA as a monolithic organisation representing a singular studio interest. How the organisation will manage to evolve this collaborative approach as industrial challenges emerge will determine the future efficacy of this industry group.

Despite these structural changes, one significant factor remains: the modes in which the MPAA/MPA continue to negotiate the common interests of many parties locally and globally. According to Pendakur: 'while these corporate giants compete fiercely with each other for talent, capital, and access to markets around the world, they also collaborate under the benevolent umbrella of the Motion Picture Association of America in trying to achieve some common goals' (Pendakur, 2008, p. 182). Yet, in the conglomerate era, identifying and acting upon common goals among the member studios proves challenging. In 2014, an aggressive hack of Sony Pictures Entertainment's computer network resulted in thousands of documents leaked, divulging everything from private corporate communications and payroll records to individual employees' personal data and email exchanges (Cieply and Barnes, 2014; Gara and Warzel, 2014).[2] The hack resulted in a massive PR fiasco not only for Sony but also for the MPAA/MPA. The organisation under Dodd's leadership was widely criticised for its slow actions and lukewarm support in the aftermath. SPE's Co-CEO Michael Lynton reportedly threatened to leave the almost hundred-year-old studio alliance, criticising it as 'out of touch and ineffective' (Verrier and Bierman, 2015). A week after the hack, Dodd eventually released a letter in support of Sony and backed by the other five studios, yet Warner Bros. CEO Kevin Tsujihara reflects, 'we could have and should have done more for Michael and Sony' (Verrier, 2014). Tensions among the members arose when Warner Bros. was the only studio willing to support Sony publicly; the others chose to remain quiet and distant. The MPAA maintains 'a rule that requires alignment of all member companies behind any significant step', which inevitably has impacted, even halted, past policy debates and initiatives (Cieply and Barnes, 2015).

In the current era, the MPAA/MPA face challenges as member priorities diverge. First, interests vary from studio to studio. These differences may play out in large-scale global production and distribution cultures but also are reflected by Sony, Fox, and Warner Bros.' prioritising of local-language productions in contrast to Paramount and Disney's limited interest therein. As one Spanish industry representative for the studios suggests, 'Paramount is not as flexible as Warner Bros. [in the local market]. Depends on the international office and they are not interested ... [Paramount] might say, "We don't want to be Warner Bros." ... different strategy in different markets' (interview with Spanish Industry Professional, 2013). Furthermore, the MPAA/MPA also must navigate internally for their members, because the diverse divisions within the parent media conglomerates may have differing, or even contradictory, business strategies. With member studios renewing

Dodd's contract through 2018, it will be revealing how the MPAA/MPA continues to maintain institutional strategies against transforming studio priorities and local market conditions.

NOTES

1. Access to Hollywood studio executives and managers is notoriously restricted, an issue Sherry B. Ortner explores in an essay detailing her ethnography work and research on studio professionals in Los Angeles. My contacts at the MPA were vital for conducting this work. My initial access to studio managers in both Latin America and Europe came from current and former MPA managers in those regions. Most notably, at one point during a meeting, former VP of MPA Latin America Steve Solot opened up his Blackberry and casually asked, 'Who do you want to talk to?' He was able to pull contacts from decades-long relationships with local studio managers in Brazil. This system of introductions illustrates a culturally specific Brazilian tradition of sponsoring introductions and sidestepping formal channels of access, called *jeitinho*. After email introductions to leading producers, distributors, and managing directors of local studio divisions, this insider 'introduction' lifted the most important industrial barrier to access and allowed me the opportunity to build my own contacts and foster relationships with sources.

2. On 24 November 2014, a group calling themselves the Guardians of Peace hacked Sony Pictures Entertainment's company computer network. Spanning a few weeks and eight data 'releases', Sony's so-called 'I.T. matter' emerged as 'the most embarrassing and all-encompassing hack of internal corporate data ever made public' according to Michael Cieply and Brooks Barnes' 'Sony Cyberattack, First a Nuisance, Swiftly Grew into a Firestorm' in the *New York Times* and Tom Gara and Charlie Warzel's 'A Look through the Sony Pictures Data Hack: This Is as Bad as It Gets' in *Buzzfeed*. Sony's erratic and contradictory response, as documents revealed in the aftermath, caused a storm of industry criticism. The leaked email inboxes of then SPE co-chairpersons Amy Pascal and Michael Lynton became a public relations nightmare. Emails included conversations disparaging a number of top creatives and actors working with the major studio, along with spreadsheets illustrating the massive pay gap between male and female Sony executives, according to Mark Seal's 'An Exclusive Look at Sony's Hacking Saga' in *Vanity Fair*.

7

Local Blockbusters and Media Franchising: Convergence and Cross-Media

Blockbuster tentpole practices and media franchising have transformed Conglomerate Hollywood production cultures. Studio-filmed entertainment divisions have concentrated and scaled back their slates to focus the majority of resources on ten to twelve big-budget, English-language titles intended for global audiences. The participation of local territory offices is vital for promoting and circulating these films outside North America. As examined in Chapters 3 and 4, local territory offices may participate through feedback loops in some aspects of the studio production process as well as oversee local distribution and marketing activities for major-event pictures. Country managers and their local teams are active participants in adapting campaigns for local audiences. Marketing materials and release patterns for Paramount's *Star Trek* rebooted franchise (2009–) or Warner Bros.' *The Dark Knight* series (2005–12) may be tailored to a local market's audience tastes, distribution culture, and exhibition infrastructure (interview with Gil, 2013; interview with Silva, 2014).

Yet franchising strategies and blockbuster production cultures are not limited to major English-language titles. Local offices are adapting and reimagining studio commercial practices to produce properties and franchises across Europe, Latin America, and Asia. This chapter explores the complexities and negotiations involved in the localisation of contemporary blockbuster and franchising practices, from institutional restructuring and corporate culture to creative decision-making and collaborative relationships between the studios and their local independent partners. What emerges is a marked tension, distinct from the English-language tentpoles, between expanding and multiplying these local properties beyond a single theatrical platform release while also containing them geographically within these mid-sized territories.

Derek Johnson challenges popular and industrial discourses that reductively dismiss media franchising as 'cultural bankruptcy' and instead suggests how this practice functions as a post-Fordist economic system characterised by cultural exchange and collaboration across industrial networks (D. Johnson, 2013, p. 29). Franchise systems rely on expansion and repeatability through serialisation and sequelisation, or the ability to extend a media property beyond one film or series into additional platforms across film, television, gaming, print, and digital media. Not only have the studios managed and tailored a number of properties in this way, but franchising has become a central strategy since the 2000s. See, for example, Universal's efforts to sustain and resurrect a fledgling *Fast and Furious* series from a direct-to-DVD third film to a globally lucrative franchise followed by five iterations – and it's still growing. Additionally, Disney's Marvel Studios has developed a strategic production process and release pattern, planning franchised film series segments over five years in advance. The *Avengers* movies and other Marvel series have tightly organised and integrated production and distribution plans known as Phase I, II, and III (Chitwood, 2014).

Johnson distinguishes between the inter-industrial and intra-industrial franchise. The former constitutes a 'transmedia extension across the social and industrial context of multiple media industries', whereas the latter serves as 'multiplication across productions in a single medium or institutional context' (D Johnson, 2013, p. 45). Sony's *Spider-Man* iterations spanning film series, games, and other platforms are an example of the inter-industrial franchise. By contrast, Marvel's plan to introduce new film spin-offs from *The Avengers* series operates as an intra-industrial franchise. Whether across multiple industries or one medium, building and expanding a story universe reflects a particular 'logic in which product innovation, decision-making processes and cultures of production becomes sites of negotiation among a range of stakeholders' (D. Johnson, 2013, p. 34). This logic relies heavily on securing and managing intellectual property, so the exchange and negotiation over creative rights for licensing and reproducing these media properties by the conglomerates emerges as a key facet for understanding twenty-first-century media industry activities.

Beyond the technological shifts shaping creative and reception practices set against the backdrop of digitisation, Henry Jenkins highlights how media convergence 'alters the relationship between existing technologies, industries, markets, genres, and audiences' (Jenkins, 2004, p. 34). On the one hand, convergence characterises the conglomerate era as driven by new media technologies offering more accessibility, affordability, availability, and interconnectivity than before as a way of connecting film, television, home entertainment, gaming, and new media platforms. On the other hand, the concentration in ownership of media companies worldwide has led to the formation of a handful of multinational operations dominating cross-media production, distribution, and exhibition practices (Jenkins, 2004, p. 33). Beyond branding logic, Jenkins contends, convergence 'represents a reconfiguration of media power and a reshaping of media aesthetics and economics' (Jenkins, 2004, p. 35). With media properties developed for longer lifespans made possible by diversified ancillary markets, production and distribution logic relies heavily on serialisation, extension, and replication to connect these various delivery channels. While the scale and scope of media franchises within local territories varies in contrast to

English-language tentpoles, as will be discussed throughout this chapter, blockbuster logic and transmedia strategies largely are impacting production and distribution processes on a local level.

Two key production practices operate at the centre of media franchising: blockbuster mentality and transmedia storytelling. Transmedia and franchising are often conflated within academic and industrial discourse, with the former characterised by world building and expansive story universes across multiple platforms. Johnson differentiates these two practices: 'Whereas transmedia storytelling suggests cultural artistry and participatory culture, "franchising" calls if not more attention to corporate structure and the economic organisation of that productive labor' (D. Johnson, 2013, p. 33). This chapter focuses on franchising efforts, corporate structures, and case studies from local studio operations – Disney and Warner Bros. – where transmedia storytelling is a key factor in developing these local properties.

Studio reliance on media franchising and building transmedia universes largely drives the post-1990s conglomerate era. Moments of industrial restructuring, institutional decision-making, and technological transformation shape how studios are producing local content for international territories. I explore two industrial cases of local franchising. The first case study focuses on Disney's *High School Musical* (*HSM*) universe, from the initial made-for-TV movie to its various local theatrical iterations in key European, Latin American, and East Asian markets. As an intra-industrial franchise, *HSM* reflects Disney's particular production culture, total marketing strategy, and reliance on its global distribution pipelines. The second case study explores the expansion of Warner Bros. Germany's unit and LLP strategy. Specifically, the local operation partnered with an independent production company helmed by a major film star to develop *Keinohrhasen* (*Rabbit without Ears*, 2007) into an inter-industrial franchise with paratextual extensions including toys and children's literature.

Based largely on industry interviews and trade coverage, the creative and economic processes surrounding these local franchises illustrate the uneven and at times contradictory nature of transnational studio networks. Ultimately, this chapter reveals the complex process of negotiation across institutional priorities, transnational production cultures, local management structures, and creative decision-making. Whether Warner Bros.' local transmedia success or Disney's rocky global expansion, each media property and its various iterations represent an experiment in localised franchising, transnational cultural flows, and a reimagining of studio commercial practices during a particular moment of local convergence.

DISNEY AND *HIGH SCHOOL MUSICAL*

Since its launch in 1983, the Disney Channel has produced and released a steady slate of original made-for-TV movies targeting the tween audience. *High School Musical*, released in January 2006, proved to be one of the broadcaster's most successful movies and launched a global transmedia franchise. Following the high school trials of friendship and first love set to an array of original pop song and dance numbers, the film features a group of then unknown young actors and a modest budget of around $4.2 million (Marr, 2007a). Over the following four years, Disney developed and extended the franchise into two sequels, several live shows, soundtracks, licensed school productions, stage versions, local-language film versions, and a universe of merchandising. As illustrated in this section, *HSM* reflects the company's shifting priorities during the 2000s towards expanding Disney operations and content both globally and locally.

In her extensive work on Disney, Janet Wasko identifies the 1980s and 1990s as a turning point for the company. In the previous decade, the filmed entertainment division released a number of theatrical flops and was slow to embrace the new home video market, especially the slow monetisation of Disney's vast film library. The installation of a new management team led by Michael Eisner in 1984 ushered in the 'New Disney'. The Eisner team refocused efforts on corporate partnerships, diversified expansion, and corporate synergy (Wasko, 2001, pp. 32–6). The massive restructuring included efforts to diversify film audiences by launching the Disney Channel and the adult-focused label Touchstone Pictures in 1983 and 1984, respectively. Furthermore, the company began an aggressive amortisation strategy to systematically release titles from the film library 'vault' to take advantage of increased home video sales. Disney's institutional expansion continued with the purchase of Miramax in 1993 and Capital Cities/ABC in 1995, characterising what many within the company coined as 'the Disney Decade' (Wasko, 2001, pp. 36–7).

On the one hand, Disney's diversification and aggressive expansion parallels larger industrial trends of conglomeration, concentration of ownership, and convergence. On the other hand, the push during that period for cross-division and cross-media strategies illustrates Disney's aim for 'total entertainment' – what Paul Grainge characterises as both 'an industrial principle' and 'cultural and textual practice' – historically central and essential in building the company's brand (Grainge, 2008, pp. 47–51). Grainge emphasises:

> if, as some argue, theatrical film is one long marketing device for a range of ancillary products (videos, DVDs, soundtracks), extra-textual experiences (theme park rides, video games) and non-filmic consumables (toys, soft drinks, fast food), then branding has become the lynchpin of a new gestalt of 'total entertainment', central to a consolidated media moment transforming the status of the motion picture as commodity and aesthetic object. (Grainge, 2008, p. 53)

Disney's management and extension of intellectual property through its characters and popular family franchises is a significant facet of the company culture. Whether

Mickey Mouse's crossover into comics and merchandising during the 1930s or the cross-promotional effort of the ABC Disneyland series to sell the new California theme park in the 1950s, Disney historically has relied on synergy and transmedia strategies. These efforts towards 'total entertainment' operate to construct and maintain a cohesive 'brand of fantasy' across multimedia platforms of magic and innocence in order to target the family audience (Anderson, 1994).

The 'New Disney' focused heavily on growing domestic divisions and audiences. Yet, like its peers, the company also began to focus institutional expansion on global audiences and international operations. By the late 1990s, the filmed entertainment division had begun to expand aggressively into the international market, which made up less than 20 per cent of overall company revenue at the time. Robert Iger, then newly hired head of international, began to restructure the local operations openly described as disconnected and unorganised. Until this period, Disney did not have a clear strategy for international expansion, which led many local offices to be inefficient and poorly coordinated. In describing the new approach to the international market, Iger later suggested, 'we're building Disney from scratch ... as Walt did in the US over 50 years ago' (Marr, 2007b). On a broader level, by employing the romantic origin story around Walt Disney, Iger contributes to a cohesive corporate image. On a more local level, an example of this 'building' local operations is the restructured Walt Disney International's Latin American offices in 1999. The region was divided into four territories – Argentina, Andean Region, Mexico, and Brazil – each led by a general manager and local office ('Disney Appoints International Team', 1999). This push to localise operations and extend the flow of content internationally directly impacted the way Disney would develop and circulate media properties during the following decade.

Structural changes intersected production efforts for particular properties. *High School Musical* emerged from Disney's convergence and globalisation efforts in the 2000s. The success of the initial film depended heavily on the company's horizontal integration and coordination between divisions to mobilise and further develop the franchise (D. Johnson, 2013, p. 42). VP of Global Original Programming at Disney Channel Worldwide Steve Aranguren said, 'if we have a show which is particularly successful, we adopt a 360-degree policy and we adapt it to all possible platforms' ('Disney Channel Worldwide', 2009). The *High School Musical* franchise exemplifies an aggressive 360 'total entertainment' policy, or, as Disney Pictures' president characterised it during the late 2000s, 'cross-collateralization' (Gubbins, 2008) across divisions. *HSM* was intended as a cohesive story universe, where paratexts – what Jonathan Gray defines as material extensions such as posters, video games, and merchandising of a media text – expand the transmedia experience under the Disney corporate umbrella (Gray, 2010, p. 20). Paratexts are extremely important for filling in the gaps between film releases and encouraging more immersive and interactive reception. According to Disney Channel Worldwide head Rich Ross, 'we were nothing short of maniacal in making sure the production extensions had the DNA of the original movie yet creatively went beyond it' (Marr, 2007a). The notion of a franchise's DNA implies a site of origin or essential core of a media property. Henry Jenkins identifies this strategy as the 'mothership approach', where all paratexts and extensions operate to complement and not cannibalise an expanding story universe (Jenkins, 2014, pp. 24–7). Whereas *HSM* books, live shows, games, and other extensions may have deepened audience engagement, Disney's logic was that these extensions would lead back to the *HSM* mothership – namely, the films. Walking into an American mall between 2006 and 2008, one could not help but notice the tween-targeted stores featuring huge displays of *HSM* merchandise. The faces of Zac Efron, Vanessa Hudgens, and other cast members were plastered on the notebooks, backpacks, and T-shirts of an entire tween generation.

Disney launched television networks under the Disney Channel division label across Europe, Latin America, Asia, and the Middle East between the mid-1990s and mid-2000s. In utilising this global distribution pipeline, Disney broadcast the first film in over thirty languages across 100 countries (Coonan, 2009). According to one industry analyst, the global release and marketing for the first film reflects Disney's traditional strategy towards the international market: 'to force feed its US products from its Burbank, CA headquarters' (Marr, 2007b). Using the metaphor of force-feeding to describe Disney's broadcast release pattern parallels earlier scholarly critiques of the media company's global presence as hegemonic. Earlier work on Disney's global presence often focused less on business operations or corporate culture and more on the uneven global flow of its properties. Scholarly work by Mattelart and Dorfman, Wasko, and others typically views Disney through a rigid political-economic lens. This approach characterises Disney's international activities through unprecedented economic power, an uneven flow of media due to control over distribution channels, or a totalising ideological impact on audiences. This perspective assumes Disney as all-powerful with cohesive corporate priorities. Yet the globalised and localised expansion of *HSM* reveals a more complicated relationship to local markets, partnerships, and audiences.

The following year, the Disney Channel broadcast *High School Musical 2*. Promoted as a special media event, the sequel featured the same cast with new songs and a larger, $7 million production budget. Disney again released *HSM 2* in territories worldwide but also adapted marketing campaigns for key local markets. As Ross emphasised at the time, for the *HSM* franchise, 'localization really matters. We're pushing deeper into various countries. With the first movie, we didn't do something special for the Netherlands. [With the sequels] we did' (Barnes, 2008). In the case of India, Disney dubbed the entire soundtrack into Hindi, released a special soundtrack with three new Hindi songs, launched a dance competition involving schools all over India utilising the *HSM* songs, and co-produced special music videos to market the film (Kamath, 2008; Marr, 2007a, 2007b). Produced by Shankar-Ehsaan-Loy, the music video 'All for One (Aaaja nachle)' features hybrid pop, hip hop, and Bollywood music and dance set in an Americanised high school with Indian dancers as cheerleaders, basketball players, and students in preppy uniforms. The video also features 'public' dance sequences in a village square area with police officers and market sellers. The Hindi lyrics are interspersed with an English-language chorus – 'all for one/let's have some fun' – and a rap sequence praising 'magical India'. The most prominent intertextual reference is the material insertion of *HSM* clips into the video's sets. For example, a giant screen sits in the town square and shows *HSM* dance sequences, complementing moments of cross-cutting between group dance sequences in the Indian location and the original American cast. By hybridising Hollywood and Bollywood production cultures, the music video serves to ground promotional materials within local media cultures and tastes but always returns these paratextual moments back to the *HSM* mothership.

Disney launched the next instalment of the franchise, aptly called *High School Musical 3: Senior Year* (2008), through a global theatrical release as opposed to the previous broadcast strategy. The film was distributed simultaneously in more than twenty international territories and grossed almost twice as much in foreign as domestic ($162 million versus $90 million) (Kay, 2008). Significantly, the third film's theatrical release outperformed similar Disney transmedia tween franchises that made the jump from television, including the Hannah Montana and Lizzie McGuire movies (Box Office Mojo, 2015). While a fourth film, tentatively titled *High School Musical: East Meets West* about a rivalry between two schools, went into development around 2008, it was never completed, as the franchise instead expanded into local markets (Addler and Branigan, 2009).

A wave of scholarly work explores large-scale shifts in the cultural industries through the lens of globalisation during the 1990s and 2000s. Arjun Appadurai differentiated the post-1989 cultural economy driven by globalised forces due to its 'complex, overlapping, disjunctive order' (Appadurai, 1990, p. 6). A disjunctive relationship between five central cultural dimensions – ethnoscapes, mediascapes, technoscapes, finanscapes, and ideoscapes – led to an uneven flow and exchange of people, media, technology, finances, and other resources within the media industries. Other scholars, such as Roland Robertson (1990) and Jan Nederveen Pieterse (2004) emphasised localisation and the hybrid dynamics of cultural exchange. Significantly, not only were Disney and other conglomerate divisions quick to adopt localisation efforts to produce and circulate media products during this time, but executives began actively to adopt these theoretical concepts internally and externally.

In this period of restructuring, the international division of Walt Disney Pictures utilised localisation language to explain these structural and institutional changes. Then worldwide studio head, Richard Cook, emphasised in 2007: 'I think it's really important for Disney in these markets to become part of their culture and be able to tell very local stories' (Krishna, 2007). In addition to an attempt to develop a localisation strategy, Disney management mobilised globalisation rhetoric as a corporate device for rebranding and neutralising international activities. Disney was working to refashion their image away from controlling corporate machine towards local creative partner.

As Disney strategically built the global circulation of the *HSM* films, the international division began to develop and co-produce local-language versions across key territories – Argentina, Mexico, Brazil, India, and China. In a 2007 interview with *The Economic Times*, a former chairman of Walt Disney Pictures suggested: 'Relying only on our Hollywood products will not help us penetrate foreign markets. Also, if Disney has to grow and become an international company, it has to start establishing its presence in local markets' (Krishna, 2007). Significantly, the localisation of the *High School Musical* franchise parallels the company's experimentation with local-language productions during the late 2000s. As outlined in Chapter 3, the local-language production strategy involves a studio territory office co-producing and/or distributing a film with a local production partner intended for the local market. Significantly, Disney was one of the last studios to adopt this strategy as well as one of the first to abandon it.

Johnson emphasises the mobility and adaptability of this particular franchise within Disney's various cross-media and transnational divisions:

> irreducible to a single media platform, this migratory property could be more easily understood as a coordinated system in which multiple profit centres worked under a shared brand name – just as the McDonald's franchise unites hamburger shops in different locales to function more efficiently and profitably under a standardised corporate umbrella. (D. Johnson, 2013, p. 37)

Initially, Disney's local production efforts centred on adapting its global franchises and production cultures to be based on animation and family films for local operations in Asia and Latin America. The company prioritised extending existing properties as a localisation strategy beyond the English-language market. One of the most significant aspects of Disney's *HSM* expansion across local markets is how it reveals the fissures or tensions in the expansion management within the 'standardised corporate umbrella', and how it struggles to operate across a diverse transnational media landscape.

Moving beyond corporate structure and language to an on-the-ground approach offers a different perspective. During the late 2000s, Disney's international division and a handful of territory offices extended the franchise for local audiences with varying degrees of success. Unlike the rosy and hopeful corporate spin circulating in the trades about localising existing content, efforts to manage *HSM* as a franchise and as Disney intellectual property proved to be an unwieldy process. In the first wave, Disney co-produced and released two different Spanish-language versions for Mexican and Argentine theatrical markets in 2008. Instead of directly translating the English script, an often failed strategy, as illustrated by a number of British television formats remade unsuccessfully in the US, the LLPs were developed from new scripts, songs, and choreography (Sanson, 2011). Significantly, Disney took advantage of its Argentine infrastructure and personnel to shoot both Spanish-language versions in Buenos Aires. The films retain stock characters similar to those found in the American version: the jock, the smart girl, the brother and sister duo, and the musical theatre nerd. In an interview with *Reuters*, Disney Latin American head Diego Lerner distinguishes the Spanish-language film from simply *HSM* adaptations and instead emphasises the process of localising the settings, music, and scripts to reflect Mexican or Argentine popular culture (Ben-Yehuda, 2008).

For the second localisation wave, in 2010, Disney co-produced and released local-language *HSM*s in Brazil and China. Disney's Brazilian division of the Walt Disney Company co-produced *High School Musical: o desafio* (*High School Musical: The Challenge*) with local independent producer Total Entertainment. Prior to this collaboration, Disney Brazil distributed only a few local films and captured just 9.4 per cent of the box office for local-language films (far less than the market share and LLP activities of other MPA Latin American members) (Guerini, 2010). Disney's São Paulo-based general manager classified this version as a 'format adaptation of the *HSM* script' (interview with Saturnino Braga, 2010). Yet, while stock characters, settings, and themes were carried over from the mothership, the Latin American LLPs were developed as localised iterations of an established franchise. All three Latin American iterations were developed from *HSM* paratexts, particularly a book extension of the franchised story universe. Similar to the Spanish-language versions, the Brazilian *HSM* adapted key aspects of the setting, script, and soundtrack towards popular Brazilian culture: soccer, samba dancing, and samba-reggae music.

HSM: o desafio largely utilised national tax incentives to finance the film. Since the introduction of these incentives in the 1990s, local offices of Sony, Fox, Disney, and peer studios routinely invested in local co-productions during the 2000s and early 2010s. Unlike many of these LLPs co-produced with *os majors* from locally developed scripts, Brazilian industry professionals categorise and imagine *HSM* differently due to its status as a Disney-studio-branded franchise. In fact, I observed

High School Musical: o desafio adapts many Disney production cultures and franchise-specific elements for this Brazilian musical

mixed accounts of local Brazilian professionals' experiences – both independent and studio – working with the Disney property from personal interviews and trade coverage. A local Disney mid-level professional distinguishes the Disney process and *HSM* from other experiences with LLPs and local studio operations – namely, as more tightly managed financially and creatively by Los Angeles executives.

HSM complicates notions of contemporary national cinema. Director Cesar Rodrigues and his producers categorise the film as *brasileiríssimo* (very Brazilian), yet also classify it primarily as a 'Disney film made in Brazil' (Globo Filmes entrevistas, 2010). In other words, a Disney franchise localised within a particular production culture and financing scheme. The film came to embody Brazilian sensibilities, as one independent producer put it, yet through a Disney business model and media property. The tight management of this property across the Latin American versions is evident from the promotional campaigns which featured identical graphic design and similar stock cast costuming and photos. *HSM: o desafio* received theatrical release but did not earn the minimum one-million-spectator marker that has come to define a successful local collaboration within the Brazilian market.

By 2010, Disney began to experiment with local animated and family fare in Russia, China, and India as well as restructuring its international production under new head Jason Reed. The local development and production unit's attempts were widely promoted in popular press and trade publications, characterised by headlines like 'Disney's *HSM* Heads to the East,' 'Magic Kingdom Woos China with Tale of an Enchanted Vegetable,' and 'Disney Aims to Breach Wall around China' (Allen,

2007). Similar to coverage of the Sony and Columbia Pictures Entertainment acquisition in the late 1980s, the common discursive strategy paints Disney as breaking new ground or grappling with the cultural difficulties of locating an operation in the Chinese market. Again, the narrative circulates vis-à-vis Hollywood studios who must overcome the culture shock of working with and inside East Asian media markets.

Disney's *HSM* initiative in China proved to be even more challenging. Filming in Shanghai, Disney teamed with local producers Shanghai Media Group and Huayi Brothers Media Corporation. The industry coverage of Disney's *Ge wu qing chun* (*High School Musical: China*, 2010) reveals the tension inherent in international divisions' trying to expand and to adapt to local markets where they lack infrastructure and have little experience in co-producing. In a trade interview, Executive VP and Managing Director of Disney Great China Stanley Cheung suggested, 'Chinese audiences enjoy great storytelling. Disney *High School Musical* China promotes classic values of teamwork, optimism, friendship, pride, and the spirit of self-discovery which made *HSM* a worldwide phenomenon and further cements Disney's position as a family entertainment brand in China' (Coonan, 2009). The emphasis on Disney's broader corporate brand and the franchise's themes as both specific and universal represent the difficulties of balancing a global franchise and local specialisation process. One widely cited anecdote illustrates how Disney's collaboration with local producers helped to achieve a more locally relevant product. In particular, earlier drafts of the *HSM* script included martial arts as the featured sport. Yet, after conversations with Chinese producers, the script changed so that the students played basketball. Interestingly, Reed, then international head, characterised the Shanghai division's localisation strategy thus: he said that it 'made [*Ge wu qing chun*] more local by making it more American' (Coonan, 2009). This distinction complicates industry lore based around cultural binaries – such as local/Eastern, global/Western, specific/universal – that drive how media content is produced and circulated by the studios.

Expansion and localisation efforts for the *HSM* franchise reflect two key aspects about the company's changing international strategies during the 2000s. First, how Disney managed and controlled franchising practices maps its growing interest in new efforts to pursue local markets. Each of the English-language films, and later each of the LLPs, was imagined as a transmedia experience that should work to complement and extend a cohesive story universe for the franchise. Disney executives imagined and fashioned the tween franchise through cross-media circulation, and such a larger, 360 strategy relies heavily on company-owned and controlled distribution platforms from theatrical distribution to television to other ancillary markets. One of the most salient examples includes the casting process for the LLPs. Due to Disney's ownership and tight management of this particular media property, the local offices and international production divisions were involved in every step from development to distribution. Prior to production, each local market launched a reality television competition to cast the film with unknown talent. Each casting competition partnered a Disney television operation with a local broadcaster to serve as promotion for the upcoming local-language film.

Second, during this period, Disney focused heavily on expanding its operations and projects within the BRIC market (Brazil, Russia, India, and China) as well as within the greater Latin American region. This reflects larger industry trends discussed throughout this book about Hollywood studios moving away from the saturated European region towards emerging markets by the 2000s. However, the uneven pursuit of *HSM* in these markets illustrates not only the difficulties in developing a company-wide LLP strategy but a strategy of expansion hinging on one particular property across diverse industrial conditions, production cultures, and audience tastes. Disney's attempt imagined local productions less as homegrown projects, as other studios have done, and more as managing and expanding a specific media property. This approach resulted in contradictions and tensions between the need for on-the-ground collaboration and flexibility with local conditions and a tightly controlled expansion and licensing of the Disney-owned *HSM* story universe and corporate culture. While the Brazilian iteration was met with lukewarm reception, the Chinese version was seen largely as a disaster. Or, as one LLP executive from a competing studio remarks, 'I asked my colleagues there [in China] about [*Ge wu qing chun*] and they were laughing. They were like we've seen *HSM* . . . and then they give us that? Why?! People were baffled. It was kind of ridiculous . . . [Disney] miscalculated. People watch and know the original. Why do you remake something poorly everyone has already seen?' (interview with International Production Executive, 2014). Among local industry managers, *HSM* functions as shorthand for Disney's failed strategy. In their last attempt to localise the franchise, Disney began to develop an Indian *HSM* in 2007 that the international division eventually abandoned to development hell.

WB GERMANY AND THE FAMILY ENTERTAINMENT FILM

In contrast to Disney's *High School Musical* strategy, which was aimed at localising a global studio property, in a number of territory offices, Warner Bros. developed specialised local-language franchises based on individual market trends and transmedia practices. Unlike Disney's late adoption and short-lived LLP strategy, Warner Bros. was one of the first studios to approach local production as a long-term strategy. Since the 1990s, and under the oversight of Executive VP of International Richard Fox, the Burbank-based division has developed and built an LLP strategy in key territories, including Brazil, Spain, Germany, Japan, and other mid-sized markets, led largely by local country managers.

In fact, Warner Bros. first developed and experimented with an LLP strategy in Germany around 1999 – what Richard Fox describes as a 'vibrant market' due to diverse content across genres and available subsidies to supplement production and distribution costs. Instead of producing and distributing one or two one-off projects as represented by earlier attempts, Fox and his colleagues proposed developing a twenty-film slate over the course of five years. From the beginning of WB's German local strategy, a few factors emerged that helped to shape their focus on local family franchise. First, as Richard Fox and other international studio executives attest, 'you don't live on these movies, especially local content, because they don't travel … so you have to make it in the country of origin' (interview with Fox, 2013). The films first and foremost were imagined as local products with circulation limited to the German market.

Second, developing a larger annual film slate of co-productions and acquisitions relied on the studio's ability to build a 'full run on video' (interview with Fox, 2013). Because these films do not travel out of the local German market, the projects relied – and continue to depend heavily – on a windowing strategy that provides a lifespan beyond theatrical. In other words, monetising home entertainment and television is key. Warner Bros. takes an on-the-ground, integrated approach to distributing these local projects across theatrical, home entertainment, and other ancillary markets that greatly shape how they choose and develop their films.

Located in the sleepy and affluent industrial hub of Hamburg, Warner Bros. Germany reflects the regional divisions among this national film industry. Hamburg is separated from the major media capitals of Berlin and Munich. Due to the fragmented nature of German film production after the 1990s reunification of East and West Germany, the industry relies heavily on regional film boards, such as Medienboard Berlin-Brandenburg, to oversee a highly subsidised production and distribution system that manifests into a particular decentralised industry structure. Local studio operations map onto the regionalised nature of the industry, with Sony in Berlin, Fox in Frankfurt, Disney near Munich, and so on. Long-time studio veteran Willi Geike, who began at United Artists after studying at a local university, has spent over thirty years at Warner Bros. and runs the centralised Hamburg office staffed by over 200 employees. Around 1995, the local office integrated its local theatrical and home entertainment division as led by German-born country manager Geike, a distinct move that significantly impacted their long-term local production and distribution activities (interview with Geike, 2013).

By the early 2010s, the German-language market was one of the most robust film industries in Europe, both in terms of annual production numbers (over 200 films) and audience attendance (between 126 and 135 million spectators) (Focus 2014). While other mid-sized markets like Spain and Italy struggled with digital piracy, declining theatrical attendance, and a weakening home entertainment sectors,

Germany's film market continued to grow across theatrical and ancillary by 2015. For example, WB Germany has co-produced over 100 local titles in the two decades since developing this strategy. The local operation, as compared to other German studio efforts and independents, has maintained a strong production and distribution position throughout this period. In 2011, one of the company's best years, WB Germany earned one-third of their annual income from local production box-office receipts. The office theatrically distributes an average of fifteen to twenty-five local titles and fifteen to twenty-five English-language studio titles annually. Notably, six to eight of the local titles are co-productions with German partners; a handful of those attract a million or more spectators theatrically each year (interview with Geike, 2013; German Federal Film Board, 2015).

As compared to other local studio operations, Warner Bros. has had the longest presence and most consistent strategy in Germany. Sony, one of the first studios involved in local-language productions by the late 1990s, saw early success with an LLP unit based in Berlin, including the 2000 horror film *Anatomie*. As discussed in Chapter 5, within five years of some successful collaborations but mostly lacklustre box-office results and a large operational overhead, Sony shuttered the operation and moved European production headquarters to Madrid. Although Sony re-established the German unit in 2008 after European LLP operations were restructured and streamlined, the Berlin operation struggles to gain a strong position in local production. Additionally, Fox International Productions entered the local production market in 2008. Today, under the supervision of head of production and development, the unit co-produces and distributes two to three German films per year, very few in comparison to the twenty to twenty-five English-language studio pictures Fox releases annually (Roxborough, 2014).

Since the 1990s, and coinciding with this increased participation of major studios in local-language production, German film-makers have produced a wave of commercial comedies, which critics early on labelled *Neue deutsche Komödie* (New Germany Comedy). David N. Coury describes how these films not only broke away from the earlier experimental and counter-cinema movements *Autorenkino* and New German Cinema but 'revitalized the German film industry' due to their connections to Hollywood narrative and conventions and continued commercial success (Coury, 1997, p. 356). These comedies often focus on relationships, families, or situational events. By the 2000s, a cycle of comedies, rom-coms, and family entertainment films came to characterise the modern German blockbuster as commercial, genre-oriented titles that attract large box-office attendance, and, in turn, the types of projects in which WB Germany seeks to invest and co-produce. In addition to genre films, key features of the most recent cycle of German blockbusters during this period include bankable stars and reliance on subsidies. First, the majority of Warner Bros.' local comedies depend on the star power of a handful of

List of Germany's highest-grossing films annually, many recently co-produced with local Hollywood studio units, displayed at the Deutsche Kinemathek in Berlin

German actors, namely Til Schweiger, Matthias Schweighöfer, and Michael 'Bully' Herbig. Besides their theatrical bankability with comedies and romantic comedies, both Schweiger and Schweighöfer wield a level of creative agency within the industry through their own production companies (Barefoot Films and Pantaleon Films, respectively), and both have signed multi-picture deals with WB Germany (Roxborough, 2012).

The local studio units put stock in these relationships, wherein each country manager and head of production for Warner Bros. or Fox emphasises the importance of building long-term partnerships with local talent. Managers and creative executives imagine and describe these relationships less in terms of short-term box-office results and more in terms of social capital and a mutually beneficial creative dynamic. The former head of production and development for FIP's German unit, Marco Mehlitz, describes creative relationships as an 'investment' (interview with Mehlitz, 2013). WB and other studio GMs emphasise the necessity of building networks and fostering these partnerships, even as the long-term investment in these relationships ultimately relies on the market logic of profitability and commercial success.

Second, national and regional subsidies support many of these films. For example, Germany has a revolving film fund, known as *Referenzprinzip*, or 'reference principle', available for local productions (German Federal Film Board, 2015; Wagner, 2012, p. 533).[1] On the national level, the Germany Federal Film Fund (DFFF) offers funds for films that spend at least 25 per cent of their production budget locally. In 2014, WB invested in five co-productions sponsored by DFFF funds, with subsidies ranging from 1 million to 600,000 euros (DFF website, 2015). On the regional level, seven funding bodies from Berlin to Hamburg grant additional incentives. As noted by many of the German producers and distributors I interviewed, these funding schemes increasingly are tied to commercial performance and reward box-office success. In studio partnerships with major local producers like X-Filme and Barefoot Films, Warner Bros. and their projects directly benefit from these subsidies and from the domestic theatrical success of each film. According to Geike, 'if you do a million in admission and you have a million subsidies in that movie, you get a million again for your next movie … [so if your films are successful] part of the budget is always a revolving capital that comes from subsidies but is now earned back and goes back into the production budget' (interview with Geike, 2013).

Because of Warner Bros.' success with local pictures and dependence on revolving subsidy support, the Hamburg unit is one of the most active studio and independent distributors domestically. Only a few years after launching the LLP strategy, in 2002 WB Germany released the most films theatrically (thirty-two titles) and captured the largest market share (21.9 per cent), more than all of the major studios and local independents. Geike suggests that because of this revolving support, WB is able to take more risks in developing local productions, whether exploring a new genre or extending a franchise through a spin-off or sequel. While Til Schweiger is best known for his comedies, the actor-producer-director worked with WB to develop and co-produce a successful spy thriller, *Schutzengel* (*The Guardians*, 2012). In fact, an English-language remake is in the development phase (Meza, 2012b). Beyond the German unit, the Burbank studio also benefits by retaining remake rights for the majority of these co-productions.

WB Germany's most successful production strategy has been the family entertainment franchise. For example, their first two series, *Der kleine Eisbär* (*The Little Polar Bear*, 2001) and *Lauras Stern* (*Laura's Star*, 2004), were based on popular German children's books. WB Germany developed both animated series with partner Cartoon Films into multiple films released theatrically and across home entertainment. Both *Der kleine Eisbär* and *Lauras Stern* are significant for two reasons. First, WB conceived and developed the family entertainment franchise as a central production strategy, whereas these films were intended to extend across distribution platforms and expand into multiple sequels. The long lifespan of a media property represents not only the convergence and conglomerate practices of the contemporary industrial moment but also how the studio negotiates limited production activities and resources inside these mid-sized markets.

Second, because both series were adapted from well-known and popular children series, studio decision-making relied heavily on preconceived concepts or pre-sold property that were seen as culturally specific and significant. This directly contrasts with Disney's approach to localise a more 'universal' property like *High School Musical*. Geike emphasised the local specificity of these animated properties and credited it to their theatrical performance:

> These [film franchises] were big successes because the local families like to have movies that are very special and based on German characters, German books, or German franchises. They are different from the big American-only entertaining animation movies. [German animated productions] mostly have a story to tell and people like them because they have educational background for small kids. (interview with Geike, 2013)

Geike makes a point of differentiating between German animated films and Hollywood ones, not only in their development process but in terms of audience reception. Yet, unlike the majority of WB's LLPs and against institutional logic of global-versus-local films, WB released *Der kleine Eisbär* internationally, where the film earned half of its gross. This is an exception, however, since most country managers consistently declare that LLPs do not travel outside their home market. But in analysing the 'does or does not travel' logic, the localness or 'cultural odour' of these media products is what limits their ability to travel yet is precisely what makes these family films successful locally (Iwabuchi, 2002). Therefore, so much of the negotiation or tension with local-language productions produced within the studio structure is bound within fluid ideas of genre, audience, cultural specificity, and geography that varies vastly from market to market.

Keinohrhasen is a key example of how WB Germany developed and expanded a localised production strategy on media franchising and transmedia practices. Originally conceived as a star vehicle for Til Schweiger, the 2008 romantic comedy follows Ludo (Schweiger), a playboy and muckraking journalist who is sentenced to community service in a city kindergarten. What results is a fish-out-of-water love story with Anna, his nerdy, uptight female counterpart at the school (Nora Tschirner). In its theatrical release, *Keinohrhasen* garnered $51 million and an audience of around 6.5 million, which is equivalent to how a successful WB studio film like *Harry Potter and the Deathly Hallows (Part 2)* (2011) performs in Germany (Kirschbaum, 2010).

Til Schweiger's character making the chicken with ears toy in *Zweiohrkueken* (2009)

Due to the film's local blockbuster performance and along with a revolving subsidy, Warner Bros. and Barefoot co-produced a successful sequel, *Zweiohrkueken* (*Rabbit without Ears 2*, 2009), released two years later. Furthermore, the co-producers collaborated on three different extensions. First, a line of toys was developed based on one of the film's plotlines, wherein Ludo sews together a scrappy, earless stuffed toy rabbit (in the first film) and stuffed toy baby chicken with ears (in the second film). Each toy is a central plot point that show's Ludo's character growth – namely, the sincerity of his feelings for the children and his love for Anna. Next, Schweiger and collaborators developed, wrote, and illustrated a children's book series based on the friendship of the rabbit and chick 'helping a friend fulfil their dream'. Paratexts from two initial films evolved into other media products as an initial blockbuster rom-com transformed into a family franchise. While the initial toy line's circulation was limited to the German market, the children's books were released internationally and translated into various local-language markets, from French to Arabic (interview with Geike, 2013).

Finally, Barefoot and WB partnered with Berlin-based Cartoon Film on a 2013 3D animated feature, *Keinohrhase und Zweiohrküken* (*Rabbit without Ears and Chick with Two Ears*). In operating as paratexts, the toys are extracted from a plotline and extended into new characters and story worlds. The rabbit and chick evolved from tie-in merchandising to a spin-off book series and finally back into an animated family film. Despite the popularity of Schweiger's rom-com films and book series, the animated feature was written off as a flop due to its poor theatrical performance – attracting around 300,000 spectators, fewer than the two million that the Schweiger comedies typically average ('Box Office', 2013).

Returning to Derek Johnson's franchising discussion, the strategy for expanding this series follows standard studio logic:

> franchise systems support serialization and sequelization to keep generating content over time – whether confined to a single medium like television or multiplied more promiscuously across media. Content is aimed at repeatability and multiplication – and

focus on the industrial relations of franchising calls our attention to the social nature of that ongoing exchange. (D. Johnson, 2013, p. 45)

By framing *Keinohrhasen* within Johnson's franchising logic, the series operates as an *inter-industrial franchise*, or a transmedia extension across various media industrial cultures and particular contexts. The film series and paratexts represent franchising logic and practices that depend on the idea of an ongoing exchange – financial, creative, intellectual property rights, and reception. Unlike many of the English-language studio franchises common to the conglomerate era, this German-language franchise operates within markedly different institutional and industrial production cultures. Shaped by studio structures and production cultures as well as local industrial contexts, the series reveals more about WB's local management culture, production strategies, and position within the German market.

The *Keinohrhasen* franchise illustrates WB Germany's increased reliance on and challenging experiences with localised franchising and transmedia practices in a local-language market. The series' evolution illustrates the complicated social relations within franchising, particularly in the case of independent partnerships with Conglomerate Hollywood. Johnson contends: 'if you look a little deeper, we see that even conglomerates like Disney and Time Warner enter into contractual agreements with independent parties seeking mutual beneficence' (D. Johnson, 2013, p. 43). Despite the mixed success and unclear future of the series, *Keinohrhasen* was beneficial to all parties in different ways and serves to complicate a view of the LLP relationship within the reductive framework of traditional Hollywood-versus-European competition (Pardo, 2007).

On the one hand, for Barefoot Films and Cartoon Films, WB provides distribution and marketing resources as well as negotiating power with television networks for more profitable ancillary agreements. On the other hand, Warner Bros. Germany relies on partners Barefoot, Cartoon, and others both creatively and financially, for local industry experience and resources. WB acted as a co-producer, contracting out creative production processes to its partners and gaining access to local production subsidies. WB's role as co-producer, as opposed to 'leading' or majority producer, is significant. Although the Hamburg unit has a team working on LLPs and relies heavily on multi-picture deals with its partnerships, these independent companies complete the majority of creative development and physical production processes. Furthermore, this franchise case relied heavily on Til Schweiger's stardom, bankability, and creative labour as producer-writer-director. This is evident especially in the case of the animated extension, where his stardom is less visible. Despite his multi-faceted creative involvement, it was not a surprise to many in the industry when this deviation – featuring the actor only as the voice of the Rabbit character – became the least successful extension of the franchise. So much of the success of contemporary

German blockbusters is interconnected with a handful of actor-producer-director stars working within commercial, family-friendly genres.

While media industry scholarship focuses more on larger convergence practices within the studios that produce major English-language tentpoles, local convergence and transmedia practices manifest themselves differently in various territories. And studio units are responding. Ultimately, while WB has creative and financial input, the local unit shapes the distribution and marketing activities for this type of franchise separately from international headquarters in the US. Geike suggests, '[our unit relies on] total release pattern and one responsible management team. We are not so divisional as the studio in Burbank. That is how the country manager concept works' (interview with Geike, 2013). WB's activities rely heavily on a self-sustaining country manager system and, specifically, the unit's integrated structure. In other words, film, home entertainment, and television operations are housed inside the same semi-autonomous local office. The integrated operations reinforced and supported an LLP strategy driven by franchising and cross-media efforts. In the case of Germany, comedies and family films have proved most successful through franchising strategies and integrated release patterns.

CONCLUSION

Studio reliance on media franchising and building transmedia universes largely drives post-1990s Conglomerate Hollywood. Moments of industrial restructuring, institutional decision-making, and technological transformation shape how studios are producing local content for international territories. Therefore, it is this liminal space between control and expansion, universality and specificity, globality and locality, consumer participation and creative management, and broader genre conventions and licensed intellectual property where local franchising practices emerge and converge.

Disney's *High School Musical* franchise reveals a larger evolution or shift in the company's international approach to localisation – everything from promotional language and corporate priorities to local territory restructuring and production cultures. Overall, an attempt to standardise and coordinate the franchise across multiple markets was not sustainable. By 2011, Disney closed its international production unit and exhausted the *HSM* franchise after the English spin-off and straight-to-DVD film *Sharpay's Fabulous Adventure* (2011) (Littleton, 2011). The following year, Disney shuttered its international production office and abandoned a wide-scale LLP strategy. For Disney, intellectual property and localising company properties drove the *HSM* franchise expansion in these local markets. Yet how Disney managed this process and then quickly abandoned speaks to the company's changing priorities to wider, global audiences – notably happening around the same time that the parent company bought Marvel Studios and Lucasfilm.

While the particular case of Warner Bros.' local franchising and merchandising efforts speaks to the specificities of the German media market in this transitional moment, it also illustrates continued assumptions and challenges within local industries. A tension exists between localisation efforts from territory office to territory office in negotiating these studio franchising and storytelling strategies, and more universal industry lore around whether these films do or do not circulate. Richard Fox suggests that '90 per cent [of LLPs in general] don't travel and it takes two to three years to get full values from the windows' (interview with Fox, 2013). In addition to executives like Fox, virtually every local country manager I met in Europe and Latin America asserts that comedies do not travel outside their local-language territory, so it is significant that the local units are investing in a notoriously culturally specific and limited genre. In turn, WB Germany must rely on integrated operations and LLPs that can reach the widest local audience, either through genre or platform. In order to build long-term franchises and partnerships, WB's local operations represent how these studio production cultures are being localised, integrated, and adapted in scope and scale for release in a limited market.

NOTE

1. According to the 'FFA Overview' (2015) brochure for producers, reference film funding is based on a 'points threshold': 'The total number of reference points for a film is calculated from the cinema tickets sold domestically and the success at nationally and internationally significant film festivals and awards.'

8

Conclusion: Local Spaces, Global Places

Localising Hollywood is the culmination of extensive industry fieldwork and interviews in which I map the changing climate of Hollywood's international operations. Over the course of my research, films were produced and released, some successful and others not. Studios introduced, altered, or entirely abandoned local production strategies. One of the most telling indications of the increased prioritisation of local markets, as argued throughout this book, was the rise of key mid-level studio managers I followed during my six-year research process. Only a year after Sanford Panitch left his post as president of Fox International Productions to run Sony's new international production division, the studio expanded his job to include overseeing Columbia Pictures as well in 2016. Furthermore, that same year, Universal merged their international production division with speciality arm Focus Features, promoting Peter Kujawski to the helm (Frater, 2015; Kay, 2015, 2016). These moves in management are significant for two reasons. First, the two executives rose through studio ranks largely due to their success running international production and distribution divisions. With this climb, each studio executive brought their knowledge, expertise, and commitment to expanding international business opportunities in key territories to the new division. Second, this signals not only the continued importance of the studios adapting content and circulation strategies to local markets but also the expansion and integration into the larger filmed entertainment group and away from the previous status of international as a separate speciality operation.

This book offers an unparalleled perspective on the intersection of local operations and transnational ambitions – on how media is shaped by a circuit of conditions including policy, economy, regulations, technology, and culture. The in-depth case studies show how industry strategies and practices for localising content may overlap across Sony, Fox, and peer divisions while simultaneously being driven by distinct institutional cultures and priorities. I illustrate how the increased importance of international markets for the major studios has led to a wave of internal, structural, and cultural shifts in recent decades. The impact of these changes is felt not only by local studio units but also by local partners and industry sectors.

We find ourselves in an instructive moment for Hollywood when global media industries are both increasingly fragmented and more interconnected than ever before. The studios continue to grapple with how to exercise multilayered media strategies to address specific audiences across local markets after a long legacy depending upon commercial English-language releases to serve mainly imagined white domestic and nondescript global audiences. A central objective for this project was to contribute to the lack of scholarship examining the complexities of Hollywood's local production and distribution efforts in the twenty-first century, as well as to interrogate often overstated, or misunderstood, industry logic around these activities and the international market itself. The tendency of global Hollywood scholarship in the past was to focus on domestic studio operations as separate from international, or to overly generalise studio activities outside North America as homogenous or streamlined. Widely circulated global films, franchises, production cultures, and circulation strategies should not be understood as separate or in opposition to country managers, local units, local-language productions, and so on. Local territory offices navigate the global blockbuster alongside local productions, both of which simultaneously operate as global-local studio products, even if to different ends. Scholars must reconsider instead how we approach these vastly diverse and evolving transnational media institutions. In other words, it is important to understand how the expansive globalisation of Hollywood increasingly materialises through its decentralised localisation.

As laid out in this book's introduction, it is worth revisiting the broader theoretical and methodological implications of this project as a potential framework to expand research on how Hollywood operations intersect local media industries. Hollywood studio strategies, professionals, and products may operate and move across traditional regional and national borders but are still bound by the specificities of local market dynamics in which they are produced and released. Media business practices, partnerships, and content creation defy traditional boundaries of the nation, categories of West versus the rest, global Hollywood versus local industry. Often local studio interests – creative and financial – align with industry sectors in a particular media hub of Berlin, London, or Rio de Janeiro. Infrastructure is built, industry sectors are developed, partnerships formed, and media products are produced and distributed. In turn, the positionality of Hollywood in these local markets and the complexities of these financial and creative relationships that develop reveal insights into institutional cultures and individual media workers for both the studios and local players.

A translocal approach incorporating multi-modal methods is necessary to fully grasp the interaction between macro-level forces and micro-level contexts. As media industry scholars, we should work not to privilege the global over the local, or a wider political economic lens over an on-the-ground industrial-cultural ethnography. But it is also equally important not to ignore the global for the local. By comparing production and distribution strategies among the six studios in a handful of local markets, a richly complex picture of how local industry conditions interact with larger global forces emerges. And it is at this intersection where human agents become key in understanding how the studios negotiate and balance internal priorities with external conditions through the process of decision-making, promotional spin, and industry lore. How industry-wide and institutionally specific strategies like local-language productions or the country manager system operate differently across each studio and individual industry is as significant as how the local managers understand and exercise their roles within these institutions.

A multi-modal approach should incorporate a variety of methods, pulling on the strengths of our interdisciplinary field by integrating larger political and economic forces and sweeping industry-wide discourses with individual studio films, promotional materials, and internal perspectives on activities, logic, and cultures from first-hand accounts. On the one hand, the major studios, like most corporate entities, are profit-minded, risk-averse, and slow to enact sweeping structural and cultural changes. On the other hand, we cannot characterise Sony and Warner Bros. as rational economic bodies; instead, they are somewhat irrational institutions run by divisions of human agents with different agendas reacting to fluctuating global and local conditions. Management visions for local productions or strategies for localised advertising and distribution often rely on shifting market conditions and how individuals choose to react. In turn, I watched many of these company practices transform in surprising ways during my fieldwork. Studio professionals as individuals or teams are human agents: their actions and decision-making are variable and fallible. Sony quickly closed all LLP operations during the late 2000s, only to change course less than a decade later. Despite the development of an industry-wide LLP strategy, albeit an inconsistent one from studio to studio, an MPA regional executive still had to convince member studios of the value and cultural capital in local training programmes. These processes are not always neat or tidy, or logical. Sometimes they are more contradictory than consistent.

As media scholars, we need to remain flexible and nimble in our own theoretical frameworks as we navigate the rapidly changing international film business. By underestimating or overestimating the six major studios' presence in the local markets, we will only view these institutions through a lens of absolute power and dominance. Hollywood studios are neither a monolithic bloc nor static institutions. Studio priorities change, people leave, divisions are restructured. Furthermore, the studios as a group are not homogenous, as many professionals in local units and the MPA attest. Institutional priorities and values vary, as is most apparent with the studios who invest heavily in local production (Sony, Fox, Warner Bros., and Universal) and those that do not (Disney and Paramount).

My project evolved as a media industry studies exercise in access. *Localising Hollywood* contributes an in-depth view of Conglomerate Hollywood which is missing from global media studies, media industry studies, and film studies. A general lack of examination or nuanced understanding of media conglomerates and the international branches of their filmed entertainment divisions has led to the relative invisibility of mid-level and other key international professionals. Local studio managers serve as linchpins at a particularly transformative moment for Conglomerate Hollywood and international operations (Havens and Lotz, 2012). Country managers and their teams offer the opportunity to explore how broader studio structures and processes intersect, or at times collide, with the development and circulation of media on the local level. Mid-level managers function as cultural intermediaries, ones who understand and leverage their own knowledge, value, and power within the larger studio structure (Brannon Donoghue, 2014a). Understanding internal studio and external industrial roles offers a particular study in circumscribed agency and negotiation within transnational media industries.

However, working with human variables can be unreliable and inconsistent for researchers. Conducting contemporary media industries research, particularly grounded in industry fieldwork, is slippery by nature and similar to chasing a moving target. Even as I gained further access inside a studio unit or developed connections to local professionals, for every two or three people I contacted, only one responded and agreed to meet me. In an extreme case, a studio's VP of Communication derailed my research activities in a particular region by essentially blocking any future access. These challenges echo Sherry B. Ortner's difficulties gaining access inside LA-based Hollywood studio offices to conduct ethnography work (2010). Typically, upon meeting with an independent or studio professional, I had to navigate their willingness to talk to an academic and anticipate what information they would actually divulge, or what they were allowed to share. John Caldwell emphasises the constructed nature and promotional stakes surrounding this method of research. He identifies the 'inverse credibility law': the higher a researcher moves up the 'industrial food chain', the more the stories emerge as 'suspect and spin-driven' (Caldwell, 2008, p. 3). Caldwell argues the reason is

> because insider knowledge is *always* managed; because spin and narrative define and couch any industrial disclosure; and because researcher-practitioner contacts are always marked by symbiotic tensions over authenticity and advantage. (Caldwell, 2008, pp. 2–3)

At times, a professional's level or position in their institution did affect their willingness to be open regarding studio operations; hence, a few interviewees were quoted by title only. Yet other factors impacted the depth of our conversations, including distinct personalities, local business traditions, or a particular studio's institutional culture. Some mid-level managers freely offered studio insider information or critical opinions about their company, whereas, at other times, higher-level media professionals, who spoke often in the press and held a position of remarkable power in their local industry, were harder to move beyond polished spin or basic descriptions of business activities. A part of my method was establishing trust and building a rapport with each contact, especially those I met many times over the span of this project. But it is not enough to identify the promotional spin and institutional lore; we must understand how Hollywood studio structures, strategies, and products operate themselves as 'social constructions'. As Serra Tinic argues, transnational media are 'products of a series of complex negotiations between policy makers, funding agencies, and the creative minds that reinterpret diverse, and often competing, conceptualisations of place in the process of cultural storytelling' (Tinic, 2005, p. 152).

Hollywood's failed ventures are just as illuminating as the successful ones, whether it be Disney's attempt to localise the *HSM* franchise or Sony's uneven and rocky LLP strategy, going from productive to shuttered to revived in less than two decades. The studios still struggle to partner and produce in rapidly growing markets like India and China, and to achieve a consistent level of success in Russia and Brazil during the 2010s. Fox, Warner Bros., and their peers work to adapt their practices to drastically different production cultures, policies, financing, and audience tastes, particularly in the Global South, where they do not maintain the same historical footprint as in other local markets. Even long-term studio presence in local industrial climates requires these units to navigate unpredictable political, economic, and cultural conditions. For example, 2016 saw the UK Brexit vote to leave the European Union as well as Brazil's presidential impeachment, economic crisis, and backlash from the poorly managed Summer Olympics. Due to London and Rio de Janeiro's positions as major media capitals and sites of business for the global film market, undoubtedly the future will lead to significant, and challenging, transformations for all local industry players. All that being the case, what can we learn from the successful commercial ventures and blockbuster co-productions, and the failed collaborations and box-office bombs? Contradictions and fissures exist within celebratory, and at times critical, narratives and can be instructive for understanding how these transnational media institutions operate.

In turn, local studio operations offer illuminating examples of how the majors brand themselves, build alliances, address local specificities, and work to adapt within an increasingly translocal business. Future research must interrogate Hollywood's locality in a nuanced manner, depicting studio operations across structural and geographical layers as both flexible and rigid. Hollywood's localisation should be examined on a wide scale – local spaces to global places – as we also should consider the complex scope of the political, economic, cultural, industrial, and technological variables involved. International studio operations provide a unique thread that, when pulled, helps unravel the diverse nature and negotiation of global media flows today, steeped as they are in Hollywood's historical industrial presence and power leveraged within increasingly complex Global North and South dynamics.

Bibliography

Acland, Charles (2005), *Screen Traffic: Movies, Multiplexes, and Global Culture* (Durham, NC: Duke University Press).

Addler, Esther, and Tania Branigan (2009), '*High School Musical* Gets Chinese Remake', *The Guardian* (23 November), accessed online (15 February 2014) theguardian.com/film/2009/nov/23/chinese-high-school-musical-disney.

Adler, Tim (2010), 'Hollywood Slams Catalan Dubbing Law', *Deadline Hollywood Daily* (7 July), accessed online (12 June 2013) deadline.com/2010/07/hollywood-slams-catalan-dubbing-law-52085/.

Allen, Katie (2007), 'Magic Kingdom Woos China with Tale of an Enchanted Vegetable', *The Guardian* (11 June), accessed online (1 March 2014) theguardian.com/business/2007/jun/11/media.china.

Anderman, Gunilla, and Jorge Diaz-Cintas (2009), *Audiovisual Translation: Language Transfer on Screen* (New York: Palgrave Macmillan).

Anderson, Christopher (1994), *Hollywood TV: The Studio System in the 50s* (Austin: University of Texas Press).

——— (1997), 'Television and Hollywood in the 1940s', in Thomas Schatz (ed.), *Boom and Bust: American Cinema in the 1940s* (Berkeley: University of California Press), pp. 422–44.

Appadurai, Arjun (1990), 'Disjuncture and Difference in the Global Cultural Economy', *Public Culture* 2(2) (Spring), pp. 1–24.

Balio, Tino (1987), *United Artists: The Company That Changed the Film Industry* (Madison: University of Wisconsin Press).

——— (1998), '"A Major Presence in All the World's Important Markets": The Globalization of Hollywood in the 1990s', in Steve Neale and Murray Smith (eds), *Contemporary Hollywood Cinema* (London: Routledge), pp. 58–73.

——— (2013), *Hollywood in the New Millennium* (London: BFI).

Banks, Miranda (2015), *The Writers: A History of American Screenwriters and Their Guild* (New Brunswick: Rutgers UP).

Barnes, Brooks (2008), 'Disney's *High School Musical* Goes Abroad', *New York Times* (8 February), accessed online (1 March 2014) nytimes.com/2008/01/28/technology/28iht-disney.1.9541311.html.

Beltrán, Mary (2013), 'Fast and Bilingual: *Fast & Furious* and the Latinization of Racelessness', *Cinema Journal* 53(1) (Autumn), pp. 75–96.

Ben-Yehuda, Ayala (2008), 'High School Musical Retunes to Suit Latin America', Reuters (12 July), accessed online (18 February 2014) reuters.com/article/us-highschool-idUSN1126047920080712.

Blake, Meredith (2014), 'Metastasis, Spanish-Language Remake of Breaking Bad, Gets Cooking', Los Angeles Times (11 June), accessed online (14 January 2015) latimes.com/entertainment/tv/showtracker/la-et-st-metastasis-spanishlanguage-remake-of-breaking-bad-premieres-20140611-story.html.

Blaney, Martin (2005), 'Germany, Brazil Sign Co-production Treaty', Screen Daily (22 February), accessed online (15 June 2016) www.screendaily.com/germany-brazil-sign-co-production-treaty/4022134.article.

——— (2013), 'Set Report: Trash', Variety (13 December), accessed online (14 January 2015) www.screendaily.com/features/set-report-trash/5064696.article.

——— (2015), 'Captain America: Civil War Benefits from New German Funding', Screen Daily (4 August), accessed online (15 May 2016) www.screendaily.com/news/captain-america-civil-war-benefits-from-new-german-funding/5091237.article.

Bordwell, David (2006), The Way Hollywood Tells It: Story and Style in Modern Movies (Berkeley: University of California Press).

Bordwell, David, Janet Staiger, and Kristin Thompson (1985), The Classical Hollywood Cinema: Film Style & Mode of Production to 1960 (New York: Columbia UP).

Box Office Mojo (2015), official website, accessed online (1 August 2015) boxofficemojo.com.

'Box Office: Til Schweiger floppt als Animator' (2013), Der Spiegel (30 September), accessed online (15 January 2015) spiegel.de/kultur/kino/2-guns-nummer-1-der-deutschen-kinocharts-cloudy-2-in-den-usa-a-925260.html.

Brannon Donoghue, Courtney (2014a), 'Brazilian Film Management Culture and Partnering with os majors: A Midlevel Approach', in Derek Johnson, Derek Kompare, and Avi Santo (eds), Making Media Work: Cultures of Management in the Entertainment Industries (New York: NYU Press), pp. 165–87.

——— (2014b), 'The Rise of the Brazilian Blockbuster: How Ideas of Exceptionality and Scale Shape a Booming Cinema', Media, Culture & Society 36(4), pp. 536–50.

——— (2014c), 'Sony and Local-Language Productions: Conglomerate Hollywood's Strategy of Flexible Localization for the Global Film Market', Cinema Journal 53(4), pp. 3–27.

Brown, Colin (2005), 'Warner Bros: A Very Local Engagement', Screen Daily (11 February), accessed online (24 May 2010) screendaily.com/warner-bros-a-very-local-engagement/4021949.article.

Buchala, Luciana (2012), 'Informe de acompanhamento do mercado; distribuição de ssalas 2009 a 2012', ANCINE, accessed online (16 September 2014) http://oca.ancine.gov.br/sites/default/files/cinema/pdf/Informe_Distribuicao_2012.pdf.

Busch, Anita, and Nancy Tartaglione (2014), 'Summer Film Budgets vs. Total Worldwide Grosses', Deadline Hollywood Daily (2 September), accessed online (30 September 2014) deadline.com/2014/09/summer-film-budgets-vs-total-worldwide-grosses-826603/.

Caldwell, John Thornton (2008), *Production Culture: Industrial Reflexivity and Critical Practice in Film/Television* (Durham, NC: Duke University Press).

Chao, Loretta, Reed Johnson, and Luciana Magalhães (2014), 'Middle Class Brazil Lifts Voice', *The Wall Street Journal* (23 September), accessed online (21 February 2015) wsj. com/articles/middle-class-brazil-lifts-voice-1411511724.

Chitwood, Adam (2014), 'Marvel Releases Official Phase 3 Timeline Image', *Collider* (17 November), accessed online (7 December 2014) http://collider.com/marvel-phase-3-timeline-image/.

Cieply, Michael (2015), 'Tom Rothman's High-Wire Act at Sony Pictures', *New York Times* (17 May), accessed online (7 July 2015) nytimes.com/2015/05/18/business/media/tom-rothmans-high-wire-act-at-sony-pictures.html.

Cieply, Michael, and Brooks Barnes (2014), 'Sony Cyberattack, First a Nuisance, Swiftly Grew into a Firestorm', *New York Times* (30 December), accessed online (1 May 2015) nytimes.com/2014/12/31/business/media/sony-attack-first-a-nuisance-swiftly-grew-into-a-firestorm-.html.

—— (2015), 'After Sony Hacking, the MPAA Considers Majors Changes', *New York Times* (5 February), accessed online (1 May 2015) nytimes.com/2015/02/06/business/media/after-sony-hacking-the-mpaa-considers-major-changes.html.

'Columbia TriStar TV Going South Will Co-produce a Slate of Programs in the Latin America Region' (1997), *The Hollywood Reporter* (18 November), available via Business Source Complete (accessed 24 May 2010).

Coonan, Clifford (2009), '*Musical* Heads to China', *Variety* (22 November), accessed online (1 March 2014) variety.com/2009/biz/news/musical-heads-to-china-1118011719/.

Coury, David N. (1997), 'From Aesthetics to Commercialism: Narration and the New German Comedy', *Seminar* 33(4), pp. 356–73.

Crafton, Donald (1999), *The Talkies: American Cinema's Transition to Sound, 1926–1931* (History of the American Cinema series) (Berkeley: University of California Press).

Curtin, Michael (2003), 'Media Capital: Towards the Study of Spatial Flows', *International Journal of Cultural Studies* 6(202), pp. 202–28.

—— (2007), *Playing to the World's Biggest Audience: The Globalization of Chinese Film and TV* (Berkeley: University of California Press).

—— (2011), 'Global Media Capital and Local Media Policy', in Janet Wasko, Graham Murdock, and Helena Sousa (eds), *The Handbook of Political Economy of Communications, First Edition* (Malden, MA: Blackwell).

Curtin, Michael, and Kevin Sanson (eds) (2016), *Precarious Creativity: Global Media, Local Labor* (Berkeley: University of California Press).

Curtin, Michael, and Jane Shattuc (2009), *The American Television Industry* (London: BFI).

DFFF website (2015), 'Approved Grants', accessed online (1 December 2014) dfff-ffa.de/approved-grants.html

'Disney Appoints International Team for Latin America (1999), *Business Wire*
(9 November), available via Business Source Complete (accessed 24 March 2010).

'Disney Channel Worldwide: Spearheading Production in Europe' (2009), Cineuropa
Industry Report: Animation (21 January), accessed online (7 July 2015) cineuropa.org/
dd.aspx?t=dossier&l=en&tid=1437&did=89032.

Dorfman, Ariel, and Armand Mattelart (2004), 'Introduction on How to Become
a General in the Disneyland Club', in Meenakshi Gigi Durham and Douglas
Kellner (eds), *Media and Cultural Studies: Keyworks* (Malden, MA: Blackwell),
pp. 144–51.

Drake, Phillip (2008), 'Distribution and Marketing in Contemporary Hollywood', in
Paul McDonald and Janet Wasko (eds), *The Contemporary Hollywood Film Industry*
(Malden, MA: Blackwell), pp. 63–82.

Du Gay, Paul, Stuart Hall, Linda Janes, Hugh Mackay, and Keith Negus (1997), *Doing
Cultural Studies: The Story of the Sony Walkman* (London: Sage).

Duarte, Luiz Guilherme (2001), *The Cable Empire Strikes Latin America: How American
Pay-TV Conquered the Continent* (Lexington, KY: vide-u).

Elley, Derek (2000), 'Review: Anatomy', *Variety* (28 August), accessed online
(15 December 2014) variety.com/2000/film/reviews/anatomy-1200463675/.

Elmer, Greg, and Mike Gasher (2005), 'Introduction: Catching up to Runaway Productions',
in Greg Elmer and Mike Gasher (eds), *Contracting Out Hollywood: Runaway Productions
and Foreign Location Shooting* (Lanham, MD: Rowman & Littlefield).

English, Rebecca (2013), 'Hermione, Eat Your Heart Out!', *The Daily Mail* (26 April),
accessed online (15 November 2014) dailymail.co.uk/femail/article-2315136/Pregnant-
Kate-Middleton-Prince-William-battle-Harry-Potter-film-studios.html.

Featherstone, Mike (1990), 'Introduction', in Mike Featherstone (ed.), *Global Culture:
Nationalism, Globalization and Modernity* (London and Newbury Park: Sage), pp. 1–14.

'FFA Overview: Brief Information about the German Federal Film Board' German Federal
Film Board (2015), accessed online (22 January) ffa.de/.

Filho, Daniel (2010), 'Entrevista com Globo Filmes' (30 August), accessed online
(30 September 2015) globofilmes.globo.com/en/noticia/daniel-filho/.

'Film Co-Production: Agreement between the Government of the United Kingdom
of Great Britain and Northern Ireland and the Government of the Federative
Republic of Brazil' (28 September 2012), accessed online (15 June 2016)
gov.uk/government/publications/ts-no72017-ukbrazil-film-co-production-agreement.

Fleming, Mike (2011), 'Disney Shuffles Calendar to Fit the "Lone Ranger" into
May 31, 2013 Release Slot', *Deadline Hollywood Daily* (13 October), accessed online
(29 April 2015) deadline.com/2011/10/disney-shuffles-calender-to-fit-the-lone-ranger-
into-may-31-2013-release-slot-182453/.

'Focus 2014: World Film Market Trends', European Audiovisual Observatory (Marché du
Filme, Cannes Film Festival).

Fong, Gilbert (2010), *Dubbing and Subtitling in a World Context* (Hong Kong: Chinese University Press).

Fortune editors (1970), *Conglomerate Commotion* (New York: Viking Compass).

Franco-American Cultural Fund website (2016), accessed online (17 March 2016) societe. sacem.fr/en/ecosystem/facf.

Frater, Patrick (2004), 'French Court Breaks off *Engagement*', *Screen Daily* (26 November), accessed online (20 May 2016) screendaily.com/french-court-breaks-off-engagement/ 4021090.article.

——— (2014), 'Fox International and Bona to Produce Chinese *Bride Wars* Remake', *Variety* (21 June), accessed online (23 June 2015) variety.com/2014/film/asia/fox-international-and-bona-to-produce-chinese-bride-wars-remake-1201239463/.

——— (2015), 'How Sanford Panitch's Move Shakes up the International Production Scene (Analysis)', *Variety* (13 April), accessed online (15 April 2015) variety.com/2015/ film/asia/sanford-panitch-fox-sony-move-analysis-1201471812/.

Gara, Tom, and Charlie Warzel (2014), 'A Look through the Sony Pictures Data Hack: This Is as Bad as It Gets', *Buzzfeed* (2 December), accessed online (15 May 2015) buzzfeed.com/tomgara/sony-hack#.fm6pgdWdD.

German Federal Film Board (2015), accessed online (22 January 2015) ffa.de/.

German Film Commission website (2014), accessed online (1 December 2015) location-germany.de/Welcome.html.

Gilbey, Ryan (2011), 'Ten Years of Making Harry Potter Films, by Cast and Crew', *The Guardian* (7 July), accessed online (24 May 2016) theguardian.com/film/2011/ jul/07/harry-potter-making-the-films-cast-and-crew.

Glenn, A. Adam (1991), 'HBO Olé Targeted to Latin America', *Broadcasting & Cable*, available via Business Source Premiere (accessed 21 January 2011).

Globo Filmes entrevistas (2010), *High School Musical: O Desafio* (22 January), accessed online (26 February 2014; no longer available).

Goldsmith, Ben, and Tom O'Regan (2005), *The Film Studio: Film Production in the Global Economy* (Oxford: Rowman & Littlefield).

Goldsmith, Ben, Tom O'Regan, and Susan Ward (2010), *Local Hollywood: Global Film Production and the Gold Coast* (Queensland: University of Queensland Press).

Goldstein, Patrick (2011), 'Is Hollywood's Mania for Remakes Spinning Out of Control', *Los Angeles Times* (14 October), accessed online (7 December 2012) latimesblogs.latimes. com/movies/2011/10/is-hollywoods-mania-for-remakes-totally-out-of-control.html.

Gomery, Douglas (1986), *The Hollywood Studio System* (New York: St Martin's Press).

Goodridge, Mike (2004), 'Warner Bros Makes History with First Ever Foreign Production Co in China', *Screen Daily* (14 October), accessed online (15 July 2016) screendaily.com/ warner-bros-makes-history-with-first-ever-foreign-production-co-in-china/4020508.article.

——— (2009), 'Putting the Foreign First', *Screen Daily* (18 June), accessed online (15 January 2015) www.screendaily.com/putting-the-foreign-first/5002620.article.

———— (2011), 'Paramount to Shut Down Worldwide Acquisitions Group', *Screen Daily* (3 June), accessed online (26 May 2015) screendaily.com/news/distribution/paramount-to-shut-down-worldwide-acquisitions-group/5028423.article.

———— (2012), 'The Stage Is Set', *Screen Daily* (31 January), accessed online (1 June 2016) www.screendaily.com/reports/features/the-stage-is-set/5037040.article.

Grainge, Paul (2008), *Brand Hollywood: Selling Entertainment in a Global Media Age* (London: Routledge).

Graser, Marc, and Dave McNary (2010), 'Reed to Head Disney's International Productions', *Variety* (10 February), accessed online (15 August 2011) variety.com/2010/film/markets-festivals/reed-to-head-disney-s-international-productions-1118015035/.

Gray, Jonathan (2010), *Show Sold Separately: Promos, Spoilers, and Other Media Paratexts* (New York: NYU Press).

Guback, Thomas H. (1969), *The International Film Industry; Western Europe and America since 1945* (Bloomington: Indiana University Press).

Gubbins, Michael (2008), 'High School Musical 3 Takes Brand-Building to New Level', *Screen Daily* (30 October), accessed online (1 March 2014) www.screendaily.com/high-school-musical-3-takes-brand-building-to-new-level/4041687.article.

Guerini, Elaine (2010), 'The Land of Promise', *Screen International* (5 August), accessed online (15 January 2011) www.screendaily.com/features/territory-focus/the-land-of-promise/5016534.article.

Hale, Mike (2014), 'Walter White, Meet Walter Blanco', *New York Times* (17 June), accessed online (13 January 2015) nytimes.com/2014/06/18/arts/television/metastasis-a-spanish-version-of-breaking-bad-debuts.html?_r=0.

Halle, Randall (2006), 'German Film, European Film: Transnational Production, Distribution and Reception', *Screen* 47(2), pp. 251–9.

Halliday, Josh (2011), 'Film Piracy Battle Heads to Court', *The Guardian* (27 June), accessed online (15 May 2016) https://theguardian.com/technology/2011/jun/27/film-piracy-battle-heads-to-court.

Hansen, Eric, and Cathy Dunkley (1998), 'SPE Makes Mark in Germany', *Hollywood Reporter* (13 February), available via Business Source Complete (accessed 30 September 2010).

Hardt, Michael, and Antonio Negri (2000), *Empire* (Cambridge, MA: Harvard University Press).

Havens, Timothy (2014), 'Towards a Structuration Theory of Media Intermediaries', in Derek Johnson, Derek Kompare, and Avi Santo (eds), *Making Media Work: Cultures of Management in the Entertainment Industries* (New York: NYU Press), pp. 39–62.

Havens, Timothy, and Amanda D. Lotz (2012), *Understanding Media Industries* (Oxford: Oxford University Press).

Havens, Timothy, Amanda D. Lotz, and Serra Tinic (2009), 'Critical Media Industry Studies: A Research Approach', *Communication, Culture & Critique* 2, pp. 234–53.

Hazelton, John (2011), 'A New Approach to International', *Screen Daily* (6 November), accessed online (7 July 2015) www.screendaily.com/features/in-focus/a-new-approach-to-international/5033960.article.

Healey, Jon (2010), 'Hollywood Wins Another Lawsuit against a Search Engine', *Los Angeles Times* (29 March), accessed online (16 May 2016) latimesblogs.latimes.com/technology/2010/03/hollywood-wins-another-lawsuit-against-an-online-search-engine.html.

Hepp, Andreas (2009), 'Transculturality as a Perspective: Researching Media Cultures Comparatively', *Forum: Qualitative Social Research* 10(1), accessed online (30 September 2015) qualitative-research.net/index.php/fqs/article/view/1221/2657.

Hesmondhalgh, David (2013), *The Cultural Industries*, 3rd ed. (Los Angeles: Sage).

Hettrick, Scott (1994), 'HBO in Brazil with Olé Spinoff of 24-Hr Premium Cable TV Network to Launch July 1, 1994', *Hollywood Reporter* (20 April), available via Business Source Premiere (accessed 13 April 2010).

Higson, Andrew, and Richard Maltby (eds) (1999), *Film Europe and Film America: Cinema, Commerce and Cultural Exchange 1920–1939* (Exeter: University of Exeter Press).

Hils, Miriam (1998), 'Babelsberg Home to SPE Unit', *Variety* (12 February), accessed online (15 December 2014) variety.com/1998/biz/news/babelsberg-home-to-spe-unit-1117467746/.

——— (1999), 'Deutsche Col-Tristar Pix Up', *Variety* (27 January), accessed online (15 December 2014) variety.com/1999/film/news/deutsche-col-tristar-pix-up-1117490699/.

'History of Leavesden Studios' (2014), Warner Bros. website, accessed online (30 September 2014) wbsl.com/about-us.

Hollinger, Hy (2005), 'Distribs Speaking Their Language', *The Hollywood Reporter* (10 May), available via Business Source Complete (accessed 24 May 2010).

——— (2007), 'New Output Era for Overseas', *The Hollywood Reporter* (2 January), accessed online (7 May 2015) hollywoodreporter.com/news/new-output-era-overseas-127032.

Holson, Laura M. (2006), 'Hollywood Seeks Action Overseas', *New York Times* (2 April), accessed online (20 January 2015) nytimes.com/2006/04/02/technology/hollywood-seeks-action-overseas.html.

Holt, Jennifer (2011), *Empires of Entertainment: Media Industries and the Politics of Deregulation, 1980–1996* (New Brunswick, NJ: Rutgers University Press).

Hopewell, John (2007), 'Sony's Spain Freeze', *Variety* (19 October), accessed online (15 January 2015) variety.com/2007/film/markets-festivals/sony-s-spain-freeze-1117974336/.

——— (2010), 'RioFilme Backs Mountain', *Variety* (10 December), accessed online (15 May 2016) variety.com/2010/biz/news/riofilme-backs-mountain-1118028836/.

——— (2013a) 'Big Players Take Control of Brazil's Market', *Variety* (26 January), accessed online (23 July 2014) variety.com/2013/film/news/big-players-take-control-of-brazil-s-market-1118064912/.

——— (2013b) 'RioFilme Fuels Brazilian Biz', *Variety* (26 January), accessed online (15 August 2014) variety.com/2013/film/news/riofilme-fuels-brazilian-biz-1118064911/.

——— (2013c), '*Trash*: A Pioneering U.K.-Brazil Co-Production', *Variety* (7 October), accessed online (15 May 2015) variety.com/2013/film/global/trash-a-pioneering-u-k-brazil-co-production-1200703240/.

Hopewell, John, and Emilio Mayorga (2009), 'Dubbing Pain in Spain', *Variety* (4 March), accessed online (12 June 2013) variety.com/2009/film/markets-festivals/dubbing-pain-in-spain-1118000810/.

Horak, Jan-Christopher (1993), 'Rin-Tin-Tin in Berlin or American Cinema in Weimar', *Film History* 5, pp. 49–62.

Horkheimer, Max, and Theodor W. Adorno (2006), 'The Culture Industry: Enlightenment as Mass Deception', in Meenakshi Gigi Durham and Douglas Kellner (eds), *Media and Cultural Studies: Keyworks* (Malden, MA: Blackwell), pp. 41–72.

Hoskins, Colin, Stuart McFadyen, and Adam Finn (1997), *Global Film and Television: An Introduction to the Economics of the Business* (Oxford: Clarendon Press).

Iwabuchi, Koichi (2002), *Recentering Globalization: Popular Culture and Japanese Transnationalism* (Durham, NC: Duke University Press).

Jaafar, Ali (2009), 'Hollywood Biz without Borders', *Variety* (17 April), accessed online (7 December 2015) variety.com/article/VR1118002564.

Jenkins, Henry (2004), 'The Cultural Logic of Media Convergence', *International Journal of Cultural Studies* 7(33), pp. 33–43.

——— (2014), 'The Reign of the "Mothership": Transmedia's Past, Present, and Possible Futures', in Denise Mann (ed.), *Wired TV: Laboring over an Interactive Future* (New Brunswick, NJ: Rutgers University Press), pp. 244–65.

Johnson, Derek (2013), *Media Franchising: Creative License and Collaboration in the Culture Industries* (New York: NYU Press).

Johnson, Derek, Derek Kompare, and Avi Santo (2014), 'Introduction: Discourses, Dispositions, Tactics: Reconceiving Management in Critical Media Industry Studies', in Derek Johnson, Derek Kompare, and Avi Santo (eds), *Making Media Work: Cultures of Management in the Entertainment Industries* (New York: NYU Press), pp. 1–24.

Johnson, Randal (1987), *The Film Industry in Brazil: Culture and the State* (Pittsburgh: University of Pittsburgh Press).

Kamath, Sudhish (2008), 'Brand Disney', *The Hindu* (6 November), accessed online (1 March 2014) thehindu.com/todays-paper/tp-features/tp-metroplus/Brand-Disney/article15392792.ece.

Kay, Jeremy (2007), '2007 Review: Hollywood Looks for Local Heroes', *Screen Daily* (21 December), accessed online (14 February 2011) www.screendaily.com/2007-review-hollywood-looks-for-local-heroes/4036400.article.

———— (2008), '*High School Musical* Ready to Rock International Marketplace', *Screen Daily* (23 October), accessed online (15 February 2014) www.screendaily.com/high-school-musical-ready-to-rock-international-marketplace/4041535.article.

———— (2009), 'Isabel Hund to Head Sony's German Production', *Screen Daily* (31 August), accessed online (30 October 2014) www.screendaily.com/news/isabel-hund-to-head-sonys-german-production-division/5005030.article.

———— (2011a), 'Fox to Distribute Cannes Entry *Miss Bala* in Mexico', *Screen Daily* (28 April), accessed online (18 June 2015) www.screendaily.com/5026740.article.

———— (2011b), 'Reed Out as Disney Reviews Local-Language Production', *Screen Daily* (20 September), accessed online (27 May 2015) screendaily.com/reed-out-as-disney-reviews-local-language-production/5032275.article.

———— (2014), 'Peter Kujawski Lands UPIP Role', *Screen Daily* (19 September), accessed online (24 May 2015) www.screendaily.com/news/peter-kujawski-lands-upip-role/5077758.article.

———— (2015), 'Columbia Pictures, China Film Co Ready My Best Friend's Wedding Remake', *Screen Daily* (26 May), accessed online (15 July 2015) screendaily.com/news/production/columbia-pictures-china-film-co-ready-wedding-remake/5088680.article.

———— (2016), 'Focus Features, UPIP to Merge', *Screen Daily* (4 February), accessed online (18 April 2016) screendaily.com/news/focus-features-upip-to-merge/5099839.article.

Kirschbaum, Erik (2010), 'Schweiger Likes Lighter Touch', *Variety* (28 August), accessed online (7 January 2015) variety.com/2010/film/news/schweiger-likes-lighter-touch-1118023420/.

Krishna, Sonali (2007), 'Walt Disney Wants to Work in the Local Dimension', *The Economic Times* (14 June), accessed online (26 February 2014) economictimes. indiatimes.com/news/industry/media/entertainment/walt-disney-wants-to-work-in-the-local-dimension/articleshow/2121405.cms?intenttarget=no.

Kroll, Justin (2008), 'Gareth Wigan: CineAsia Visionary of the Year', *Variety* (5 December), accessed online (30 September 2010) variety.com/2008/film/markets-festivals/gareth-wigan-1117996969/.

Kunz, William M. (2007), *Culture Conglomerates: Consolidation in the Motion Picture and Television Industries* (Lanham, MD: Rowman & Littlefield).

Lang, Arthur, and Steven de Csesznak (1914), 'New Fields for American Film', *The Moving Picture World* (24 October), p. 468.

Lang, Brent (2011), 'Why America Doesn't Count at the Box Office Anymore', *The Wrap* (28 July), accessed online (1 December 2012) thewrap.com/movies/article/hollywoods-global-expansion-more-theaters-more-markets-more-profits-29574/.

———— (2016), 'Box Office: *Star Wars: Force Awakens* Will Top *Jurassic World*, *Titanic* on New Year's', *Variety* (1 January), accessed online (1 May 2016) variety.com/2016/film/box-office/star-wars-force-awakens-box-office-3-1201670535/.

Lang, Brent, and James Rainey (2015), 'New Sony Chief Tom Rothman on His Plan to Get the Studio Back in the Game', *Variety* (2 June), accessed online (1 July 2015) variety.com/2015/film/news/sony-tom-rothman-first-interview-1201509519/.

LaPorte, Nicole (2004), 'Local Pix Pique H'wood Interest', *Variety* (12 September), accessed online (19 July 2015) variety.com/2004/film/markets-festivals/local-pix-pique-h-wood-interest-1117910235/.

Leigh, Alan (1999), 'Think Locally', *Hollywood Reporter* (1 October), available via Business Source Complete (accessed 12 April 2015).

Lev, Peter (2003), *The Fifties: Transforming the Screen, 1950–1959* (History of the American Cinema 7) (New York: Charles Scribner's Sons).

Levin, Jonathan (2010), 'Next Summer's Blockbusters: *Marmaduke* and a *Footloose* for the New Millennium', *Slate* (8 January), accessed online (7 December 2012) slate. com/blogs/browbeat/2010/01/08/next_summer_s_blockbusters_marmaduke_and_a_footloose_for_the_new_millennium.html.

Lindvall, Helienne (2010), 'Film Industry Seeks BT Blocking Order in Newzbin2 Piracy Case', *The Guardian* (16 December), accessed online (15 May 2016) https:// theguardian.com/technology/2010/dec/16/mpa-bt-newzbin2?INTCMP=SRCH.

Littleton, Cynthia (2011), 'Disney Sets *High School Musical* Spinoff Series', *Variety* (17 February), accessed online (15 March 2015) variety.com/2011/tv/news/disney-sets-high-school-musical-spinoff-series-1118032486/.

Lobato, Ramon (2012), *Shadow Economies of Cinema: Mapping Informal Film Distribution* (London: BFI).

Lodderhose, Diana (2012), 'Leavesden Studios Opens for Biz', *Variety* (11 June), accessed online (15 January 2014) variety.com/2012/film/news/leavesden-studios-opens-for-biz-1118055312/.

Lynton, Michael (2007), 'Globalization and Cultural Diversity', *The Wall Street Journal* (4 September), accessed online (10 April 2015) wsj.com/articles/SB118885657159716199.

Marich, Robert (1995), 'WB, Sony Plan Latin Cablers Announces Plan to Launch Cable Networks in Latin America', *Hollywood Reporter* (25 January), available via Nexus Lexus (accessed 25 April 2010).

Marr, Merissa (2007a) 'Can *High School* Last Forever?', *The Wall Street Journal* (17 August), accessed online (15 February 2014) wsj.com/articles/SB118731875446900663.

——— (2007b), 'Small World', *The Wall Street Journal* (11 June), accessed online (15 February 2016) wsj.com/articles/SB118151608951430635.

Massey, Doreen (1992), 'A Place Called Home?', *New Formations* 17, pp. 3–15.

McDonald, Paul (2007), *Video and DVD Industries* (London: BFI).

——— (2008), 'Britain: Hollywood, UK', in Paul McDonald and Janet Wasko (eds), *The Contemporary Hollywood Film Industry* (Malden, MA: Blackwell), pp. 220–31.

——— (2015), 'Piracy and the Shadow History of Hollywood', in Paul McDonald, Emily Carman, Eric Hoyt, and Philip Drake (eds), *Hollywood and the Law* (London: BFI/Palgrave), pp. 69–101.

McIntosh, Joanna (2015), 'Re: MPAA Comments Regarding the 2016 National Trade Estimate Report on Foreign Trade Barriers' (28 October), MPAA website (accessed 1 April 2016).

McNary, Dave (2015a), 'Universal Crosses $5 Billion at Worldwide Box Office', *Variety* (17 July), accessed online (28 July 2015) variety.com/2015/film/news/universal-crosses-5-billion-worldwide-box-office-2015-1201543005/.

—— (2015b), 'Universal, Working Title Extend Production Deal to 2020', *Variety* (5 June), accessed online (1 July 2016) variety.com/2015/film/news/working-title-universal-extend-production-deal-2020-1201513185/.

—— (2016), 'Lionsgate Launching GlobalGate Local-Language Film Consortium', *Variety* (2 May), accessed online (24 May 2016) variety.com/2016/film/news/lionsgate-globalgate-local-language-movie-consortium-1201764636/.

Melnick, Ross (2015), 'Hollywood Embassies, Labour and Investment Laws and Global Cinema Exhibition', in Paul McDonald, Emily Carman, Eric Hoyt, and Philip Drake (eds), *Hollywood and the Law* (London: BFI), pp. 154–80.

—— (2016), 'Salisbury Stakes: Twentieth Century-Fox, Segregated Cinemas, and the Making of an International Crisis in Colonial Zimbabwe, 1959–1961', *Cinema Journal* 55(3), pp. 90–116.

Mermigas, Diane (1995), 'Sony Division Bouncing Back; SPE's Programming Key in Global Cable Growth', *Electronic Media* (25 September), available via Business Search Complete (accessed 24 May 2010).

Meza, Ed (2009), 'German Firms Compete in VFX Industry', *Variety* (15 May), accessed online (15 May 2016) variety.com/2009/digital/features/german-firms-compete-in-vfx-industry-1118003756/.

—— (2012a), 'National Treasure Morphs into International Player on the Make', *Variety* (4 February), accessed online (15 January 2015) variety.com/2012/film/markets-festivals/national-treasure-morphs-into-int-l-player-on-the-make-1118049300/.

—— (2012b), 'Remake for *Guardians*', *Variety* 36 (21 February), p. 6.

Miller, Toby (1996), 'The Crime of Monsieur Lang: GATT, the Screen, and the New International Division of Cultural Labor', in Albert Moran (ed.), *Film Policy: International, National and Regional Perspectives* (New York: Routledge), pp. 71–84.

Miller, Toby, Nitin Govil, John McMurria, Richard Maxwell, and Ting Wang (2005), *Global Hollywood 2* (London: BFI).

Miller, Toby, and Richard Maxwell (2007), 'Film and Globalization', in Oliver Boyd-Barrett (ed.), *Communications Media, Globalization, and Empire* (Bloomington: Indiana University Press).

Mingant, Nolwenn (2007), 'Hollywood's Global Outlook: Economic Expansionism and Production Strategy', *Revue LISA* 5(3), pp. 99–110, accessed online (18 April 2015) lisa.revues.org/1615.

———— (2010), *Hollywood à la conquête du monde: marchés, stratégies, influences* (Paris: CNRS).

———— (2011), 'A New Hollywood Genre: The Global-Local Film', in Rohit Chopra and Radhika Gajjala (eds), *Global Media, Culture, and Identity: Theory, Cases, and Approaches* (New York: Routledge), pp. 142–55.

———— (2015), 'A Peripheral Market? Hollywood Majors and the Middle East/North Africa Market', *The Velvet Light Trap* 75 (Spring), pp. 73–87.

Mohr, Ian (2006), 'U Digs Gardener Guy', *Variety* (26 July), accessed online (14 July 2015) variety.com/2006/film/features/u-digs-gardener-guy-1200338990/

Mommaas, Hans (2009), 'Spaces of Culture and Economy: Mapping the Cultural-Creative Cluster Landscape', in Lily Kong and Justin O'Connor (eds), *Creative Economies, Creative Cities: Asian-European Perspectives* (New York: Springer), pp. 45–60.

Monaco, Paul (2001), *The Sixties: 1960–1969* (History of the American Cinema 7) (New York: Charles Scribner's Sons).

Moran, Albert (ed.) (1996), *Film Policy: International, National and Regional Perspectives* (New York: Routledge).

———— (2011), *TV Formats Worldwide: Localizing Global Programs* (Bristol: Intellect).

Mosco, Vincent (1996), *The Political Economy of Communication* (London: Sage).

Motion Picture Association of America (MPAA) website (2015), accessed online (15 April 2016) mpaa.org/our-story/.

Motion Picture Association of America (2016), 'Theatrical Market Statistics 2016', accessed online (1 April 2017) www.mpaa.org/wp-content/uploads/2017/03/MPAA-Theatrical-Market-Statistics-2016_Final.pdf.

Mueller, Matt (2011), 'Rio Int'l Film Fest Winners', *IndieWire* (19 October), accessed online (24 May 2016) indiewire.com/2011/10/rio-intl-film-fest-winners-rio-seeks-more-premieres-like-twilight-more-fast-fives-and-woody-allen-184378/.

Murphy, Patrick D., and Marwan M. Kraidy, (2003), *Global Media Studies: Ethnographic Perspectives* (New York: Routledge).

Nathan, John (1999), *Sony: The Private Life* (Boston, MA: Houghton Mifflin).

Negus, Keith (1997), 'The Production of Culture', in Paul du Gay (ed.), *Production of Culture/Cultures of Production* (London: Sage), pp. 67–118.

O'Brien, Chris (2016), 'Netflix's New French TV Series "Marseille" Represents a Big Bet on Local Content', *Los Angeles Times* (4 May), accessed online (24 May 2016) latimes.com/entertainment/envelope/cotown/la-et-ct-netflix-marseilles-20160504-snap-story.html.

O'Brien, Kevin (2004), 'Fade-Out for a German Film Studio?', *New York Times* (7 June), accessed online (15 October 2014) nytimes.com/2004/06/07/business/worldbusiness/07iht-movies07_ed3_.html.

Ohga, Norio (2008), *Doing It Our Way: A Sony Memoir*, trans. Brian Miller (Tokyo: International House of Japan).

Oren, Tasha, and Sharon Shahaf (2011), 'Introduction: Television Formats – A Global
    Framework for TV Studies', in Tasha Oren and Sharon Shahaf (eds), *Global TV
    Formats: Understanding Television Across Borders* (New York: Routledge).
Ortner, Sherry B. (2010), 'Access: Reflections on Studying Up in Hollywood', *Ethnography*
    11(2), pp. 211–33.
Owczarski, Kimberly A. (2008), '*Batman*, Time Warner, and Franchise Filmmaking in the
    Conglomerate Era' (University of Texas-Austin, unpublished PhD dissertation).
Pardo, Alejandro (2007), *The Europe–Hollywood Competition: Cooperation and Competition
    in the Global Film Industry* (Pamplona: Ediciones Universidad de Navarra).
Pendakur, Manjunath (2008), 'Hollywood and the State: The American Film Industry
    Cartel in the Age of Globalization', in Paul McDonald and Janet Wasko (eds), *The
    Contemporary Hollywood Film Industry* (Malden, MA: Blackwell), pp. 182–94.
Petersen, Anne Helen (2014), *Scandals of Classic Hollywood: Sex, Deviance, and Drama
    from the Golden Age of American Cinema* (New York: Plume).
Pflanner, Eric (2004), 'Hollywood Turning to Non-English Fare', *New York Times* (24 May),
    accessed online (15 January 2015) nytimes.com/2004/05/24/business/worldbusiness/
    hollywood-turning-to-nonenglish-fare.html?_r=0.
Pieterse, Jan Nederveen (2004), *Globalization and Culture: Global Mélange* (Lanham, MD:
    Rowman & Littlefield).
Pollack, Andrew (1997), 'Entering US Broadcasting, Sony Buys Telemundo Stake', *New
    York Times* (25 November), accessed online (15 April 2016) nytimes.com/1997/11/25/
    business/the-media-business-entering-us-broadcasting-sony-buys-telemundo-stake.
    html.
Porter, Michael E. (2000), 'Location, Competition, and Economic Development: Local
    Clusters in a Global Economy', *Economic Development Quarterly* 14(1), pp. 15–34.
Pulver, Andrew, and Mark Brown (2015), 'Warner Bros' Josh Berger Appointed Chair
    of BFI', *The Guardian* (22 December), accessed online (15 May 2016) https://
    theguardian.com/film/2015/dec/22/warner-bros-josh-berger-appointed-chair-of-bfi.
Punathambekar, Aswin (2013), *From Bombay to Bollywood: The Making of a Global Media
    Industry* (New York: NYU Press).
Purdum, Todd (2012), 'Getting Reel', *Vanity Fair* (April), accessed online (1 June 2016)
    vanityfair.com/news/2012/04/chris-dodd-sopa-pippa-mpaa.
Ramos, Juan (2014), 'On *Metastasis*', *Mediático* (18 August), accessed online
    (15 March 2015) reframe.sussex.ac.uk/mediatico/2014/08/18/vlog-ep-1-metastasis/.
Reckard, E. Scott (1992), 'Japan's Deals in America: Did the Empire Strike Out?', *Associated
    Press* (16 January), available via Business Source Complete (accessed 24 May 2010).
Rêgo, Cacilda M. (2005), 'Brazilian Cinema: Its Fall, Rise, and Renewal (1990–2003)',
    New Cinemas: Journal of Contemporary Film 3(2), pp. 85–100.
'Rio: mais cinema, menos cénario' (2015), official Facebook page, accessed online
    (1 February) https://facebook.com/maiscinemamenoscenario/info?tab=page_info.

Robertson, Roland (1990), 'Mapping the Global Condition: Globalization as the Central Concept', in Mike Featherstone (ed.), *Global Culture: Nationalism, Globalization and Modernity* (London: Sage), pp. 15–30.

Robins, Kevin (1991), 'Prisoners of the City: Whatever Could a Postmodern City Be?', *New Formations* 15, pp. 1–22.

Rolfe, Pamela (2014), 'Spain Passes Much-Debated Intellectual Property Law', *The Hollywood Reporter* (30 October), accessed online (16 May 2016) hollywoodreporter. com/news/spain-passes-debated-intellectual-property-745130.

Rosser, Michael (2014), 'Warner Bros Names Harry Potter Global Franchise Development Team', *Screen Daily* (30 July), accessed online (15 May 2016) www.screendaily.com/ news/warner-bros-names-harry-potter-team/5075735.article.

Roxborough, Scott (2012), 'Warner Bros. Germany Signs Four-Picture Deal with Matthias Schweighofer', *The Hollywood Reporter* (6 February), accessed online (15 January 2015) hollywoodreporter.com/news/warner-bros-germany-Matthias-Schweighofer-287241.

———— (2014), 'Fox Boosts German Production Team with Magdalena Prosteder and Anna Maria Zundel', *The Hollywood Reporter* (7 January), accessed online (15 May 2015) hollywoodreporter.com/news/fox-boosts-german-production-team-668807.

Rucinski, Tracy, and Iciar Reinlein (2011), 'Spanish Piracy Law Draws U.S. Investments: Minister', *Reuters News* (22 July), accessed online (2 August 2015) reuters.com/article/ us-spain-piracy-idUSTRE76L32A20110722.

Salisbury, Mark (2016), 'Training: Visual Effects', *Screen Daily* (29 March), accessed online (15 June 2016) screendaily.com/features/training-visual-effects/5101867. article.

Sanson, Kevin (2011), 'We Don't Want Your Must-See TV: Transatlantic Television and the Failed *Coupling* Format', *Popular Communication: The International Journal of Media and Culture* 9(1), pp. 39–54.

———— (2015), 'Corresponding Geographies Remapping Work and Workplace in the Age of Digital Media' Television & New Media 16:8, pp. 751–768.

Sarda, Juan (2012), 'Spanish Exhibitors Respond to VAT Increased on Cinema Tickets', *Screen Daily* (18 July), accessed online (5 June 2015) www.screendaily.com/spanish-exhibitors-respond-to-vat-increase-on-cinema-tickets/5044479.article.

———— (2014), 'Paramount Takes Tad 2, Capture the Flag', *Screen Daily* (21 July), accessed online (15 April 2015) www.screendaily.com/news/distribution/paramount-takes-tad-2-capture-the-flag/5075432.article.

———— (2015), 'Spain: Overview – A Torrid Affair', *Screen Daily* (4 February), accessed online (15 April 2015) www.screendaily.com/features/territory-focus/spain-overview-a-torrid-affair/5082702.article.

Sassen, Saskia (2001), *The Global City: New York, London, Tokyo*, 2nd ed. (Princeton, NJ: Princeton University Press).

Schamus, James (2000), 'Holiday Films: The Polyglot Task of Writing the Global Film', *New York Times* (5 November), accessed online (12 April 2012) nytimes.com/2000/11/05/movies/holiday-films-the-polyglot-task-of-writing-the-global-film.html.

Schatz, Thomas (1988), *The Genius of the System: Hollywood Filmmaking in the Studio Era* (New York: Henry Holt & Co.).

——— (1993), 'The New Hollywood', in Jim Collins, Hilary Radner, and Ava Preacher Collins (eds), *Film Theory Goes to the Movies* (New York: Routledge).

——— (2008), 'The Studio System and Conglomerate Hollywood', in Paul McDonald and Janet Wasko (eds), *The Contemporary Hollywood Film Industry* (Malden, MA: Blackwell), pp. 13–42.

Scott, Allen J. (2005), *On Hollywood: The Place, The Industry* (Princeton, NJ: Princeton University Press).

Seal, Mark (2015), 'An Exclusive Look at Sony's Hacking Saga', *Vanity Fair* (March), accessed online (15 May 2015) vanityfair.com/hollywood/2015/02/sony-hacking-seth-rogen-evan-goldberg.

Sebok, Bryan (2009), 'Convergent Consortia: Format Battles in High Definition', *The Velvet Light Trap* 64, pp. 34–49.

'Sept Launched for Sony TV Channel' (1997), *The Business Times Singapore* (21 August), available via Business Source Complete (accessed 24 April 2010).

Shackleton, Liz (2014), 'Fox, Bona Team for Bride Wars Remake', *Screen Daily* (20 June), accessed online (15 March 2015) screendaily.com/territories/asia-pacific/fox-bonateam-for-bride-wars-remake/5073410.article.

Shaw, Lisa, and Maite Conde (2005), 'Brazil through Hollywood's Gaze: From the Silent Screen to the Good Neighbor Policy Era', in Lisa Shaw and Stephanie Dennison (eds), *Latin American Cinema: Essay on Modernity, Gender and National Identity* (Jefferson, NC: McFarland & Company).

Sinclair, John (1999), *Latin American Television: A Global View* (Oxford: Oxford University Press).

Sklar, Robert (1994), *Movie-Made America: A Cultural History of American Movies* (New York: Vintage).

'Sony Launches Local Production Initiative in Mexico' (2003), *Screen Daily* (15 July), accessed online (15 August 2013) www.screendaily.com/sony-launches-local-production-initiative-in-mexico/4014190.article.

'Sony Pictures Creates International Motion Picture Production Group' (2007), *PR Newswire* (30 April), accessed online (15 September 2014) prnewswire.com/news-releases/sony-pictures-creates-international-motion-picture-production-group-58893427.html.

'Sony Pictures Unveils Moviemaking Unit in Asia' (1998) *Reuters* (28 September), available via Business Source Complete (accessed 16 August 2010).

Steinhart, Daniel (2013), 'A Flexible Mode of Production: Internationalizing Hollywood Filmmaking in Postwar Europe', in Petr Szczepanik and Patrick Vonderau (eds), *Behind the Screen: Inside European Production Cultures* (New York: Palgrave Macmillan).

Stewart, Andrew (2012), 'Hollywood B.O. Rides O'seas Boom', *Variety* (14 January),
     accessed online (1 December 2012) variety.com/2012/digital/news/hollywood-b-o-
     rides-o-seas-boom-1118048578/.

Stilson, Janet (1994), 'Americans Plan Rival Film Channels in Brazil', *Multichannel News*
     15(7) (25 April), available via Business Source Complete (accessed 18 April 2010).

Straubhaar, Joseph (1991), 'Beyond Media Imperialism: Asymmetrical Interdependence
     and Cultural Proximity', *Critical Studies in Mass Communication* 8, pp. 1–11.

———— (2007), *World Television: From Global to Local Communication and Human Value*
     (Thousand Oaks, CA: Sage).

Studio Babelsberg official site (2015), accessed online (15 June 2016) studiobabelsberg.
     com/en/.

Sweney, Mark, and Josh Halliday (2011), 'High Court Forces BT to Block File-Sharing
     Website', *The Guardian* (28 July), accessed online (16 May 2016) theguardian.com/
     technology/2011/jul/28/high-court-bt-filesharing-website-newzbin2.

Szalai, George (2013), '"White House Down": Sony's Second Summer Flop Arrives Amid
     Call for Spinoff', *The Hollywood Reporter* (30 June), accessed online (13 January 2015)
     hollywoodreporter.com/news/white-house-down-sonys-second-577784.

Takayama, Hideo, Michael Hastings, Christian Caryl, George Wehrfritz, John Sparks,
     and Kay Itoi (2005), 'Sony Is Not Japan', *Newsweek* (21 March), accessed online
     (1 June 2011) newsweek.com/sony-not-japan-114375.

Tartaglione, Nancy (2003a), 'France Mulls Granting U.S. Majors Access to State Funding',
     Screen Daily (18 December), accessed online (20 May 2016) www.screendaily.com/france-
     mulls-granting-us-majors-access-to-state-funding/4016575.article.

———— (2003b), 'Jeunet's *Long Engagement* Gets French Approval', *Screen Daily* (9
     September), accessed online (20 May 2016) www.screendaily.com/jeunets-long-
     engagement-gets-french-approval/4014918.article.

———— (2003c), 'Warner Bros', *Engagement* Stirs French Debate', *Screen Daily* (1 August),
     accessed online (20 May 2016) www.screendaily.com/warner-bros-engagement-stirs-
     french-debate/4014397.article.

———— (2004a), 'French Producers Hit by Warner Funding Wrangle', *Screen Daily* (9
     November), accessed online (20 May 2016) www.screendaily.com/french-producers-hit-
     by-warner-funding-wrangle/4020860.article.

———— (2004b), 'Warner Bros. Faces French Uncertainty', *Screen Daily* (14 October),
     accessed online (20 May 2016) www.screendaily.com/warner-bros-faces-french-
     uncertainty/4020501.article.

———— (2005), 'French Culture Minister Addresses Engagement Controversy', *Screen
     Daily* (17 May), accessed online (20 May 2016) www.screendaily.com/french-culture-
     minister-addresses-engagement-controversy/4023167.article.

———— (2013), 'Studios Translate Local Language Movies into Lucrative Global Business',
     Deadline Hollywood Daily (5 May), accessed online (15 July 2014) deadline.com/2013/05/
     studios-translate-local-language-movies-into-lucrative-global-business-490513/.

———— (2014), 'Warner Bros Studios Leavesden to Expand in UK; "Tarzan" Swings into Residence', *Deadline Hollywood Daily* (30 June), accessed online (28 May 2015) deadline.com/2014/06/warner-bros-studios-leavesden-to-expand-in-uk-tarzan-swings-into-residence-797821/.

———— (2015), '"Furious 7" Box Office Hits $801.5M Global; "Paul Blart 2", "Longest Ride" New Overseas', *Deadline Hollywood Daily* (13 April), accessed online (13 May 2015) deadline.com/2015/04/international-box-office-furious-7-china-record-longest-ride-insurgent-paul-blart-1201408563/.

Tartaglione, Nancy, and Anita Busch (2015), '*Ultron* Outpacing *Avengers* & *IM3* with a Final $439.8M; *F7* Fuels Up – Intl B.O. Update', *Deadline Hollywood Daily* (4 May), accessed online (15 July 2015) deadline.com/2015/05/avengers-age-of-ultron-imax-furious-7-international-box-office-china-1201419976/.

Thompson, Anne (2015), 'Why Universal Is Breaking Box Office Records', *IndieWire* (20 July), accessed online (1 August 2015) indiewire.com/2015/07/why-universal-is-breaking-box-office-records-185979/.

Thompson, Kristin (1985), *Exporting Entertainment: America in the World Film Market, 1907–34* (London: BFI).

———— (2007), *The Frodo Franchise: The Lord of the Rings and Modern Hollywood* (Berkeley: University of California Press).

Thussu, Daya Kishan (2007), 'Mapping Global Media Flow and Contra-Flow', in Daya Kishan Thussu (ed.), *Media on the Move: Global Flow and Contra-Flow* (New York: Routledge), pp. 10–29.

Tinic, Serra (2005), *On Location: Canada's Television Industry in a Global Market* (Toronto: University of Toronto Press).

Trumpbour, John (2002), *Selling Hollywood to the World: U.S. and European Struggles for Mastery of the Global Film Industry, 1920–1950* (Cambridge: Cambridge University Press).

'TVA, WB, SPE, etc.' (1994), *Business Wire* (20 April), available via Business Source Complete (accessed 24 March 2010).

Ulaby, Neda (2012), 'Fox International Finds That Not Everyone Wants to Buy What Hollywood Sells', *NPR Monkey See* (19 January), accessed online (23 May 2015) npr.org/sections/monkeysee/2012/01/19/145447855/fox-international-finds-that-not-everyone-wants-to-buy-what-hollywood-sells.

Verrier, Richard (2014), 'In MPAA Statement, Hollywood Studios Show Support for Sony after Attack', *Los Angeles Times* (16 December), accessed online (16 May 2016) latimes.com/entertainment/envelope/cotown/la-et-ct-sony-hacking-studios-mpaa-statement-20141216-story.html.

Verrier, Richard, and Noah Bierman (2015), 'MPAA's Chris Dodd Is Facing Industry Upheaval and Clashing Studios', *Los Angeles Times* (15 March), accessed online (16 May 2016) latimes.com/entertainment/envelope/cotown/la-et-ct-chriss-dodd-mpaa-movie-studios-20150317-story.html.

Villarreal, Yvonne (2016), 'Univision Teams with Netflix, Announces New Slate of Programming', *Los Angeles Times* (17 May), accessed online (24 May 2016) latimes.com/entertainment/envelope/cotown/la-et-ct-univision-netflix-upfront-20160517-snap-story.html.

Wagner, Brigitta B. (2012), '10 August 1994: One Month after Founding X-Filme, Filmboard Berlin-Brandenburg Paves Way for New Productions in the Capital', in Jennifer M. Kapczynski and Michael D. Richardson (eds), *A New History of German Cinema* (Rochester, NY: Camden House), pp. 530–6.

Wasko, Janet (2001), *Understanding Disney: The Manufacture of Fantasy* (Cambridge: Polity).

——— (2003), *How Hollywood Works* (London: Sage).

Wasko, Janet, and Mary Erickson (eds) (2008), *Cross-Border Cultural Production: Economic Runaway or Globalization?* (Amherst, NY: Cambria).

Wasser, Frederick (2008), 'Ancillary Markets – Video and DVD: Hollywood Retools', in Paul McDonald and Janet Wasko (eds), *The Contemporary Hollywood Film Industry* (Malden, MA: Blackwell), pp. 120–31.

'Welcome to Tinseltown, Mr. Morita' (1994), *The Independent* (10 April), available via Business Source Complete (accessed 24 February 2010).

'When Corporate Cultures Collide' (1992), *Electronic Media* (2 March), available via Business Source Complete (accessed 24 March 2010).

'Will Sony Make It in Hollywood?' (1991) *Fortune* (9 September), available via Business Source Complete (accessed 20 January 2010).

Willmore, Alison (2012), '*Miss Bala* Filmmaker Gerardo Naranjo Will Direct the Pilot for FX's *The Bridge*', *IndieWire* (20 September), accessed online (17 June 2015) indiewire.com/2012/09/miss-bala-filmmaker-gerardo-naranjo-will-direct-the-pilot-for-fxs-the-bridge-diane-kruger-to-star-44782/.

Wiseman, Andreas (2011a), 'Christian Grass Steps Down from Role at Universal', *Screen Daily* (6 July), accessed online (28 May 2015) www.screendaily.com/christian-grass-steps-down-from-role-at-universal/5029557.article.

——— (2011b), 'International Box Office 2010 Wrap', *Screen Daily* (13 January), accessed online (15 March 2014) www.screendaily.com/box-office/international-box-office-2010-wrap/5022291.article.

Wyatt, Justin (1994), *High Concept: Movies and Marketing in Hollywood* (Austin: University of Texas Press).

Interviews

Antón, Carlos (2013), EGEDA, President, interview by author, 5 June, Madrid, Spain.

Artacho, Estela (2013), FEDICINE, President, interview by author, 7 June, Madrid, Spain.

de la Tour, Vincent (2013), General Manager, Fox Films Germany, interview by author, 19 June, Frankfurt, Germany.

de Macedo, Iona (2011), Former Vice President of Production for Latin America and President of Columbia Films Producciones Españolas, interview by author, 17 January, Madrid, Spain.

Dock, Olivier (2013), Vice President, MPA EMEA, interview by author, 14 June, Brussels, Belgium.

Former International Executive A (2015), Warner Bros., interview by author, 24 February, phone.

Former International Executive B (2011), Sony Pictures Entertainment, interview by author, 11 February, Madrid, Spain.

Former International Executive C (2011), Sony Pictures Entertainment, interview by author, 15 August, phone.

Former International Sales Executive (2011), Sony Pictures Entertainment, interview by author, 24 August, phone.

Former MPA Executive (2013), interview by author, 15 September, phone.

Fox, Richard (2013), Executive Vice President of International, Warner Bros., interview by author, 21 August, phone.

Geike, Willi (2013), President and Managing Director, Warner Bros. Germany, interview by author, 25 June, Hamburg, Germany.

Gil, Montse (2013), Vice President and General Manager, Paramount Pictures Spain, interview by author, 10 June, Madrid, Spain.

Independent Producer A (2010), interview by author, 1 September, Rio de Janeiro, Brazil.

Independent Producer B (2013), interview by author, 17 May, Cannes, France.

International Production Executive (2014), interview with author, 26 February, Los Angeles.

International Studio Executive A (2014), interview by author, 20 February, Los Angeles.

International Studio Executive B (2013), interview by author, 1 June, Madrid, Spain.

Kokourina, Anna (2013), Vice President of Production, Fox International Productions, interview by author, 25 September, phone.

———— (2014), Vice President of Production, Fox International Productions, interview by author, 27 February, Los Angeles.

Ledwith, Jack (2014), Senior Vice President of International Distribution, Universal Pictures, interview by author, 21 February, Los Angeles.

Local Studio Manager (2010), interview by author, 15 September, São Paulo, Brazil.

Lustau, Miguel (2013), General Director, Twentieth Century-Fox España, interview by author, 7 June, Madrid, Spain.

Marcich, Chris (2016), Former President of International, Motion Picture Association, interview by author, 18 March, phone.

Mehlitz, Marco (2013), Former Head of Production and Development, Fox International Productions Germany, interview by author, 21 June, Berlin, Germany.

MPA Territory Manager (2013), interview by author, 17 June, Brussels, Belgium.

Noguerones, Pablo, (2011), General Manager, Warner Bros. Spain, interview by author, 28 January, Madrid, Spain.

———— (2013), General Manager, Warner Bros. Spain, interview by author, 4 June, Madrid, Spain.

Peregrino, Jorge (2010), Senior Vice President of Distribution for Latin America and Caribbean, Paramount Pictures, interview by author, 25 August, Rio de Janeiro, Brazil.

Robles, Begoña (2013), Director of Production, Warner Bros. Spain, interview by author, 11 June, Madrid, Spain.

Sá Leitão, Sergio (2010), Former President, RioFilme, interview by author, 31 August, Rio de Janeiro, Brazil.

————— (2013), Former President, RioFilme, interview by author, 18 May, Cannes, France.

Santiago, Ilda (2014), Executive Director, Festival do Rio, interview by author, 25 July, Rio de Janeiro, Brazil.

Saturnino Braga, Rodrigo (2010), General Manager, Sony Pictures Brazil, interview by author, 15 September, São Paulo, Brazil.

Silva, Cesar (2014), Vice President and General Director, Paramount Pictures Brasil, interview by author, 1 August, Rio de Janeiro, Brazil.

Silver, Aviva (2011), Director, MEDIA programme, interview by author, 3 February, Brussels, Belgium.

———— (2013), Director, MEDIA programme, interview by author, 18 June, Brussels, Belgium.

Solot, Steve (2010), Rio Film Commission and former VP MPA Latin America, interview by author, 22 August, Rio de Janeiro, Brazil.

Spanish Industry Professional (2013), interview by author, 7 June, Madrid, Spain.

Studio Managing Director (2013), interview by author, 10 June, Madrid, Spain.

Trindade, Diler (2010), President and Executive Producer, Diler & Associados, interview by author, 31 August, Rio de Janeiro, Brazil.

Uriol, Pedro (2011), Executive Producer, Morena Films, interview by author, 28 January, Madrid, Spain.

Wainer, Bruno (2010), General Director, Downtown Filmes, interview by author, 9 September, Rio de Janeiro, Brazil.

Werber, Clifford (2015), Co-Founder and CEO, Globalgate Entertainment, interview by author, 6 March, phone.

Winther, Eloisa (2014), Director of Production, Sony Pictures Brazil, interview by author, 14 August, São Paulo, Brazil.

Index

A

ABC/Capital Cities, 33t3.1, 136

Adland, Charles, 58–59n4

Adorno, Theodor, 20

Africa, 15, 21, 64

African Consolidated Theatres, 21

African Queen, The (1951), 23

After Earth (2013), 78

Amazing Spider Man, The (2012), 78

Amazing Spider Man 2, The (2014), 40

Americanisation, 27. *See also* culture

Anatomie (Anatomy, 2000), 99, 146

ancillary markets, 30, 35, 36, 136, 145. *See also* home entertainment technology

ANCINE, 90

Anderson, Christopher, 21

Anna Christie (1930), 17, *18*

Ant-Man (2015), 97

AOL (America Online), 33t3.1

Appadurai, Arjun, 139

Aranguren, Steve, 137

Argentina, 58n3, 137, 141; foreign investment, 37

Artacho, Estela, 119

Article 3 (Brazil tax incentive). *See* Brazil

Asia, 14, 15, 21; local-language productions, **44–56**. *See also specific countries*

audiences (film): active *vs.* passive, 5, 27; African-American, 1; decline of numbers, 28; expansion of, 30; female, 1; global, 1, 19, 20, 29, 58–59n4, 133; Latino, 1; local, 56–57, 71, 133; manipulation of, 20; suburban, 20; targeted, 1; urban, 15

audiences (television), **37–40**

Australia, 15, 21; Gold Coast, 89, 111n4

Avengers: Age of Ultron (2015), 63, 97

Avengers franchise, 134

B

Balio, Tino, 4, 28

Banks, Miranda, 7

Barefoot Films, 148, 151

Batman (1989), 35

Bayona, Juan A., 79

Bekmambetov, Timur, 52

Belgium, 63

Beltrán, Mary, 43

Benelux, 57, 63–64

Ben-Hur (1959), 23

Berlin, 94; media hubs, 87

Berlin-Brandenburg region: media hub, 94

blockbusters, 22, 28, 29, 43, 97, **133–53**; blockbuster logic, 135

Boespflug, Francis, 120

Bollywood, 88, 139

Bordwell, David, 18, 29

Braga, Rodrigo Saturnino, 77

Brazil, 21, 52, 58n3, 137, 141, 144, 158; Article 3 (Brazil tax incentive), 78, 80, 89, 120, 122; Brazilian film theatre, *16*; Cinema Novo, 26; economic crisis, 158; foreign investment, 37; Hollywood co-productions, 26; international media hub, **89–93**; local studio operations, **62–84**; local-language productions, **44–56, 73–83**, 141–42, *142*; piracy, 126; presidential impeachment, 158; screen quotas, 26; spiritual dramas, 74–75; Summer Olympics, 158

Breaking Bad, 39

BRIC market (Brazil, Russia, India China), 56, 144

Bride Wars (2009), 52

Bridge, The (2011), 54

Bridge of Spies (2015), 95, 97

Browning, Tod, 17

Brussels office of MPA, 116

Burton, Richard, 25, *25*

C

Cairo, 88

Caldwell, John, 7, 157–58

Cannes Film Festival, 53, 82, 128

capitalism, 5, 27, 115; cultural protectionism *vs.* free trade, 117, 122

Captain America: Civil War (2016), 96, 97

Caribbean, 15

Cartoon Films, 151